JOURNEY TO PEACE

A True Story of Forgiveness and Reconciliation

JOURNEY TO PEACE

*A True Story of Forgiveness
and Reconciliation*

Adam Joe Lawton

Matador
9 Priory Business Park,
Wistow Road, Kibworth Beauchamp,
Leicestershire. LE8 0RX
Tel: (+44) 116 279 2299
Fax: (+44) 116 279 2277
Email: books@troubador.co.uk
Web: www.troubador.co.uk/matador

ISBN 9781780883182

British Library Cataloguing in Publication Data.
A catalogue record for this book is available from the British Library.

Typeset by Troubador Publishing Ltd, Leicester, UK
Printed and bound in the UK by TJ International, Padstow, Cornwall

Matador is an imprint of Troubador Publishing Ltd

This book is dedicated to the memory of the twenty men who gave their lives in HMS *Sheffield* in May 1982 in the defence and liberation of the Falkland Islands. They willingly made the supreme sacrifice that others may live in the peace and freedom of their choosing. May they never be forgotten.

Our sons for their country they fought so proud,
now they lie in the deep with the sea for a shroud.

(Unknown)

David Balfour	34	Lieutenant Commander
David Briggs DSM	25	Petty Officer Marine Engineering Mechanic
Darryl Cope	21	Catering Assistant
Anthony Eggington	35	Weapons Engineering Artificer 1st Class
Richard Emly	36	Sub Lieutenant
Robert Fagan	34	Petty Officer Cook
Neil Goodall	20	Cook
Allan Knowles	31	Leading Marine Engineering Mechanic
Lai Chi Keung	31	Laundryman No1
Tony Marshall	31	Leading Cook
Anthony Norman	25	Petty Officer Weapons Engineering Mechanic
David Osborne	22	Cook
Kevin Sullivan	35	Weapons Engineering Artificer 1st Class
Andrew Swallow	18	Cook
Michael Till	35	Weapons Engineering Artificer 1st Class
Barry Wallis	26	Weapons Engineering Mechanician 1st Class
Brian Welch	34	Master At Arms
Adrian Wellstead	26	Leading Cook
Kevin Williams	20	Cook
John Woodhead DSC	40	Lieutenant Commander

CONTENTS

AUTHOR'S NOTE

This book was started in 2001, nineteen years after the original events took place. It took many years to complete and it is purely a personal recollection. All my diaries were lost in HMS *Sheffield*, and at the time it was not an event I wished to recall, nor keep detailed accounts of. I never re-started my diaries; consequently my recollection of events may differ from those of others who were there. Even the following day in 1982, our accounts were different.

All the characters are real and all the events took place. I cannot vouch for the authenticity of the actions I did not take part in. They have been repeated here verbatim, as they were imparted to me. To the best of my recollection, this story is accurate and I have tried to tell it as truthfully as possible. Whatever my thoughts or feelings about people and/or events mentioned, they are as I felt at that time, good or bad. My feelings may have changed since then.

It took me twelve to eighteen months or so (mid 2002 – end 2003) to go the full circle after my trip, and reach the point where I am today. By undertaking my 'Journey to Peace' I confronted, in person, the demons that had haunted me and negatively affected my life, and I subsequently exorcised those ghosts. Doing so has made me a much stronger, more resilient and more thoughtful person. I have dispensed with my aggression and am now a lot more understanding, forgiving and tolerant. I look back now at the 'people' I have been and I don't recognise some of them.

I have a lot of people to thank for helping me through some of these times. Firstly, my very supportive friends in both Britain and Australia, I owe them more than they realise. I could name them, but will not, for they know who they are.

I owe so much to my loving sister who helped me through much of the suffering and trauma, without knowing what had happened, and who took so much of the burden on herself.

Finally and most importantly, my mum and dad, for their patience, fortitude and magnificence in understanding. They suffered as much as I did and in some ways more, because unlike me, they did not have the opportunity to confront and close the subject once and for all.

If this book helps one other sailor, soldier, marine or airman come to terms with the life changing events we all shared so long ago and so far away, then I will have achieved my objective.

ACKNOWLEDGEMENT

Lieutenant Commander Nick Batho.

This man has been vilified for a long time by many people. After maintaining a dignified silence for 25 years he spoke out. Nick has had the courage and integrity to stand up and make a statement admitting he made a "gross error of judgement" in leaving his post in the operations room of HMS *Sheffield*. In war mistakes will be made, such is the nature of war. Despite what I felt towards him in the years after the loss of *Sheffield*, I have learned forgiveness for him, as I did for the enemy pilots responsible for the loss of the ship. I bear Nick Batho no ill will and admire his humility and the profound sense of sadness he has confessed too. I hope all those involved in the events of 1982 can now draw a line underneath this and move on.

FATE

"You're a very lucky young man."

I was just 17, and had recently graduated from radar training. The rest of the class and I were kicking our heels, waiting to get to our first ships. All the talk was of where various ships were going and what they were doing. One sailor, Beckett, had finished his course a couple of weeks ahead of us and had been drafted to HMS *Sheffield* a Type 42 destroyer. He took great delight in telling us that in a couple of weeks he'd be joining the ship which was deploying to the Indian Ocean, the Persian Gulf and places like Mauritius. We were *green* with envy. In the trainees' administration office, the Divisional Officer, Lt Young, was sorting out the final paperwork with the Chief Petty Officer in charge of training, ready to send his next batch of young sailors off to their new life on the ocean wave.

I came off duty at 4pm and as soon as I walked into Flint Block, the trainees' accommodation, I was told to report to the administration office. I thought I must be in trouble, again. I was marched in front of Lt Young and stood to attention until invited to 'stand at ease'.

"Do you have a draft yet Lawton?" the Divisional Officer asked me.

"No sir" I replied.

He studied the papers in front of him. "You're from Norfolk aren't you Lawton?"

"Yes sir," I said.

"You don't sound like you're from Norfolk."

"Originally I'm from Yorkshire sir," I told him.

"Oh! That's a coincidence," he said.

"What's a coincidence sir?"

"Sheffield is in Yorkshire and you're joining her on 9th November. Ten days later she deploys for six months in the Gulf and Indian Ocean. Some cracking runs ashore to be had there Lawton. You're a very lucky young man."

"But I thought Beckett was going to the *Sheffield*, sir. He's been onto everyone about where the ship is going."

The DO lifted his head and stared at me for a moment.

"He was going to join her but he's gone sick-on-shore and is unfit for sea service. So you're taking his place. Good luck. Dismissed."

I stood there gaping, not knowing what to say. Lt Young went back to signing papers. Without looking up, he said, "Lawton, I said you were dismissed. About turn, quick march!"

"Yes sir, thank you sir," I said, and wheeled about.

I took the stairs three at a time up to the mess.

"Guess what fellas!" I said. "Beckett's gone sick and I've got the *Sheffield* in his place. Six months fun in the sun – woohoo!"

"You lucky bastard!" one of them said. The others were less polite.

On the morning of Monday 9 November 1981, the four ton lorry trundled to a stop at Fountain Lake Jetty. I jumped out, caught my kitbag as it was thrown out after me, and watched as the wagon rumbled off.

Directly in front of me was a gangway, its large banner announcing: HMS *Sheffield*.

PROLOGUE

The missile streaked across the wave tops at the speed of sound. A single metallic sliver, packed with high explosive and spouting smoke. It shimmered against the dull blue of the South Atlantic swell, its warhead primed, its homing radar locked onto the British destroyer.

CHAPTER I

What's it all About?

... there are no public holidays to remember the living.

Each November on Remembrance Day we think about those who have made the ultimate sacrifice, those who have laid down their lives for their country. We glorify and pay homage to the sacrifice of a nation's younger generation. Those who have fallen in battle have done their duty. For them, the war is over, irrespective of the brutal way in which it ended. Whether it was quick or slow is of comfort only to the living.

What most forget or have no concept of, is that whilst the nation rejoices on that tidal wave of national pride with bands playing and flags waving, many of the men and women marching before them are still fighting a war – a silent unmentioned war, one which will never be won on a dark and lonely battlefield in a far flung corner of the world. For some, when the guns stop, the fighting really starts, as generations of war veterans can testify. Worldwide, there is significant anecdotal evidence which confirms that veterans of conflict have significantly greater psychological problems than a similar cross-section of the population as a whole. You do not have to bleed to be wounded. And there are no public holidays to remember the living.

Many seek solace in drink and drugs. They lose their jobs, their homes, their families and ultimately, their lives. In 1982 in the South Atlantic campaign, two hundred and fifty five British servicemen died. In the last twenty five years, it is believed, though figures cannot be confirmed, that a greater number, possibly as many as 300 of the surviving veterans, have taken their own lives. There were only two members of HMS *Sheffield* ships company who were younger than me. One is now in psychiatric care – the other is dead, having taken his own life.

1

Some of those involved in the Falklands conflict became high profile public figures afterwards, and their stories became known. But how much is known of the suffering endured by the men who returned, by their wives, parents, children? How many youngsters who were babies at the time have grown up with a dad who was 'strange', not like other kid's dads? How many have witnessed their mothers being beaten, and when they were big enough, been beaten as well? These too are victims of war, a war which was 'over' more than thirty years ago. The suffering and after-effects of war go on privately in homes all over the world, as I and many others can testify.

The effects of physical wounds can often be overcome with medical expertise, patience, and care. But the mental scars, the pain etched upon the memory, the horror the eyes have seen, the suffering and agony that has been witnessed is less easy to erase and takes significantly longer to overcome. For some, that day never comes. Their lives disintegrate, and too frequently end prematurely.

There are many stories to come out of war; courage, heroism, bravery, call it what you will. But all too often, these stories finish when the shooting does. The stories of the aftermath are very rarely told.

For each person who dies in conflict, how many other lives, of family, of friends, are affected? If a whole group of men from one regiment, one ship or one village is lost, imagine for a moment the attendant suffering. There must be millions of people around this world who live daily with the effects of war. What becomes of the wounded, those who lose limbs, or eyesight? How can we account or compensate for this level of suffering, knowing that these people live with a constant reminder of how and where they acquired their disability?

The effects of war differ, depending on which service you are in. Pilots, because of the range of their targets can be more detached from the personal side to war. That's also true in the Navy. An aircraft or another ship is destroyed when it is just a blip on a radar screen. But the target itself is not just a ship; it's a ships company, men who have bonded together over the months and years to form a close knit community, a community of pride. And the ship itself becomes part of that community; the men become attached to it, an integral part of it. Those who have not experienced such things will find it hard to understand. When you lose your ship, you lose your home, your community, your family. That's why some of us have found it so hard to deal with.

To quote Regimental Sergeant Major Peter Ratcliffe, DSM, a senior and highly experienced soldier:

If politicians had the job of upholding their own promises to defend far flung corners of the empire which are highly unlikely to ever make the pages of a holiday brochure, then we would very quickly become a nation of isolationist pacifists.

Eye of the Storm – Michael O'Mara Books, 2000

CHAPTER 2

Sailing South for the Winter

27ᵗʰ – 30ᵗʰ March 1982

HMS *Sheffield* had been away for five months in the Persian Gulf on the Armilla Patrol. We had been protecting British shipping during the Iran-Iraq war, and were en-route home to Portsmouth. Our last port of call was Gibraltar for three days before participating in Exercise *Spingtrain*. Every year in March/April a large contingent of Royal Navy warships and Royal Fleet Auxiliaries ('RFAs' large stores ships and tankers which re-supply ships at sea) gather in Gibraltar to carry out an exercise simply called *Springtrain*, after the period of the year in which it is held. This exercise is carried out in the Atlantic Ocean in the approaches to the Mediterranean Sea. Also participating are submarines and aircraft. The exercise consists of a number of submarine hunting exercises (CASEX); anti-air warfare defence exercises (ADEX); surface action group exercises (SAGs) culminating in high seas firings of Sea Dart missiles.

Sheffield was a Type 42 destroyer, commissioned in 1975 and the oldest of her class, under the watch of Captain Sam Salt RN, who had recently assumed command whilst we were undergoing a leave and maintenance period in Mombasa, Kenya. As *Sheffield* entered Gibraltar, I was on the bridge roof. This was one of the highest points of the ship's super- structure, and had a flat top to make it easy to stand still. Immediately behind us was the huge fibreglass dome housing the 909 fire control radar. There was a large Union flag painted on the roof to identify the ship from the air. I was accompanying 'The Jimmy', the First Lieutenant, who was second in command, and it felt to me, a 17 year old Junior Seaman, as though he was a million rungs higher up the naval ladder than I was. The air was thick with the smell of sea salt, and it was absolutely freezing.

Being a ceremonial entry we were all lined up along the decks in our best sailor suits. When warships pass each other, they are required to 'salute'. This is carried out by means of blowing the 'still', an eight second blast on the bosuns 'call', a type of whistle with a chain, draped around the neck and underneath the blue sailor's collar, and used since the days of sail for issuing various orders. The Quartermaster and Bosun's Mate wear Bosuns calls tucked into the front of their tunics and when the salute is required, the order is given to 'pipe the still'. The Jimmy was holding a plan of the harbour, every piece of berthing space was full. The ships more senior to *Sheffield* which we would have to pipe, were marked in red. Those more junior to us, which would be piping *Sheffield,* were in blue. The flags we were flying for harbour entry snapped and cracked at the halyards. The Royal Navy has always been extremely keen on ceremony and maintaining its traditions. I glanced over to the communications ratings who would haul down and hoist the flag signals; they were shivering, and I could see them silently cursing the wind. Despite the bitter cold, we were under a sky of brilliant azure blue as we turned onto the final course to pass through the breakwater and into Gibraltar harbour.

The Jimmy addressed me: "Junior Seaman Lawton, all eyes will be on *Sheffield* as we enter, so let's put on a good show and show them why we're the Deputy Squadron Leader." It was the first time he'd ever addressed me by my rank and not just by my surname, as was typical of the senior officers. Knowing that the Flag Officer Gibraltar would be watching us, as would Rear Admiral Woodward, the Flag Officer First Flotilla (FOF1), I pulled myself up to my full five feet six inches and puffed out my thirty four inch chest, feeling as important as every other man on the ship and a real part of the Navy.

There was a frenzy of four-second pipes, salutes and about turns. At the far end of the dockyard on the left hand side, was the last available berth for *Sheffield*, with *Active* who had accompanied us on the Gulf patrol to secure outboard of us. We nosed in just ahead of the two Type 22's, *Broadsword* and *Battleaxe*, the new all-missile frigates fitted with the point defence missile, Sea Wolf. Behind them was *Glamorgan* who, since our last meeting in the Gulf when she had run aground, had returned to Portsmouth for repairs and was now fully operational. All the ships' companies stopped what they were doing and stood to attention to face us as the salutes were piped between the ships. The order was given for *Sheffield* ships company to fall out from ceremonial entry and prepare to berth.

The first heaving lines were thrown, a long line the thickness of a skipping rope looped into small coils with a solid 'monkey's fist' (a tightly woven ball of rope, with a weight inside) on the end to carry the weight of the rope to the jetty. The inboard end was secured to the ship's main berthing ropes and heaved ashore by the dockyard workers, then secured to bollards on the jetty. As the first rope was secured ashore, the Union Jack was run up at the jackstaff at the bow of the ship, and the White Ensign transferred from its seagoing position on the foremast, to the ensign staff at the aft end of the flightdeck.

Joining *Sheffield* just before she deployed from Portsmouth, I'd been at sea for only five months and was looking forward to my first return from deployment. I left the bridge and quickly made my way to where the gangway was being secured aft to prepare for the first of many ceremonial visits by the Captain. I'd never seen so much gold braid on uniforms and so many 'brass-hats'. Joining the Navy was truly a fantastic decision, which had extracted me from the potentially humdrum existence of college, or a series of dead-end jobs.

Across the harbour from us was *Antrim*, another of the County Class destroyers and sister ship to *Glamorgan*. She was flying the flag of Flag Officer First Flotilla Rear-Admiral John 'Sandy' Woodward, *Sheffield's* first CO in 1975. Outboard of her was *Brilliant*, sister ship to *Battleaxe* and *Broadsword*. There were thirty warships, a number of Royal Fleet Auxiliaries and two very unfortunate American ships in Gibraltar, all for Exercise *Springtrain*. The place was chaos.

I had been ashore in Gib' on the way out to the Gulf and even though still legally under age, I had been in the pub with the rest of the mess. Nobody asked my age, I didn't volunteer it. Most pubs were three or four deep at the bar this time around, none of the staff had the time or inclination to enquire if everyone was old enough. I felt like a real sailor, ashore with my mates, throwing down the beer, singing raucous songs and staggering down the main street of Gib', weaving my way back through Ragged Staff Gate, trying to look as if I were sober when passing the Ministry of Defence coppers. Some of the brainier kids at my school were still swotting for their 'A' levels, some were driving tractors around Norfolk's farms, some were still on the dole two years after leaving school. Not me! I was in the service of Her Majesty, one of the honoured, the privileged. I'd arrived and it felt fucking great!

So many ships in harbour meant a great deal of ceremony with ship's captains calling on each other. On these occasions, the gangway staff of quartermaster and bosuns mate would be joined by officer of the day and other duty staff. The QM and BM wore bosuns calls and would 'pipe the side' on these ceremonial occasions.

Each morning at 8.00am, the ceremony of 'colours' would be observed. A sailor standing at the jackstaff would call "colours sir" to the officer of the day. He in turn would order "make it so". The bosuns mate would then sound eight bells on the ship's bell which hung next to the gangway. As soon as this was complete, the OOD would order "pipe the still" and an eight second blast would be sounded on the bosuns call. Then the White Ensign would be raised aft, and the Union Jack would be raised for'ard. The ringing of the ship's bells and shrieks of the bosuns calls carried for miles across Gibraltar roads. Very few other Navies in the world could have put on such a show. Everyone on all the ships and in the dockyard stopped what they were doing to observe the ceremony – it was as if the world stood still.

Trouble Brewing

On 19th March, some Argentine scrap metal merchants landed illegally on South Georgia and raised the Argentine flag. HMS *Endurance*, the ice patrol ship, embarked some Royal Marines from the garrison in Stanley, the capital of the Falkland Islands, and she then dispatched to Grytviken, in South Georgia.

Ashore in Gibraltar we had heard scraps of information about diplomatic problems in the Falkland Islands, which in our ignorance, we imagined were up off Scotland somewhere. The first sign that the situation might be more serious was when the nuclear powered submarine, HMS *Superb* disappeared overnight from Gibraltar. It was thought to have set course for the South Atlantic (which later proved not to be the case). There were rumours but nothing was substantiated.

All our ships sailed as programmed on March 30th and headed for the exercise areas. I was back on the bridge roof for the departure from Gibraltar, where I watched as HMS *Active* was pulled away from us by two harbour tugs. We shrilled the eight second 'still' on our bosuns calls and the two captains saluted each other. The Yeomen of Signals from each ship were on their respective bridge roofs talking to each other in semaphore and the white ensign was raised at the masthead. Under a grey overcast sky, one by one the ships slipped their berthing ropes and turned for the breakwater, and the exit to Gib' harbour. The *whoop-whoop-whoop* of the sirens as the ships came astern from their berths gave me goose pimples. With a distance of about a mile between ships, as far as I could see there were warships in line astern. It was a stirring sight; a scene to resurrect Nelson himself, and my heart was bursting with pride.

I looked down from the bridge roof to the bridge wings. These extended out from either side of the main bridge superstructure to the full extent of the ship's width. On each wing was a compass repeater and the kind of navigational and directional aids which were also found inside the bridge. This meant the captain could 'drive' the ship from either bridge wing during replenishments, anchorings, and other ship evolutions. Extending aft from the wings, on the same level, was the Gunnery Direction Platform (GDP), which housed 20mm Oerlikon machine guns, fifteen inch Aldis signal lamps and the 'LAS' sights used to aid local and visual control of the ship's weapons when they weren't being radar controlled. All the ships proceeded to the exercise areas to carry out High Seas 'Sea Dart' Missile Firings, and to participate in other anti-submarine exercises. We were to return to Portsmouth on 6th April, having spent five months away from home.

We were the last destroyer in the exercise to fire. I was in the operations room manning the 966 long range air picture radar. "Target 2610 bearing two niner zero," called the Anti-War Warfare Officer (AAWO), "take 2610 with Sea Dart." The target indication operator rolled his tracker ball strobe over the top of the target and injected the search to the 909 target indication radar. The 909 searched and locked onto the target. We acquired the target at maximum range and a flashing dotted line extended out to the target, indicating to those watching the radar that it had been acquired. We tracked it right across the radar scope, the flashing dotted line moving with the target. The AAWO informed the air warfare teams both onboard and on the other ships that we had acquired the target 'Birds affirm 2610'. I listened to air team count down the target's range and initiate the missile firing sequence,

"Check safety Sea Dart, bearing two niner zero."

"Clear visual," said the Missile Gun Director (Visual) on the gunnery direction platform.

"Clear blind," said the Missile Gun Director (Blind) in the operations room.

"Launcher correct," said the officer of the watch on the bridge, leaving only Captain Salt to give his approval.

"Command approved," he called from his chair in the centre of the operations room.

The AAWO then took back the engagement. "Sea Dart…." He paused. "Engage."

There was a tangible sense of excitement as the Sea Dart Controller flicked the switch. Within micro-seconds, there was a huge roar and a palpable thud as the ship was forced downwards in response to the missile's launching.

The solid fuelled rocket booster ignited and propelled the missile away from the ship at astonishing speed, 2.5 times the speed of sound. The kerosene fuelled Odin ramjet motor then kicked in and fuelled the missile all the way to the target. "Birds away 2610," called the AAWO across the radio circuit to the other ships. With each sweep of the slow-moving 966 radar, the missile appeared to jump across the sky. As long as the 909 fire control radars remained locked-on to the target, it couldn't escape.

I watched with increasing excitement as the range of the missile opened from the ship and closed on the target blowing it to bits. On my radar screen the target disintegrated into thousands of pieces and plunged into the sea.

"Target splashed," called the AAWO. A great cheer went up around the operations room crew. We had just carried out the longest Sea Dart missile engagement in history, and the pride amongst the men in that room, at that moment, was something you could reach out and touch.

Then, oddly, the message came from Admiral Woodward aboard *Antrim*. "Bravo Zulu[1] *Sheffield*, good shooting but do not fire again." Needless to say, given the success of the operation, we all wondered why. Later, when we went off watch, I went up to look at the Sea Dart launcher. It was black, scorched, and all the paint had been burnt away – clearly it was a formidable weapon.

For the exercise, the Operations department had gone into defence watches, six hours on, six hours off. On the morning of Friday April 2nd I came on watch at 2am. Shortly after that, the CASEX (anti-submarine exercise) we were conducting with other ships and submarines was cancelled and all ships set course south-west (210 degrees) at twenty eight knots.

---

[1] Bravo Zulu or BZ for short means "excellent performance." Origins disputed.

Immediately after 'call the hands' at 06:45, Captain Salt came onto the main broadcast. He told the ship's company we would not be going home.

Earlier that morning, we were told, an Argentine invasion force had arrived off the Falklands, and had invaded and occupied the islands. Half the ships of the *Springtrain* force were deploying to the South Atlantic as part of an advance Task Force. They would await the arrival of the carrier battle group which had received orders to assemble that day, and sail by the following Monday (three days away). *Sheffield* and *Active* were ordered to pair off, with the former de-storing the latter of as much ammunition and provisions as possible.

In addition to warships being re-fuelled and re-stored at sea by tankers and stores ships, they also frequently carry out Replenishments-at-Sea (RAS) with each other to transfer stores and personnel. We closed *Active* to carry out a RAS. Given the nature and volume of the stores to be transferred, we would need to use the thickest and strongest rope available called a 'heavy jackstay', which would support the weight of all the ammunition to be transferred across. The ships closed to within sixty feet of each other and whistle blasts were sounded to signify the first lines were about to be fired over. These were fired from a standard 7.62mm Self Loading Rifle (SLR), the standard-issue British military weapon of the day. A device called a 'RAS Dildo' (so called because of its uncanny resemblance to a marital aid) was slotted over the muzzle of the rifle with a long thin line attached. It was fired across to the receiving ship, whose RAS team then heaved it in, and the larger thicker lines were attached and pulled across until both ships were joined by the jackstay on which all stores would be passed, a distance line to indicate how close the ships were and a communications line for the two captains to speak to each other.

The 4.5 inch shells for the MK VIII gun were brought across by the pallet load. Each one weighed 105lbs and was humped down the upper deck to the gun hoist on sailors' shoulders. At the aft end of the ship, the helicopter was returning all empty pallets and containers by Vertical Replenishment (Vertrep).

We also rendezvoused with *Blue Rover* which had been our tanker for the gulf patrol, and topped up with fuel, the process being very similar to that of a heavy jackstay, with the exception of a fuel hose being attached. As the tanker pulled away from us she was playing one of my favourite songs, the Julie Covington hit, *Don't Cry For Me Argentina*. No one on either of the ships could have known the irony.

I was totally confused by what was going on. We'd been away, we'd done our time, we were due home. I wanted to get down the pub with all my mates wearing my 'been there, done that' t-shirts from all the tropical paradises we'd just been to. I doubted most of them would have even heard of Mauritius or Diego Garcia. Most of them had never left Norfolk! I wanted to regale them with tales from the south seas of monstrous piss-ups, bar scraps with the yanks, lurid encounters with dusky maidens (irrespective of the inaccuracy of the latter).

My next thought was, 'what a pisser. My sister comes all the way back from working in Portugal to welcome me home, and this happens.' Then my thoughts switched to Mum and Dad, not knowing what the papers and TV would be saying at home. When the Navy rang to tell them not to come to Portsmouth to meet the ship, what would they actually say to them? Also, I was about to miss being on leave for my eighteenth birthday and I got a serious cob on over that. Not for one moment did I think about fighting, shooting, killing, ships sinking or any of the other things that were to follow in the next 74 days. Instead I groused to my messmates in 2F that this was messing up everything I'd planned for my first post-deployment social activities. They were not sympathetic. "That's life in a blue suit, Jack!"

The advanced Task Group of *Antrim, Sheffield, Coventry, Glasgow, Brilliant, Broadsword, Yarmouth, Plymouth, Arrow* and accompanying RFAs transited between the Canary Islands at night and in total radio silence. Our ship's electricians had rigged up strings of fake light bulbs around the ship, giving anyone having a casual glance at the sea, the impression of us being just another floating gin palace enjoying the ambient spring evening, albeit at twenty eight knots. We assumed the fake identity of the m.v. *Aleutian Developer*, and should we be called on VHF Channel 16, had concocted the story that we were a Liberian registered freighter, full of agricultural machinery and bound for Luanda, Angola. We even took a false callsign of GJQM.

The Navigating Officer, Lieutenant Adrian Nance from Hull, had instructed the bridge radio operator RO Deacon to take his time answering any calls, and not to be too efficient. He wanted to portray the exact opposite of what you might expect from the bridge of a warship. The pace of life onboard picked up significantly. I was busy keeping watches on the bridge, while the captain was holding a lot more meetings with his warfare officers. The signal traffic increased, especially the confidential and secret messages, and for me, it felt exciting. Maybe we would gain some actual operational experience, a step-up from protecting tankers in the Gulf, a job that we had just done for five months. That it might turn into full-blown hostilities never entered my head. I was too young, too naïve to acknowledge the seriousness of what was going on.

Russian spy ships (AGIs) were already tailing our advance task group as we proceeded south west at high speed, and were no doubt reporting our position back to the Soviet Union and onto the Argentinians. After clearing the Canaries we came across a large navigation buoy bobbing around and seemingly marking nothing. After checking charts and manuals and establishing that it had probably broken free from its mooring it was engaged with gunfire and sunk.

CHAPTER 3

Ascension Island

Tuesday 6ᵗʰ April 1982

The day we should have been arriving back in Portsmouth, I was on the bridge as we came into anchor at Ascension Island. The bridge had an array of consoles and the ship's 'wheel' was on the port for'ard console. The 'wheel' was no longer the two man device of the days of sail but a small two-gripped handle, similar to that of an aircraft's controls. At the back of the bridge was the chart table and radar for use by the officer of the watch. It was very humid, so the bridge windows were wound open by their huge and highly polished brass handles. Captain Salt was on the bridge wing as the Navigator counted down to the anchorage point. "Three cables, two cables, one cable, now please sir," the Navigator called. "Let go," said Captain Salt calmly. The Yeoman of Signals dropped his flag, and a member of the cable party on the fo'c'sle swung the sledge hammer and made contact with the retaining clasp holding the anchor, which splashed and ran out into the crystal clear ocean.

To the uninitiated, the layout of a warship can be a confusing maze of compartments, hatches and passageways. Anything that runs from the bows to the stern (front to back) is considered running 'forward (for'ard) to aft'. Ships' compartments are lettered from for'ard to aft, 'A' being in the bows. Anything running across the ship is termed 'athwartships', starboard being right, and port left. These can be sub-divided and numbered odds to starboard and evens to port. No wonder people get confused! There are no maps like there are on the London Underground, and newcomers learn the location of anywhere and everywhere by unique 'location marking'. *Sheffield* had a single level upper deck which could be walked all the way around. All warship decks are numbered, '1' being the upper deck, '2' the next, and so on. Each section is sealed off from the next by steel watertight doors which can be closed in the event of fire and/or flooding. Hatches between decks are the same, so entire compartments and whole sections of the ship can be sealed off. All these hatches are marked with an 'X', 'Y' or 'Z' which signifies their place in the ship's watertight integrity and the operating conditions in which they were to be open or closed.

When a ship is in a normal peacetime cruising state, it is said to be in 'State 3, Condition X-ray'. The 'state' refers to the readiness of the ships company for action, state 3 being normal cruising watches. The 'condition' refers to the ship itself meaning that only those openings at, or below the waterline, or the very front or back of the ship (likely collision points) remain closed, except when a man actually passes through them. 'State 2, Condition Yankee' means the ship has gone to 'defence watches' of six hours on/off with half the ship's company closed up at their defence stations in the operations room, damage control HQ, or fire and repair party posts. The next level of hatches marked 'Y' are now closed. The final state, 'State 1, Condition Zulu' signifies a ship going into Action Stations. Every man aboard is closed up at his action station and every hatch and door in the ship is battened down with all eight clips.

Because of the heat, the ships company changed back into tropical uniforms of cotton short sleeved shirts and shorts. The day was spent at anchor, re-painting parts of the ship. Anything that was white was painted grey. The entire Seaman department was turned too, an unusual occurrence as there is always at least one watch of four, off duty. I was over the side on a plank stage, painting out the pennant numbers so the ships could not be recognised. The water below us was crystal clear and warm, so at least it wouldn't be so bad if I fell in, except maybe for the sharks. Working a plank stage was one of the Ships Husbandry tasks I had to complete in my Seamanship Task Book for promotion to Able Seaman, one more tick in the box for me. It is usual to wear overalls when painting, but the weather was sweltering, so I decided against it, and by the time we'd finished, my legs and working boots were covered in grey paint. There had been no finesse in this, just a paint tray, a big wide roller and lots of 'Battleship Grey' Dulux topcoat. I had to wash my legs in turpentine.

The only Type 42 that could be recognised from the others was *Sheffield*. On the top of either side of her funnel were 'Mickey Mouse ears.' These were added after she was built, to deflect the smoke from the engines away from trailing directly aft into the mainmast and to reduce her infra-red signature. A wide black stripe was painted over the top of the funnel and down the ship's side. This was to assist any pilots in identifying the British Type 42s from the identical Argentine Type 42s ARA *Santisima Trinidad* and ARA *Hercules*. Both the Argentine ships had been in Portsmouth just before we sailed, they had been training their operations room crews in the warfare training models in HMS *Dryad*, the training base I had joined *Sheffield* from. They too had 'Mickey Mouse ears' on the funnel, and the irony was not lost on me this time.

I looked over to where *Coventry* and *Glasgow* were anchored. They now looked identical without their pennant numbers. The black stripe over the top looked completely bizarre. Just as I was pondering the effect of this, the men who had been painting our own stripe came down from the top of the funnel. "There, that'll give the fuckers something to aim at now," they laughed. "Is it beer o'clock yet?" I was gagging for a beer but there's no way I'd be allowed one whilst under the age of eighteen. I wandered around the upper deck. All the bollards and fairleads used for berthing the ship, which were usually immaculately white, were now the same grey as the rest of the superstructure and ship's side. I was sure in a couple more weeks we'd be back in Portsmouth cursing the day all this re-painting was done, only to have to change it back again, and no doubt it would be the juniors (me) getting volunteered for it again.

Anchored in the warm waters, the mullet swarmed around the discharge overboard pipes, eating all the effluent as it was pumped overboard. Some of the ships company were fishing for them with great ease. Why would you want to eat a fish whose main diet was your own turds? That night I settled for the standard naval diet of sausage and chips. The junior rates servery was midships in the port passageways. We lined up with a steel tray with various compartments, (not unlike prison) and ate in the junior rates dining hall which was the whole width of the ship bar the passageways that ran around 2 deck. The JRDH was over the after engine room so the constant hum of machinery accompanied our meals. The ship was fitted with two Rolls Royce Olympus Gas Turbines (Concorde engines) which could drive her in excess of thirty knots, and two smaller Tynes for cruising speed.

At lunchtime the dining hall was still full of shields, plaques and the two trophies for Sea Dart and the 4.5 inch gun firings. By the time the evening meal was served, all the cabinets were empty and the glass taped up. I finished my meal and walked back for'ard to 2F mess. All along the passageways, the damage control teams were testing all the fire hydrants and breathing apparatus. I went to the heads (toilets) at the for'ard end of the ship. The damage control lockers were uncovered and all the gear was being checked and tested. It was still warm when I went back on the upper deck. I don't know whether more ships had arrived at anchor whilst I'd been below decks, or they were already there and I hadn't previously noticed. Helicopters buzzed around overhead like angry wasps. I committed the cardinal sin of leaning on the ship's guard rails whilst pondering all I'd seen during the day. First aid equipment, fire fighting, damage control, all the things that are brought to immediate readiness when preparing a warship for battle. Were we really preparing for battle?

"Get off the fucking guard rails you wanker," screamed Petty Officer Turnell as he marched stiffly down from the fo'c'sle. I quickly slipped away. As I climbed up to the boat deck, two of the communications ratings had huge white ensigns laid out on the deck. "What are they?" I asked. "Battle ensigns," came the response. "What are they used for?" I asked in all sincerity. "For battle of course," one of the ratings said. "We hoist them either side of the mainmast when we go into action. That way, if the ensign on the foremast (the usual place it flew at sea) is blown away or the mast is damaged, we can still be identified."

I looked up at the foremast. Blown away? I thought that only happened in the days of Nelson when the cannon fire brought the masts and sails crashing down to disable the ship. We couldn't be preparing for that – could we?

I climbed up onto the gunnery direction platform and stared out at Ascension. Set midway between Brazil and Africa, it looked like a lump of hot barren rock covered in black volcanic sand. It is in fact an extinct and remote volcano eight degrees south of the equator. We were anchored on the western side which is nothing but heaps of volcanic ash. The eastern side is by all accounts quite green and tropical, although I never saw it. On the side we were on were more satellite dishes than you'd find on the average council estate. The 'beaches' consisted of black volcanic sand, although they had some impressive surf. Although a British-owned island and part of the South Atlantic Remote Territories group, (the remainder being the Falkland Islands themselves, South Georgia, South Thule, South Sandwich Isles, Tristan da Cunha and St Helena), it was one of the last outposts of the now almost extinct British Empire. The place was leased to the US military as a satellite tracking base. The name of the little airfield was *Wideawake* (although with a runway 10,000 feet long, I'm not sure 'little' is entirely accurate), and never was an airfield more appropriately named. In those hectic days it had more arrivals and departures than the busiest airport in the world, London–Heathrow. It looked as if the entire RAF Victor tanker and Vulcan bomber fleet was arriving, together with Phantoms. The whole of the RAF must have been mobilised to get this operation underway. I couldn't understand why the Vulcan bombers were there. Even with my relatively uninformed knowledge I knew the islands were 5,000 miles away and there wasn't a bomber around that could fly that far without multiple air-to-air refuellings. We simply didn't have the aircraft or the logistics to get a bomber there and back. I just thought it was the crabs not wanting to miss out on the action, or more likely wanting to sit in their deck chairs drinking Pimms, claiming to be part of the Task Force that recovered the Falkland Islands. There were lots of them stationed around our villages on the Broads. Many of the RAF drank in the pub I lived in from 1975 – 80, typical Brylcreem and moustache boys. I'd always found them rather "tally ho chaps, look after Nigger[1] for me."

Proceed South with All Despatch

I had attended only one briefing so far and knew that the Falklands were eight thousand miles from the UK. I still hadn't found out their significance and why the Argentinians had even invaded in the first place. We were making preparations to fight a war and I had no idea as to why it had actually started. I imagined that many other teenagers had felt that way over the last seventy years.

That afternoon I was summoned to the Regulating Office. When I arrived there were two other of the ships company both under eighteen. We were confronted with a stern-faced Master-At-Arms, who told us very matter-of-factly, "go and pack your kit. All the seventeen year olds are getting off until their birthdays. You'll stay here until you turn eighteen, then join another ship that will bring you down, if it's not all over by then and you miss it all."

I waited for the MAA to break into a smile to indicate the 'bite' that he was having us on. It didn't come.

"But Master," I wailed, "you can't be serious. You can't kick us off here, we're needed. I'm part of the port watch air team, and it's not fair."

---

[1] The black Labrador owned by Wing Cdr Guy Gibson who led the infamous Dambusters raid in 1943.

The MAA had already turned back to his desk. "Come back here with your kit when you're packed, you won't need it all."

I was gutted and almost wanted to cry with frustration. I got back to 2F mess and sat looking dejectedly at the others securing the mess for action, and laughing about giving a good kicking to a bunch of dagoes and their banana republic. Two of them chorused the words from 'Banana Republic' which had been a hit for The Boomtown Rats in 1980.

"What's up sprog?" one of the lads asked.

"We've got to get off, here at Ascension, me and the other under eighteens. There's three of us."

The only response was, "Well if you can't take a joke, you shouldn't have joined up Jack." They all laughed at my misfortune – typical military sense of humour.

There was a knock at the door; it was one of the other juniors. "Relax Joe," he said. "The Joss was having us on a bite."

"Bastard," I swore, under my breath. I went back to the Regulating Office to find the Jossman and his side-kick Leading Regulator Scouse Roberts red faced and pissing themselves laughing at the distress they'd caused me and the other juniors.

When I got back to 2F mess; it had changed radically and was now totally barren. Previously each of the nine bunks had a curtain which could be drawn across for a thinly veiled attempt at privacy and a bit of darkness. There had been posters of tropical destinations and pictures of pin-up girls. 2F mess was the Emergency Operating Theatre and doubled as the ship's secondary first aid point if the sick bay was damaged or full of casualties. The cupboards were open as the ship's two medics and some of the cooks and stewards who provided first aid teams at action stations carried out inventories of all the medical supplies. "Field dressings, morphine, bandages, splints," the ship's doc counted off. I suddenly found myself feeling nervous. That equipment would be required for wounded people. For that to happen it would mean we were going to be hit by something – rockets, bombs, gunfire. I hadn't planned for this. There were only nine of us in the mess, which was a bit of a change from the usual junior ratings messes of thirty or forty men that I'd been used to. Was it going to be any of these nine men laid on the floor with their crimson liquid life pumping out of them? Maybe I should take the Master-At-Arms at his word and start packing.

Then came something else. All the ship's company was ordered to make

18

a will if we didn't already have one. We were each allowed two postage stamps to send two letters home.

A will, my will? You only wrote those when you got really old, or really sick, not when you were still a teenager, not when you weren't even eighteen. First I didn't see the point; I had no intention of getting killed. Then I thought back to what I'd seen; field dressings, battle ensigns, morphine, fire fighting and damage control gear, bandages. Shit, maybe this could be really serious. I sat down with the will form and picked up my pen, my hand shaking uncontrollably. For the first time I really thought what it might be like if my time came. I looked around the mess, the spotlessly clean, pristine, orderly mess. Would it always look like this? It was the Emergency Operating Space to be used if the Sick Bay was knocked out, the secondary casualty station. Strangely, any emotion I felt at the thought of getting killed was only for those I left behind. I finally managed to hold the pen steady. I wrote one letter to Mum, Dad and Toni, which basically said *Don't fret, it should all be OK, and we'll be home in a couple more weeks.* I didn't know whether I believed it or not, I wasn't well enough informed to know any more. I also wrote to Aunty Joan, Mum's best friend – *If I don't come home, please give the enclosed letter to Mum and Dad.* The enclosed letter started like many of the 'You're reading this because I'm dead...' letters written by men en route to conflict. It told them not to be sad but proud that I died fighting for a country I was proud of and believed in. I meant it. I tried not to think about Aunty Joan handing it over. We were a very close family, they would be devastated. Mum and Dad had been so proud when I joined up, so proud when they attended my passing out parade after training. The thought of their potential suffering really upset me. I didn't want anyone else to see it.

It was then the BBC World Service reported that the commander of the Argentine military junta, General Leopoldo Galtieri had said, "*A country run by two women* (Her Majesty The Queen, and Margaret Thatcher) *will never send their sons so far to fight and die. That gringo woman* (Thatcher), *she will never fight.*" He wouldn't be the first, nor the last, to underestimate the Brits. Galtieri himself was struggling to hold on to power. Large numbers of the population had lost their fear of the brutal regime which had a habit of murdering those of its citizens who proved a nuisance in their anti-government protests. The Argentinian economy was faltering, inflation was out of control, the government needed a distraction to galvanise the nation and regain the people's respect. The obvious solution was to retake the Falkland Islands, a source of international dispute over sovereignty since the 18th century. Galtieri and his cronies appeared on the balcony of the presidential palace, Evita style, to the jubilant masses gathered below, to proclaim, "…we will never again lose the Malvinas". This would prove to be a spectacularly naïve misjudgement on his part.

Captain Salt went over to *Glamorgan* with the captains of all the other ships present. Admiral Woodward was holding a council of war with his battle commanders. I was in the operations room and heard two of the warfare officers talking. "The Captain has received the 'rules of engagement' and will be briefing us shortly." Rules of engagement are the guidelines under which you can open fire, whether defensively or offensively. At that moment, I felt I would have liked to have known what they were, how far south we would have to go before we could fire at something, or what the Argentinians had to do to provoke us into it. I never did find out. I didn't need to know.

The fleet padre did the rounds of the ships, holding an Easter service. I heard congregation numbers were significantly higher than he was used to. I didn't go, for a couple of reasons; I still didn't really believe it was going to come to battle, and I'd never been remotely religious so thought it was a bit late to start cashing in favours. Birds fly south for the winter, but we were sailing. The task group weighed anchor and we proceeded south west at high speed. Every now and again, a Russian Bear long-range maritime patrol aircraft would stalk the group, no doubt reporting back our position. I wondered what preparations the Argentinians were making for combat. Did they think we'd sail all the way down there, or turn back half way? Did they really believe that we were prepared to fight? I didn't know whether we actually were or not, and I didn't even know whether the Falklands were worth fighting for. Were their ships rigging for action, stripping their messdecks, checking their damage control and first aid gear? Were there fresh faced young lads wondering about what was to come in the next few weeks, or were they too full of bravado at giving the gringos a good kicking if they tried to get 'their' islands back?

The day after we sailed from Ascension, Admiral Woodward came across to the ship to address the ship's company, as he did with all the ships in the group. He didn't mince his words. He told us quite clearly that we may well be facing genuine hostile action and not only should the ship be prepared and ready in all respects for war, but we too, should be mentally ready for the things that battle brings – whatever they were (apart from the trouser crapping and mind numbing terror I imagined). He actually said there was a possibility that ships could be hit, and take casualties and that some of those present might be killed in action. I swallowed nervously. Looking around, there suddenly seemed to be an awful lot of very young people present. If they were anxious, they hid it well. The Admiral also reminded us that we were all volunteers and happy enough to accept the Queen's shilling and now was the time Her Majesty needed re-paying and there would be no one who could escape it. Captain Salt, at just 5ft 5ins, stood next to the Admiral, who towered over him. But the captain was a charismatic man with a personality and leadership style which made him seem seven feet tall. He commanded enormous respect from the ships company. The final part of the speech (and I can't remember who said it) reminded us that whatever we faced in the coming weeks, we should remember that first and foremost we were sailors in the Royal Navy. It was expected that when the time came to acquit ourselves in battle, we should do so in the finest traditions of the service and of the many generations of sailors who have gone before us – whatever the personal consequences for us, might be.

In the Royal Navy there are three priorities for men aboard a ship in action: 1) ship; 2) self; 3) shipmates; in that rigid and inflexible order. The ship comes first. She is the platform upon which the fight, and the lives of the other men, depend. Self comes second – by a very long way.

In Naval training I had learned of many heroic men who, even when their ships were almost battered into submission, with fires raging, few weapons working, many of the ship's company dead and dying at their guns, had once again turned to face the enemy and fought on, in the absolute certainty that it would be their final action and they would soon be sunk and killed. In late 1939 Admiral Henry Harwood had engaged the German battleship *Admiral Graf Spee* in the South Atlantic, with three smaller British ships, HMS *Ajax* (in which he flew his flag), *Exeter* and *Achilles*. The British ships had used the Falkland Islands as a refuelling and re-supply base. From there they had set sail to chase *Graf Spee* all the way to Montevideo, where she was eventually scuttled. The casualty figures aboard the British ships were high, but they had fought on against a far bigger, more powerful enemy whose guns had a greater range and could engage them long before they got within range for their own guns to return. They had sailed on into a barrage of fire, taking hits and casualties, yet unable to fire back because their shells would have fallen far short, into the sea. Were we about to see a re-enactment of that? *Sheffield* sailing towards the far bigger, more powerful, and far better armed Argentinian cruiser, *General Belgrano*?

CHAPTER 4

Operation Paraquat – The Re-taking of South Georgia

After we were dismissed, I thought about Captain Salt leading the ship into action. Unlike the RAF, who wave the pilots off then retire to the mess for a beer and await their return (or not), or Army commanders, who give orders from the rear (as is tactically sensible), when a naval captain takes his ship into battle, he has as much chance of being killed as any and every other man aboard. An exploding bomb or missile does not recognise rank, or discriminate in its victims. Its sole purpose is to kill as many men aboard that ship as possible, to either entirely destroy and sink the ship, or to render it inoperable through casualties and damage. One of the favourite songs of sailors ashore is the Roger Whittaker hit, 'The Last Farewell.' The lines to the second and third verses begin:

"I heard that there's a wicked war a-raging, and the taste of war I know so very well,

Even now I see the foreign flags a-raising, their guns a-fire as we sail into hell,"

"Though death and darkness gather all around me, and my ship be torn apart upon the sea."

Of all the men I'd sung those songs with, there wasn't a man amongst them who had actually ever seen action. There were very few WWII blokes left in the Navy, although there were a few from the Korean War. In a couple of month's time, would I be back in the City Arms in Portsmouth (our local) singing it for real and telling my own war stories? Or would it all go horribly wrong and descend into the darkness, chaos and confusion that war actually is and the song so beautifully portrays?

I was desperate to find out what was so special about these islands that no one had heard of. Why did they want them so badly that they would invade? Why would we dispatch the biggest naval armada since 1944? There seemed to be no sense in any of it.

The paint locker in the very forward part of the ship was to be used as a storage space for all the extra bags of gizzits[3] that had been acquired in the last five month trip. All the paint was taken down to the flight deck and quarterdeck and ditched into the wake, all at twenty eight knots. To ensure the tins sank, we punctured them. It was the most multi-coloured wake I'd ever seen.

More and more of the ship was secured for action. If it wasn't bolted down or an integral part of the ship's fixtures and fittings, it went west. The ships of the advanced group gathered together for a massive RAS with *Fort Austin* and the tankers. We embarked our maximum capacity of Sea Dart missiles and 4.5 inch shells for the Mk VIII gun. As the latitudes grew greater, the weather grew worse. Many albatrosses were following us now, riding the air currents without ever having to flap their wings. The albatross is a magical bird, it has the largest of the sea birds' wingspans – up to 6 feet for the wandering albatross. For some reason they made me feel safe, secure, that everything would be OK, as if they were watching over us. I just hope nobody killed one, as in Samuel Taylor Coleridge's 'Rime of the Ancient Mariner'.

Every day we tuned into the BBC World Service and listened to the diplomatic trans-Atlantic shuffle going on between Britain, Argentina and the Americans who were trying to mediate the situation. Argentina was trying to drum up support from within South America. The UN had passed a resolution demanding their immediate withdrawal and cessation of aggression. We heard on the BBC World Service (our major source of information) that Argentina had rejected the UN proposal(s) and was not willing to withdraw troops or negotiate. It didn't sound as if a peaceful settlement was likely, but neither did I think it would come to war. We hadn't been to war for decades. Sure the squaddies went to Northern Ireland (and lots got killed) but this was the Navy! All we did was jolly around the world – just like the pictures in the careers office window.

The ship's operations room was the electronic nerve centre of the ship. Unlike the old World War II ships which were always fought from the bridge, modern warships are fought from the operations room. *Sheffield* was

---

[3] Naval slang for 'presents'.

fitted with a long-range air warning radar on the bridge roof, which looked like a large bedstead. It rotated slowly, detecting aircraft out to a range of two hundred and fifty six miles. On the foremast was a smaller navigational radar, and aft, atop the mainmast, was the main navigation and target indication radar. The operations room was in perpetual darkness with only the dull orange glow of the radar screens to illuminate the operator's faces. The solid line of the returning electronic pulse on radar screens rotated clockwise, illuminating contacts as it painted across them, but unlike the Hollywood movies, it did not give off a 'ping' as it detected the contact.

When an unidentified contact is detected on radar, it is allocated an electronic identity and track number such as 'Unknown Aircraft (UA) 2345'. The contact is then interrogated by an electronic pulse called 'Identification Friend or Foe' (IFF). In a combat situation such as the Falklands, all friendly ships and aircraft would be transmitting this permanently to identify themselves as friendly forces.

If there is no friendly emission, and there are no known friendly aircraft in the area or on that bearing, then the aircraft will be considered potentially hostile. If the aircraft maintains an attack profile towards the ship, then the ship will take defensive measures. All of the defensive and offensive measures in the air warfare theatre are controlled by the Anti-Air Warfare Officer (AAWO) who is responsible to the command.

Every warship has a passive electronic sensor (UAA1) which detects radar emissions. If an attacking aircraft is transmitting on radar, the UAA1 will detect this and the radar will paint on a screen. The operator rolls a tracker ball (similar to a modern PC 'mouse') over the radar image and analyses it. Every radar has properties as individual as DNA. By analysing its parameters, such as pulse repetition frequency, aerial rotation speed, band-width and transmission frequency it is possible to identify the radar as belonging to a ship, aircraft, or missile, together with the nation of origin, thereby defining it as friendly or hostile. When a ship is illuminated by radar, it is called a 'racket'. If a hostile racket correlates with an unidentified aircraft, it can be confirmed that the aircraft is adopting an attack profile.

The first line of defence is always friendly air units such as Sea Harriers. However, if they are not on station, or are too far away, the Task Force relies on mutual self defence. In the event of Argentine Super Etendards or their search and attack radars codenamed 'Handbrake' being detected, all ships were to go to action stations and launch 'chaff' from 3 inch rocket launchers. This is similar to 'window' which was used in WWII, and consists of blooms of metal strips which form clouds intended to fool a missile's homing radar and seduce the missile away from its actual target – the warship. Each ship had two launchers consisting of eight criss-crossed barrels launching the chaff in different directions so they would 'bloom' in a comprehensively defensive pattern around the ship.

In addition to the defensive chaff, the ship would attempt to shoot down the attacking aircraft. This was, in practice, extremely difficult for a Type 42 destroyer to do. The main armament of the T42 is the high altitude, long range Sea Dart anti aircraft missile. These missiles were designed for combating Russian bombers of cold war era, not a sea skimming missile, travelling at the speed of sound, six feet above the sea. The Sea Dart missile is guided by a 909 radar positioned for'ard on the bridge roof and aft on the hangar roof on a T42. An able seaman in the operations room indicates the target to the guidance radar by injecting the target's track number to the weapons computer. The 909 will 'search' and then 'acquire' the target. Once the target is acquired, the missile is fired and guided towards the target. However, the 909 was not designed to track and acquire targets at sea level, and when this was attempted it would momentarily 'lock-on' to a wave top and then reset and so on and so on.

The T42's are also armed with a 4.5 inch Vickers Mk VIII gun. This was designed for shore bombardment and anti-surface roles, although it could also be used for anti-aircraft purposes. However, the chances of hitting a high-speed, low level target were virtually nil. Only the brand new, almost prototype Type 22 frigates *Broadsword* and *Brilliant*, which were fitted with the point defence weapon Sea Wolf, had any hope of hitting a sea skimming missile.

Admiral Woodward flying his flag in *Glamorgan* turned the ship northwards to rendezvous with *Hermes* and move his flag and staff to her. He detached *Sheffield, Coventry, Glasgow, Brilliant, Arrow* and RFA *Appleleaf* and ordered the captains to 'proceed south with all despatch'. More stirring stuff – a real high speed steam into battle! If only I'd known.

Late April

The UK government imposed a two hundred mile 'Total Exclusion Zone' around the Falkland Islands on 12th April. They warned that any

Argentine ship found within that TEZ would be attacked. Although they never stated it, the inference was that nuclear powered hunter-killer submarines were already on station.

The Task Group changed course and we headed due south to the Falkland Islands dependency of South Georgia. All ships were in radar and radio silence now and lookout was being kept on the bridge wings. I was on the starboard side. The weather was atrocious and freezing. The waves were enormous, and even in full foul weather gear, I was soaked in minutes. As the ship struggled up the side of the mountainous seas I could feel gravity forcing me against the deck. Then we would pivot over the crest of the wave and hurtle headlong down into the wave trough. As the bows nose-dived into the trough of the wave, the ships in company could see our propellers come clear of the water. I could see theirs as they too ploughed on into the teeth of the stormy seas. The ship would shake and shudder, creaking and groaning under the force of the waves and the weight of thousands of tons of sea water. With two enormous five-bladed propellers driven by Rolls Royce engines pushing us on, the ship's bows struggled up, bursting out from under the sea with white foam cascading over the fo'c'sle and down the ship's waists. Frequently as we ploughed downwards, the water would envelope me, finding a way into every zip and opening. I was hanging on for dear life, sodden wet through. Every time there was a slight respite I would scan the seas with my binoculars only to see nothing but angry foaming torrents. There was no way a submarine could ever surface in this. I wondered if the lookout on the port bridge wing was fairing any better. I didn't think it was possible that we could conduct a naval battle in this weather. I glanced at my watch – we were doing an hour on the bridge wing before going below; I still had 50 minutes to go. From the corner of my eye I saw some movement and looked at the bridge window. One of the bridge staff was beckoning me over – maybe they had a coffee for me. The watertight door opened slightly and the officer of the watch asked me whether I'd seen anything. A blast of warm air and the smell of hot chocolate hit me in the face – it was ecstasy. I closed my eyes to savour the moment. "Lawton, Lawton – have you seen anything?" I opened my eyes; the door was about one inch ajar. "No sir, I haven't seen anything." The bridge door slammed shut and a monumental wave broke over me. I've never been so cold, wet and miserable in my life. We were heading still further into the most inhospitable waters there are, and not only that, but at the worst time of the year, in the certain knowledge that both the state of the seas and the weather were likely to deteriorate even further. I was thoroughly pissed off and longed to be back in the cosy warmth of my mum and dad's Broadland cottage. The nearest the Task Force came to finding a submarine was any number of whales, which to a sonar, (and the operator) look remarkably like a submarine. Numerous whales were 'prosecuted to destruction'. I didn't think King Neptune would be very impressed.

The ships *Plymouth, Brilliant, Antrim, Endurance* and RFA *Tidespring*, detached ahead for the assault on South Georgia, leaving our Captain, Sam Salt in charge of the advance battle group. I couldn't believe what was happening; we were attacking a submarine with real depth charges and rockets. The Marines, SBS and SAS were ashore engaged in a battle. My pulse quickened and my mouth became dry. Surely now we'd come this far, the Argies would realise that we meant business and the might of the Royal Navy was about to be upon them. No one fucked with us – we were British! We had now proved that we were willing to fight. We had called their bluff. Surely it was time for them to pack up, go home and give us our islands back – wasn't it?

I listened to briefings coming back from the initial assault, then the crashing of helicopters onto frozen glaciers, and the possible loss of half the SAS force.

At first it appeared that Operation Paraquat, the first phase of the recovery of the Falklands and their dependencies, was going to be a disaster. Thanks to some magnificent flying by Lt Cdr Ian Stanley in *Antrim's* Wessex 'Humphrey', everyone was recovered safely and South Georgia was re-taken with no loss of British lives. The Argentine submarine *Santa Fe* was also attacked and captured. The two task groups rendezvoused and RFA *Tidespring* detached back to Ascension with Argentine PoWs for repatriation to their mainland. It was to be one of the last times that British warships would sail in line astern with their guns trained on enemy positions ashore and fire broadsides to bombard an enemy with 'salvos'.

The carrier battle group of *Invincible* and *Hermes* with their escorts of assorted destroyers, frigates, RFAs and 'Ships Taken Up From Trade' (STUFTs) caught up with us in the last few days of April. Every minute of every day was now spent conducting air defence exercises against the Sea

Harriers from *Hermes* and *Invincible*. The ship would go to action stations at all times of the day and night and we practiced, practiced and practiced again until we could be fully closed up and locked down in under five minutes.

The Royal Navy Task Force was now assembled and ready to commence the execution of Operation Corporate – the recovery and restoration of the Falkland Islands and their dependencies.

CHAPTER 5

It's War!

Saturday 1st May 1982

Morning watch, 02:00 – 08:00; I was manning the 966 long range Air Picture radar. At 07:00 two aircraft appeared from the north-east. They were identified by the Air Picture Supervisor as a Victor tanker, refuelling a Vulcan bomber. This was the first of the 'Blackbuck' missions en route to dropping twenty one 1,000lb bombs on Stanley airfield, to stop the Argentinians using it as a fighter base. I was amazed; I never thought it logistically possible.

The Vulcan bomber XM607 of 44 Squadron was piloted by Flight Lieutenant Martin Withers, who was flying into history by conducting the longest bombing mission in the history of aerial warfare. This was also the first Vulcan ever to drop a bomb in anger. This massive operation featured a round trip of 8,000 miles in an aircraft with a range of 2,500 miles and took just under 16 hours. It required 15 tankers to get the bomber to the islands and back, 17 separate air-to-air refuellings, of which seven were to the Vulcan itself, the remainder to the Victors refuelling each other. Flt Lt Withers received the Distinguished Flying Cross for this magnificent feat of airmanship, and the pilot of the Victor, Squadron Leader Bob Tuxford was awarded the Air Force Cross. Over the extraordinary 16 hour mission, the tanker had transferred enough fuel in and out of its tanks from the other tankers and to the bomber to power a fleet of 20 family saloon cars around the entire circumference of the globe.

We had placed computerised latitude and longitude reference points on the capital Stanley, and also on Goose Green, Fox Bay and Pebble Island. I tracked the Vulcan as it neared the islands and it passed through the reference point on Stanley, turned around and headed back out. We were expecting fighters to be launched to chase the offending bomber but they never appeared. We were listening for the appropriate codeword on a radio circuit, of the four possible codewords of 'Pitfall', 'Nitre', 'Superfuse' and 'Rhomboid' but the voice that came through repeated 'Superfuse, Superfuse, Superfuse' which I took to mean the raid had been a success.

Apparently, the general expectation was that if the runway hadn't been entirely destroyed, Argentinian fighters would launch and try to chase the bomber. If that happened, we were to engage them and shoot them down. The tension was electric, but no fighters appeared and we felt enormous disappointment.

The watch changed over at 08:00. We had an action messing breakfast and went to dawn action stations at about 09:00. Most of our radar air-tracking team were 3 inch rocket loading crews for our off-watch action station. We sat up in the hangar trying to get as much sleep as possible, but obviously it's not easy trying to sleep wearing action working dress, overalls, anti-flash, with a lifejacket, gasmask and survival suit hanging off you. I wondered how long it would take to settle into a wartime routine. Then I wondered if there was such a thing as routine in war?

In the hangar, a radio speaker circuit had been tuned into fighter control frequencies for us and flight maintainers to listen to the air battle. Suddenly a 'whoosh' caught us completely unawares as 3-inch chaff rockets were launched. We were halfway up the waist to re-load the launchers before the re-load klaxon had even sounded. The 4.5 inch gun also opened fire with chaff Charlie, as a Sea Harrier pilot had locked onto an enemy aircraft which had jettisoned an underwing fuel tank. As it fell away, the Harrier pilot thought he had launched an Exocet, and missile release was called. I don't mind admitting, it put the fear of God into me.

As I clambered up the ladder to the chaff rocket launching deck, the launchers were already rotating inboard for us to reload the barrels. I had been rehearsing all my drills and actions in my head over and over, determined not to screw up. The thing I feared most was suddenly finding I didn't have the courage to face up to a situation, and having to live forever afterwards with the shame.

Remembering the speech after we left Ascension about acquitting ourselves in the highest traditions of the Royal Navy, I was determined that no matter what we faced I would never do anything to bring shame or disrepute on myself, the ship or the Navy. Telling myself that made me feel a bit better, a bit braver, a bit more bullet-proof.

31

Heart pounding, I stood up on the re-loading platform and slid the rockets home one by one. At the bottom of the launch tube is an electrical plug which screws into the back of the rocket. The socket on the back of the chaff rocket was protected by a plastic cover that simply unscrewed. Two were stuck solid, probably with cold and salt. The other loader was desperately trying to unscrew them so we could fire another salvo, but our hands were freezing. "Smash the fucking thing off!" yelled the Leading Seaman Gunner in charge. One swift blow to each, and they were off. We secured the plugs into the sockets, and trained the launchers outboard, ready for the next attack.

The destroyer *Glamorgan* and the frigates *Arrow* and *Alacrity* went in to bombard Stanley airfield and targets around the town. They came under attack from Mirage IIIs and Daggers, dropping 500lb and 1,000lb bombs. All missed, but the ships sustained underwater damage from the bombs exploding in the sea. Able Seaman Ian Britnell took shrapnel during a strafing attack on *Arrow* and became the first casualty wounded in action in the war. The aircraft were engaged by the ships although none were hit, but they were caught by the Sea Harriers and shot down. I found myself wondering what it was like for the GDP crews on the three ships. Faced with real enemy aircraft for the first time, there couldn't have been anyone onboard who was a veteran of a real conflict. It would have been a baptism of fire for everyone. At least they had all faced it together, but they had still taken incoming fire, even though no one had been killed. The nervousness and dry mouth kicked in again.

Although I'd witnessed the Vulcan bomber dropping 21,000lbs of bombs and watched a Sea Harrier shoot down an enemy aircraft on radar, it still didn't truly register that we were at war. The thought struck me that here we were, trying to kill each other, purely because politicians couldn't sort things out. The whole thing seemed totally surreal.

I went back on watch in the operations room at midday. Two unidentified air contacts were picked up. The Sea Dart system acquired and tension mounted, but the contacts turned away just outside missile range. I was thoroughly disappointed. More hostile aircraft were detected and the Sea Harriers were vectored onto them to carry out an intercept.

That evening the Sea Kings searched for the *ARA San Luis*, the sister submarine to *Santa Fé* that we had sunk at South Georgia. Despite dropping numerous depth charges and torpedoes, no submarine kills were claimed.

In the early hours of the second day, the sub-hunting Sea Kings happened upon a patrol boat which opened fire on them. The vessel *Alferez Sobral* was apparently searching for the air crews shot down the previous day. Lynx helicopters from our sister ships, *Coventry* and *Glasgow* attacked her with Sea Skua missiles, but she escaped.

The day dawned with the usual dawn action stations and probing attacks by fighters and bombers from the Argentinian mainland. Captain Jorgé Colombo, the CO of the 2nd Escuadrilla Aeronaval de Caza y Ataque and Carlos Machatanz took off from Rio Grande to attack the Royal Navy Task Force with Exocet missiles. Neither aircraft could successfully complete the air-to-air refuelling required for the mission, so they returned to the Argentinian mainland to await their next opportunity.

The submarine HMS *Splendid* had been stalking the 16,000 ton Argentinian aircraft carrier ARA *Veinticinco de Mayo* (previously the RN carrier HMS *Venerable*) but had lost sight of her, depriving her captain, Commander Roger Lane-Nott, the opportunity of being the only British submarine CO ever to sink an enemy aircraft carrier.

That evening as the First Lt gave his evening 'sitrep' on action within the Task Force, the main point of the day was that the British nuclear submarine HMS *Conqueror,* sister ship of *Splendid,* had torpedoed and sunk the Argentinian heavy cruiser ARA *General Belgrano.* The 13,645 ton *Belgrano* was a well-armed cruiser with more firepower than any of our ships, and the Argentinian Navy's second largest ship after its aircraft carrier *Veinticinco de Mayo.* It was the largest warship sunk since 1945. She probably wouldn't have even known *Conqueror* was there.

To begin with we cheered; the Royal Navy had struck the first killer blow of the war. Our jubilation was short-lived however, as we shared the realisation that there were twelve hundred Argentinian sailors either dead, or freezing to death, in the South Atlantic. They may have been the enemy, but they were still fellow sailors, and every one of them was someone's son. If they weren't rescued quickly, in the temperatures at these latitudes, they would never survive the night. The potential human cost could be catastrophic – hundreds of households in Argentina would be getting the dreaded knock on the door.

I had thought the Argentinians must have been mad to think we wouldn't do something to show we meant business. I'd been convinced that they would see sense and withdraw, and give us our islands back. Two days of war had done little to cure me of my naivety, but the *Belgrano's* fate had a sobering effect.

Belgrano had previously been the USS *Phoenix* and had survived the attacks at Pearl Harbour. This was the first time since the end of WWII that a submarine had fired torpedoes in war, and the first time a nuclear-powered submarine had done so in anger. They had lived up to their lethally efficient name, 'hunter-killers.' The Argentinian Navy withdrew and did not put to sea for the rest of the war.

Those of us gathered in the dining hall looked at each other. None of us had thought it would go this far. Most imagined it would be a bit of a jolly and a bit more time for some 'bronzy bronzy[4]' at Ascension Island, before getting home a couple of weeks late. Now though, we realised that there was more to 'signing-up' than learning a profession and seeing the world. From here on, the guns did all the talking. *Fucking hell*, I remember thinking, *where's it going to stop*? It had been a bit of a squabble, some sabre rattling, and we'd bombed Stanley airfield to show them that we could. I had never imagined it would come to this.

So why had I joined up? The pictures in the careers office window showed sailors in white suits on wonderful beaches with girls in grass skirts, and it looked very tempting. There was little or no work where I lived; my dad had been to sea and he told me great stories. I didn't remember anything about dying in a burning ship thousands of miles away from home. I didn't join the Navy to kill people, and I certainly didn't join to get killed within six months of joining my first ship. What if it came to that? What if I found myself in that face to face situation? Could I do it? We'd been through training, good training – the best in fact. But had we been trained to kill people though?

I wondered what my mates at home were doing – probably going down the pub, or to the seafront. Whatever it was, it wouldn't have included contemplating their own mortality and wondering whether they were going to live through the next couple of months.

Monday 3rd May 1982

As usual, the Task Force went to action stations at dawn and the off-watch radar teams tried to get as much sleep as possible in the hangar. Predictably the Argentinian fighters were attempting daily incursions to try and penetrate the outer ring of the Task Force's defences. I had adjusted to

---

[4] Naval slang for sunbathing

this so although no less worrying it became easier to accept. Each raid was met by our Sea Harriers and they would engage in some dogfights, with the Sea Harriers keeping the upper hand. That evening during action messing on *Sheffield*, 'air raid warning red' was sounded and we all dropped our trays of stew where they were, and ran to our action stations. After the raid had been dispersed, we returned to the dining hall to find everything gone. The only trace was a notice in thick felt pen – *Your cups are in the sink, your scran is in the bin. Love L/S Bob Mullen. Killick i/c Port Watch E.I.P. (Exocet Impact Party)*

Prophetic.

Tuesday 4ᵗʰ May 1982

I came off watch at midday. The Carrier Battle Group was seventy miles south east of Stanley. Because of the Exocet threat, the frigates *Brilliant* and *Broadsword,* with their point defence Sea Wolf missiles, stayed in close to the carriers at the very centre of the protective screen. Close by and requiring equal protection were some of the RFAs. Without them, the warships would have no fuel, ammunition, or food. The second ring of defence was formed by *Glamorgan, Antrim* and the frigates. Then twenty miles out ahead of the main units, directly in the line of threat were the three Type 42 'picket' ships including *Sheffield* with their high altitude, long range Sea Darts.

Picket ship is a lonely and vulnerable place to be, but necessary for the survival of the carriers, and hence the whole of the Task Force. Frigates and destroyers are considered expendable, to ensure the survival of the high value units.

In the operations room of HMS *Invincible*, Able Seamen Mark Booth and David 'George' Forster, from my radar training class only six months earlier, were manning the 1022 long range air warning radar. This radar was of a technically superior quality to the older 965/966 fitted to the T42's. On Booth's display, two contacts appeared and he reported them through to the Air Picture Supervisor, who in turn reported them to Lt Cdr Robinson, the Anti-Air Warfare Officer. Robinson dismissed them as 'spurious.' Booth and Forster insisted the contacts were real but Robinson said they were 'chasing rabbits'. Robinson left his own position and came over to the displays manned by Booth and Forster. By the time he got there, in two sweeps of the radar, the contacts had disappeared. Robinson told the AB's they were 'riding a bike' (whatever that meant). They tried to convince the Lt Cdr that the contacts were real, but the senior officer would not have two relatively new ABs argue with him. He told them to shut up and get on with their jobs. Meanwhile Corvette Captain Augusto Bedacarratz and Frigate Lieutenant Armando Mayora raced towards their target in their 'spurious' and undetected Super Etendards.

Of the three Type 42 destroyers out on 'picket duty' ahead of the main Task Force, *Sheffield* was on the far left flank. *Coventry* was in the centre and *Glasgow* on the right. *Coventry* picked up the contacts that Booth and Forster on *Invincible* had seen, and asked *Invincible* both to confirm weapons status, and for 'weapons free', which would give the ship the authority to use her own weapons without further permission from the control ship. Lt Cdr Robinson, as controller of the Task Force air defences, refused to give 'weapons free' status, and repeated to *Coventry* what he had told the *Invincible* air team, that the contacts were spurious.

When a radar transmits, it sends electronic pulses which hit a target and then bounce back to the transmitting point causing the target to 'paint' on the radar operators screen. As it hits the target it leaves its own electronic fingerprint and the 'target' can tell it has been detected. When you are detected by an enemy radar painting across you, you are said to hold a 'racket.'

Glasgow then detected a 'racket'. She had been illuminated by the search radar fitted in the nose of the enemy's Super Etendard, codenamed 'Handbrake'. The bearing of this transmission correlated directly with the position of the contacts *Coventry* had held, the same two seen by the ABs aboard *Invincible*. Unbeknown to *Sheffield*, she too had been illuminated by this radar searching. Unfortunately, Captain Salt had been ordered to transmit a message via satellite (SCOT) to the Ministry of Defence in Whitehall, and the band on which the satellite transmitted caused interference with *Sheffield's* electronic support measures (ESM), as the transmission band/wavelength was identical to the one the Argentinian fighter bombers used, rendering the UAA1 inoperable. The passive electronic listening equipment that would detect the Etendard search radar was then blind and ineffective, until the satellite transmission was complete. This was not deemed to be a risk because *Invincible*, with its superior equipment fit, was close by. Ships of the Task Force were expected to rely on her for early aircraft detection. This time though, it allowed the enemy aircraft to close under the radar envelope undetected.

The aircraft had been detected by both *Coventry* and *Invincible*. *Coventry* had asked permission to engage and had been denied by *Invincible*. The man co-ordinating the anti-air warfare protection for the Task Force had not seen it with his own eyes and refused to believe his operators.

The correlating racket detected by *Glasgow* had been discounted as spurious by the force anti-air warfare officer in *Invincible*. The AAWO in *Glasgow* was beside himself with concern, calling *Invincible* and telling the Force AAWO "*Negative, it is not a spurious raid, THE FORCE IS UNDER ATTACK,*" almost shouting at the carrier's operations room. The two missile-carrying aircraft forged ahead towards *Sheffield*, still below her radar envelope, whilst she was temporarily blinded to their own radar detections of her. Even without her sensors, *Sheffield* should have received the information from other ships via voice and electronic data link. So why had she not fired chaff? The order to fire this or any other form of air defence is given by the Anti-Air Warfare Officer in *Sheffield's* case. The AAWO, from his AAW plot in the operations room, controlled the ship's air defences. The information about the inbound enemy aircraft was being passed out on a radio circuit manned only by the AAWOs of the other ships and could not be heard by anyone else in the operations room. The only man who could have received the information wasn't there listening to it.

The AAWO and another officer, Lt Peter Walpole, the Officer of the Watch (OOW), will tell you he was on the bridge checking a discrepancy with the cloud base. The official MoD statement admits the AAWO was not present in the lead up to the attack, but says he was 'closed up elsewhere, performing other AAWO's duties'. I spent many years in AAW teams in ships' operations rooms; the only place of duty I ever saw for an AAWO was his AAW plot in the operations room. The AAWO has subsequently admitted making a gross error of judgement by being absent from the operations room as two enemy aircraft closed. He returned when he heard the tannoy across the ship's PA system – "*AAWO, op's room AAWO!*"

This broadcast was made when the two Super Etendards climbed to fifteen hundred feet to launch their missiles. As they did so, they appeared on *Sheffield's* own radars for the first time at a range of twenty three miles. Immediately the radar operators initiated computerised tracks onto the aircraft to begin target indication procedures and attempt to shoot down the aircraft.

"*All positions stand to.*" The weapons teams swung into action. "*4.5 load load load.*" Able Seamen Hiscutt and Bartlett, in the 4.5 inch gunbay, loaded the first shell into the gun hoist. It travelled up into the turret and was loaded into the breech ready to engage the incoming targets. The Sea Dart missile hydraulics prepared to load the missiles onto the launcher for firing. The 909 fire control radars were searching for their targets, trying to lock on for missile guidance. However, the targets were too low; the 909s couldn't acquire and re-set.

The few seconds it took to initiate the electronic tracks were just long enough to allow the Argentinian pilots to feed the coordinates of *Sheffield* into the missile's homing computers. The pilots fired their missiles and dived in tight turns to avoid being shot down. To their horror, the operators aboard *Sheffield* saw two new contacts in front of the aircraft, which the next rotation of the radar showed had travelled half the distance from the point of origin to the ship itself. It could mean only one thing – inbound missiles.

The weapons systems were standing to, the procedures were underway to initiate defensive measures, but because of the stringent chain of command protocol laid down in the Royal Navy, the ship could not open fire until the command was given by the appropriate warfare officer. When the PWO realised things were already crucial, he put out the broadcast for the AAWO to return to the operations room. When he arrived, he saw what he described as 'a confused plot'.

One of the ESM operators had crash-stopped the SCOT transmission and saw a contact on his screen. He had time to roller his tracker ball strobe over the contact, and to press the 'analyse' button on the console. As the parameters of the radar illuminating the ship appeared.

"That's an Exocet warhead!" he exclaimed.

Three seconds later, our world changed forever.

CHAPTER 6

Impact and Damage

The first I knew about the attack on HMS *Sheffield* was a colossal explosion and the 20mm Oerlikon opening fire. The missile impacted the galley area (location marking 2J) and I was in 2F mess, which was two compartments for'ard. Simultaneous to the sound and force of the explosion, the mess door disintegrated and lay in bits on the deck. The doors of the medical cabinets blew off, and the contents were flung around the mess. Then, the place filled with acrid smoke.

One of the Leading Seamen in the mess shouted, "We've been hit!"

Yeah, no shit! I thought, as I pulled on my overalls. *How quick are you?* Oddly, there was no panic, but there was obviously a strong sense of urgency. I knew instinctively what to do. *Anti-flash hood and gloves on. Get to off watch action station on the 3 inch rocket deck.* I was about to leave when a Steward, Ricky Morana staggered in, covered in blood. I stared at him. He was the first serious casualty I had ever seen, and it shocked me to the core.

"What happened?" I asked him. He said a missile had hit the wardroom. At first sight, he looked like he had a shark's dorsal fin growing out of the top of his head, but closer examination revealed a lump of metal the size of my fist. Blood was pumping out of the wound. My first instinct was to lay him down, and as I did so, one of the first aid party came in and took over. I raced out of 2F mess and turned aft to go up to my off-watch action station. At that point, I had no idea what had hit us, or the extent of the damage or casualties. I couldn't get the vision of Ricky out of my head, but despite the horror, I was strangely calm. I learned later that the impact had sent millions of razor sharp shards of steel into compartments adjoining the area the missile had hit. Ricky's dorsal fin was one of many shrapnel injuries that resulted.

The Exocet is a formidable weapon. The name comes from the Latin

Exocoetus, meaning Flying Fish. The missile is five metres long, with a diameter of 35 centimetres. It has four clipped delta fins forward and four raked clipped tip moving fins at the rear. It flies at 1100 km/h (mach 0.97) and weighs 855kg, and it carries a 165kg high explosive fragmenting warhead. Its guidance system is inertial in mid-course, with an active radar phase in the terminal stages of flight. It is also fitted with a radar altimeter to control its sea-skimming trajectory.

The kinetic deceleration of a weapon of this magnitude travelling at this speed is the equivalent of a 75 ton locomotive travelling at 60 mph, crashing into a solid wall and coming to a dead stop within ten feet. After being launched from the aircraft, the missile quickly drops to between six and eight feet above the sea and rapidly accelerates at close to the speed of sound, skimming over the wave tops, following a course programmed in by the pilots. At 10km from the target, the missile's own radar system picks up the target and homes in. Exocet is propelled by a compound comprising a substance simply called RDX mixed with nitrocellulose and nitro-glycerine. This is what gives it its highly toxic smoke.

When the Exocet slammed into *Sheffield's* side, with virtually no warning, and with catastrophic explosive force, it hit six feet above the waterline, amidships, tearing a hole 120 square feet, and gouging its way through the centre of the ship. It vaporised everything in its path, causing immense damage. The fire main was cut in half, rendering all fire fighting hydrants useless. The For'ard Engine Room and For'ard Auxiliary Machinery Room were devastated, and the stokers in there at the time were horribly burned. The Galley and Junior Rates' Dining Hall took the brunt of the impact, killing everyone there instantly. A massive and roaring fireball raced along 2 deck for'ard and aft down the starboard side, it blew out the galley shutters on the port side, and raced for'ard along there too.

The Main Communications Office, the Damage Control Headquarters (HQ1) and the Machinery Control Room were all wrecked, causing burns and other injuries to a number of sailors. All chilled water to the ship's weapons and sensors was severed, rendering the fighting capability of the ship inoperable.

Within seconds of the impact, *Sheffield* had become a floating, burning, hulk. Thick acrid toxic smoke spread throughout the ship as the fire raged out of control, burning wires and cables as the un-spent missile propellant burnt off at 3,500 degrees. Several watertight hatches were blown clean off their hinges, bent and buckled, unusable. The spread of fire and smoke was un-stoppable, and we found getting to our actions stations totally impossible. No one could move from for'ard to aft inside the ship, the only way through was via the upper deck. Some of the sailors made their way out through the escape hatch underneath the 4.5 inch gun.

The one constant in a warship is noise. There is always the background hum of engines, air conditioning etc. Immediately after the impact though, there came the whine of everything shutting down, and then followed an eerie silence, which could have lasted only a split second, but which felt like a hundred years. And then, the emergency lighting came on, and the silence was broken by the 'rat a tat tat' of the 20mm Oerlikon machine gun. The lighting confirmed that the place was actually filled with thick, black, toxic, smoke, and from somewhere came the cry, "*Fire! Fire! Fire!*"

The watertight bulkhead between 2F and 2G had been blown open and two of the damage control party were attempting to close it but it was buckled by the heat and the explosion. I moved beyond them and went into the operations room passage. The door had been blown off and John Galway was lying on the operations room floor with blood pouring from his head. As I got to the aft end of the passage, the smoke became even thicker, and I could see flames ahead, so I turned to head back for'ard. I bent down low, where the oxygen is supposed to be clearer, but it wasn't true here. At one point, I had my face against the floor and still couldn't breathe. I fought to quell the rising sense of panic, the smoke was sweet and sickly, it burned my throat and hurt my lungs to breathe. I tried to breathe more lightly or more shallowly, nothing worked. The English language does not contain words to describe how I felt. Most of all, I was pissed off thinking at the age of seventeen it was all going to be over, before I was legally old enough to even drink, or to vote for the government that had sent me to my fate. I was convinced I wasn't going to make it out of the inferno the ship had become, and was terrified at the thought of drowning as the destroyer sank. A quick and painless death where the lights simply went out, with no feeling or awareness of what was actually happening would have been infinitely more preferable. I thought about all the films I'd seen and military books I'd read about men in combat readying themselves for death when they realised that their end was both inevitable, and imminent. What did they do to ready themselves? Repent for their sins? I hadn't lived long enough to commit more than a couple, so that didn't take long.

There is no accurate way of describing the inside of a warship after it's taken a direct hit from a missile specifically designed to destroy it. The fire, the heat, the smoke, the dead, the injured – the impenetrable darkness. Then there is the possibility of the ship's magazines blowing up and the ship sinking almost instantly. The absolute reality is that your life expectancy may be measured only in minutes, or possibly even seconds. It's impossible to escape the thought that any second, another missile impact might come, another searing explosion, with metal fragments ripping through your flesh. With that thought comes the possibility that your last seconds alive are going to be spent in a tangled scream of scorching metal, and indescribable agony.

I inched my way for'ard and across to the port side on 2E cross passage. There was a two man Chief Petty Officer's cabin here occupied by the Chief Bosun's Mate (Buffer) and another Chief. I heard someone shouting for the first aid party to come to the Buffer's cabin. Laid on the floor of the cabin was a man I thought was dead. Initially, I thought it was the Chief Bosuns Mate, Buffer himself. He was covered in blood and slime, a bit like a new born baby. It looked as though his overalls had been cut into neat inch-wide strips, like maypole ribbons, but a closer look told me it was his skin.

The man was CPO John Strange from the engine room where the missile had entered. The passageway from the cabin, back to the engine room escape hatch where he climbed out, was covered in blood. Chief Mechanician Strange had been bending over a piece of equipment in the For'ard Auxiliary Machinery Room when the missile hit. He regained consciousness on the steel floor plates of the room, where he found the entire room was ablaze. At that moment, he must have thought he had passed through the Gates to Hades. He was surrounded by fire, and dazed as he was by the force of the impact, he had no way of knowing what had happened.

Despite suffering first degree burns to 70% of his body, the Chief was able to get to the for'ard port corner of the engine room, where he managed to locate the escape ladder. He clawed his way up three decks to locate the escape hatch, but when he got there, he found it clipped firmly closed. With his skin hanging off him in ribbons, he hung onto the ladder with one hand, and knocked the clips off with the other, then hauled himself out into the port side passageway on 2 deck, where he crawled for'ard. The images of this man, and those of Ricky Morana, stay with me, tattooed on my memory.

Leading Radio Operator Eddie Whittaker had been on watch in the

Main Communications Office. Needing to answer the call of nature, he left the MCO and turned aft down the starboard passageway. The next compartment along was 2J, the Main Galley, where he stopped to chat with the on-watch chefs to see how scran was coming along for the evening, then continued aft to the junior rates heads. Eddie was the last person to see those men alive.

Seconds later the missile impacted two feet below where Eddie had been standing. The galley and dining hall disappeared in a maelstrom of high explosive and fragmented steel. The Main Communications Office, where his watch had been at their posts, was all but destroyed, and his men badly injured. The starboard passageways were impassable, a furnace of missile fuel and toxic smoke.

I carried on making my way aft on the port side until I reached the port operations room door, where I heard someone shout, "*turn off the radar displays!*" It transpired that the chilled water cooling systems had ruptured and the displays were over-heating. I immediately realised we had no weapon systems with which to defend ourselves against further attack. The hatch leading from the operations room down to the computer room, from where the ship's weapons and sensors are controlled, was closed and locked, as the weapons maintainers led by Lt Cdr Woodhead made a valiant effort to restore power to the ship's computers.

Neither he, nor any of his team of weapon maintainers, would survive. He was posthumously awarded the Distinguished Service Cross.

Fire and smoke made it impossible to go any further aft on 2 deck. On the port side the ladder up to 1 deck officer's cabin flat had disintegrated. I turned for'ard again to make my way to the fo'c'sle escape hatch. The smoke was getting thicker and with no fire main, the fire was advancing up the port side where I was, and probably up the starboard side too.

When I got back to 2E cross passage, virtually everyone from the for'ard part of the ship was trying to get out of the escape hatch under the 4.5 inch gun. There was no panic but it was taking time and people seemed to be struggling. Eventually, it dawned on someone why. "*Take your lifejackets off!*" came the shout. We all had our lifejackets, gasmasks and survival suit bags around our waists, and though that is required in wartime, they were jamming in the hatchway. As soon as they were slipped off, the line of men moved swiftly and efficiently out onto the fo'c'sle.

AB (M) André Lahiff, who had been in 2F with me, said as we reached the upper deck, "*have you seen the hole in the starboard side?*" I ran and looked over the starboard side, where thick black smoke poured out of a ragged missile entry hole, the funnel, and the main mast exhausts. Anywhere that smoke could escape from within the ship – it was doing so.

One of the officers told me to stand on the breakwater to keep a look out for approaching ships or aircraft. I saw two aircraft approaching low and fast from the starboard bow and shouted up to the Gunnery Direction Platform, "*Alarm aircraft!*" The gunners stood to with only the Oerlikon and machine guns with which to defend the ship. I have never felt so exposed, so vulnerable, as I felt at that moment. Fortunately the aircraft were Sea Harriers. They screamed overhead, banking in a tight turn to port, so low you could see the pilot's faces. They continued circling in a CAP figure-of-eight circuit, obviously to protect the helicopters which would inevitably arrive from the main Task Force to evacuate the wounded.

For a moment, I felt a slight twinge of relief that the remainder of the Task Force was covering us, but then I looked aft at the impenetrable pall of smoke pouring out of the missile entry hole, the funnel and the exhausts. The ship's company had rigged some hoses on the upper deck and were playing them on the bulkheads, from which clouds of steam erupted because of the intense heat inside. It seemed the fire was spreading out of control, and the ship was in critical trouble. I wondered how the fire-fighting teams inside were doing, and whether they'd be able to contain the spread of the fire. Was HQ1 (the damage control HQ) still operational and manned? Unless we contained the fire, we'd soon be ablaze from stem to stern. The South Atlantic ocean looked cold, uninviting, unforgiving, and I didn't fancy going over the side if we started to sink.

CHAPTER 7

Abandon Ship!

The *thwock thwock thwock* of heavy helicopter blades interrupted my thoughts as a flurry of Sea Kings carrying Royal Marine medics descended from HMS *Hermes*. More and more of the injured were now laid out on the fo'c'sle against the bridge screen awaiting evacuation to the hospitals of the aircraft carriers. One of the officers stood up on the after breakwater next to the Sea Dart launcher, guiding the choppers in. One of the pilots touched down the port wheel of his aircraft on the small square platform on top of the 4.5 inch gun. He then pivoted the helicopter around so the door was over the fo'c'sle and the aircrewman came down to begin evacuating the injured. I watched as Radio Operator Mark Bagnall was being winched up, his skin black, and his clothes stripped neatly into one inch ribbons. His hair had turned bright orange and wiry and was stuck up like an afro – he looked like Beaker from the Muppets.

Petty Officer 'Slinger' Woods had been in the main communications office when the missile impacted, he had a bad head wound and was sat on the deck leant against the bridge screen with dressings around his head and face. The Doc, Ged Meager was wrapping field dressings and bandages around his head and face.

The ships company did their best to battle with the fire, but with the water main blown out, it was virtually impossible. We had submersible pumps over the side and even buckets tied onto string to throw against the ship's side in an attempt to cool the metal of the hull. Petty Officer Dave 'Basher' Briggs kept returning below to retrieve fire fighting gear, but he was eventually overcome by smoke. He was pulled out, and Doc Meager administered CPR and mouth to mouth. Sadly, despite the Doc's valiant efforts, he didn't make it. The last time I saw Basher, he was wrapped in a blanket on the fo'c'sle. I knew he was dead. I wondered how many more had been killed in the missile impact, knowing it was likely to be many. An

Exocet is designed to destroy a ship and to take as many of the ships company as possible with it.

Basher was posthumously awarded the Distinguished Service Medal. Petty Officer Meager got the Queen's Gallantry Medal. In these circumstances, personal safety was not a consideration. War was making ordinary men carry out extraordinarily heroic acts.

Smoke appeared on the horizon, coming from two different directions. One was from the area the choppers had arrived from, the other not. I shouted up to warn the GDP, almost instantly realising the futility of this. If it was a heavily armed enemy warship, we had no defences anyway.

The ships began a zigzag approach. One turned to port and I made out the low sleek outline of a Type 21 frigate. To my enormous relief, they were friendly! HMS *Arrow* was ringing on full speed, as was the old Type 12 HMS *Yarmouth*. Time was playing tricks; I couldn't tell whether *Arrow* arrived in minutes or hours.

On the horizon behind the Type 21, I saw the masts of another Type 42, one of our sister ships. I wondered what was going on inside her. For the moment I forgot about our burning ship. *Arrow* crossed our stern and turned tightly to starboard to bring her alongside our portside. Her ships company were on the upper deck with hoses charged, ready to commence boundary cooling the ship's side. It looked like they were getting ready for a sail past and handover, as we had done when we handed over to HMS *Cardiff* on the Armilla Patrol, weeks ago. This time though, the sailors were not waving and holding up jokey banners. They were clad in white anti-flash hoods and gloves and laden with lifejackets, gas masks and survival suits. Their upper deck guns were all manned by men in steel helmets and the Sea Cat launcher was loaded with all four missiles. I had never seen a fully loaded Sea Cat launcher before. It was a sobering sight.

Arrow's Captain, Commander Paul Bootherstone, executed a magnificent feat of seamanship, bringing the frigate alongside and securing her to *Sheffield*. The damage to both ships was minimised by the numerous large rattan fenders suspended from any point onto which they could be secured. Normal peacetime regulations were out of the window. Usually, securing a fender to the guardrail would have got you into trouble with the Buffer, and earned you serious remedial seamanship training.

As water from *Arrow's* hoses started to spray onto the ship's side, clouds of steam poured off. Even the deck was heating up, despite the freezing sea water flooding onto it. We had only been ablaze a matter of minutes, but it was obvious the fire had a major hold throughout the central part of the ship.

As HMS *Yarmouth* went to action stations and steamed towards us, the Exocet fired by Armando Mayora passed over her flight deck and ditched in the sea ½ mile astern of HMS *Alacrity*. Yarmouth's Wasp helicopter arrived and started evacuating the wounded ship's company, then *Yarmouth* came alongside starboard side to, her bows at the after part of the ship, with her fire fighting crews on the fo'c'sle pouring fire-suppressing foam into the hole made by the missile. An immense amount of water was coming into *Sheffield* now, but with no one to regulate the flow or containment, the engine rooms had a free flow of water sluicing around inside.

Next, torpedoes were detected in the water. *Yarmouth* brought her anti-submarine mortars into action. The first salvo was fired across the top of us. There were more Sea King helicopters; I wasn't sure whether they were for casevacs[5] or were sub-hunters. *Yarmouth* fired another salvo of her mortars, followed by a torpedo mortar. One of the Sea Kings closed the torpedo launch area hunting for the submarine.

At this point, about two and half hours after we'd been hit, the ship's side of *Yarmouth* was getting too hot. The lines were slipped and she moved away astern. She prepared to receive our ship's company by helicopter and reversed away from us. She had fired twenty four mortar bombs, a number of torpedoes, and her own helicopter had joined in the prosecution of the submarine that had been trying to torpedo her, us, and *Arrow*.

I remained on the fo'c'sle for a couple of hours and helped with fire fighting, relieving the hose crews as directed by one of the damage control senior ratings. The Doc had us put some of the wounded into stretchers, following which they were carried down to the flight, where they were evacuated. After the wounded had left, I stayed on the flight deck. Five hours later, Captain Salt was on the fo'c'sle. The First Lt leaned over the bridge wing and told him, "*Sir, it is about time you started considering saving the ships company, and not saving the ship.*" By now, the fires had reached the Sea Dart missile, the 4.5 inch shell magazine for'ard, and the torpedo magazines aft.

The ship's company began moving aft to the flight deck to prepare to abandon ship. Captain Salt went up to the hangar roof above the flight

---

[5] casualty evacuations

deck with the Marine Engineering Officer and the First Lt. From there the captain ordered that everyone be taken off the ship. I couldn't believe it was actually happening. We couldn't abandon ship, that sort of thing didn't happen; it was Second World War stuff, not modern Navy stuff. By now we were ablaze from stem to stern. I heard someone say, "*The magazines are on fire.*" I have seen footage from World War II, and photographs from World War I, of warship's magazines exploding – there is very little of the ship, and very few people left.

The ship's company made their way aft to the flight deck where some were going off by chopper, some to *Yarmouth*, some to *Arrow* and some over the side into the sea.

A rope had been secured up from the quarterdeck of *Arrow* to our flight deck. A group of men were holding the rope and Leading Seaman Bob Mullen was taking charge. I stood by with an axe, ready to chop the rope if ordered. *Arrow's* engines started to rev up and the swell was increasing. I swung the axe to chop the rope but was told to stop and it would be slipped from the *Arrow*. I ran across to the starboard side of the flight deck, took a run up, and jumped. One of *Arrow's* crew caught hold of my wrists like a trapeze artist. Another reached over and grabbed the waistband of my trousers, pulling them right into my arse and crutch, which of course hurt immensely and I was unceremoniously dragged onboard. As *Arrow* pulled away from *Sheffield*, I turned round to see her for the last time. Captain Salt was in a helicopter strop being winched up to a chopper, and she, once a proud, slick warship, a sleek efficient destroyer, was reduced to a burning chaotic wreck.

"Name?" I stood looking blankly at the man clad in full anti-flash in front of me.

"Name! What's your fucking name, rate and number sailor?"

I was trying to process the information; my mind and brain swimming. "Er... Lawton, Seaman Radar, Joe Lawton, D190104G. No, it's Adam. My name's Adam," I stammered.

"Are you OK mate, are you hurt?" asked the member of *Arrow's* survivor reception team.

"No I'm OK, I think. My nickname's Joe. My real name's Adam."

Another sailor took hold of me by the arm and pulled me to one side.

"Take your anti-flash off," he ordered. I removed the long white gloves and hood. I hadn't realised how tight the elastic had been around my face and head, it felt good to get it off.

"Are you injured, are you bleeding, does it hurt anywhere?" asked the sailor. I noticed he was wearing a Red Cross armband.

"I think I'm OK. I was winded when we jumped and banged my knees and hips on your ship's side, but I don't think I broke anything."

I was aware that the ship was moving at high speed. Type 21's could really shift. She heeled hard over one way, and then the other, taking a zigzag plan back into the safety of the screen of other ships. The submarine may still have been in the area.

"OK, this way." One of the ship's company was directing the survivors who had just been picked up through the hatchway. "Ditch any wet clothes here, get a hot shower if you need one. There are clean dry clothes at the other end." Some of the sailors were filing through the showers, it was now after 19:00, and we'd been fighting the fires on *Sheffield* for over five full hours. We were all filthy, soaking and stinking of smoke. Each of us was issued a box of survivor's kit, a pair of overalls and white plimsolls; a whole new set of worldly goods.

Later, we sat down in junior rate's messes at waterline level, with the hatches battened down. The 4.5 inch gun right above us opened fire. Not one of us said a word; we simply sat there and looked at each other, and I'm sure we were all thinking the same thing. 'Surely, not again. Not twice in one day?' We were then told that the intention was to sink *Sheffield* with gunfire, which *Arrow* would do with high explosive shells, whilst *Yarmouth* provided anti-submarine cover. Before firing commenced though, the order was rescinded, and *Sheffield* was left to burn herself out as a decoy.

At some point during the night, crammed into a small space in the mess, I finally drifted off to sleep.

CHAPTER 8

A Family's War

Tuesday 4th May 1982

9.00pm GMT

I grew up in a little village called Hickling in the heart of the rural Norfolk Broads. It's a tranquil and picturesque hamlet, the essence of English village life. At 9pm on the evening of the 4th May in a cottage down a leafy lane, my family had sat glued to news reports from the South Atlantic, like thousands of families all over the UK at that time.

Just over a month previously, my nineteen year old sister Toni had come back from working in Portugal to welcome me home after a six month deployment to the Persian Gulf. A phone call from the Naval Base in Portsmouth had advised my family not to go to Portsmouth to meet the ship as planned, as the ship was being 're-deployed'. The Navy would say no more than that but my family knew where the ship was going, as did the other two hundred and sixty nine families of the ship's company.

As my family watched, the newscaster Ian McDonald came on to present the ITN news. In his usual 'Dr Doom' tone, he read the following statement: "*Today, in the course of her duties, inside the total exclusion zone around the Falkland Islands, HMS Sheffield, a Type 42 destroyer, came under attack by Argentine aircraft. Late this afternoon she was hit by a missile and set on fire. The fire spread out of control and when there was no longer any hope of saving her she was abandoned and later sank. Casualties are not yet known, but are expected to be heavy. All those who abandoned her have been picked up.*"

There was a split second of stunned silence, which Toni broke when she ran from the living room to my bedroom in floods of tears. My mum Judi followed, trying to console her as she battled her own dread that I might already be dead.

My dad Brian waited until the news had finished then switched the television off. He comforted my mum and sister as best he could until they fell into an uneasy sleep, then he took himself off to the porch, where he sat alone all night, so that if the dreaded knock came, he would be the one to answer it. As a policeman, he had too often delivered news of the death of a child, and knew it for the most distressing of a police officer's tasks. If it came to it, he wanted to make sure he would be the one to tell his own family. On this bitterly cold night, he sat outside by himself until morning, not daring to sleep. As an ex-Merchant Navy officer himself, he knew all too well I might not be returning from my first trip to sea.

In the village pub, which was just across the road from our house, the same news came on the TV in the bar. "Young Lawton's on that ship," one of the locals said in the silence that followed. One of the other men put down his pint then walked out in tears. He had lost all four of his older brothers in the last war.

The following morning, Dad walked to the village shop to get the newspaper. He wasn't alone, but he found people avoiding his gaze, because none of them knew what to say. Back in the family home at 9am, the telephone rang. Dad answered. A voice identified itself as calling from the office of Naval Family Services and asked Dad to identify himself. The caller went on to ask for details of my full name, rank and service number, and also asked where the ship had just been. When the caller was satisfied that my father was who he said he was (my officially nominated named next of kin), they told him they had received a signal from the Task Force that my name was amongst the list of the survivors who had been picked up. They could offer no further information as to whether I had been wounded, or what ship I was on. They could only confirm that I was alive. Dad asked them to double check this information and call back. When he put the phone down, he turned to my mum and sister, who stood at his side, and said simply, "He's alive."

Later, the Navy rang back and confirmed the earlier information, said that there were no other sailors of similar names aboard, and I was definitely one of the survivors. Mum and Toni threw their arms around him, and all three stood and cried tears of relief.

Soon afterwards, Dad walked back up to the village shop and asked for a bottle of gin. The owner apologised and said he could only sell alcohol during pub opening hours, which wasn't until 11am. A short and mostly one-sided conversation took place. Less than two minutes later, Dad left the shop carrying a bottle of gin and a bottle of brandy!

Those of us who had been rescued were told we were to be transferred to two of the huge Royal Fleet Auxiliaries – RFA *Resource*, an ammunition ship, and RFA *Fort Austin*, a stores ship, with whom we had conducted the five ship RAS in the Gulf and on the way south.

A Wessex helicopter hovered over the back of HMS *Arrow's* flight deck. It was too big to fit on the small frigate fore and aft, so the pilot turned it athwartships and brought it down to sit across the flight deck. This was certainly a piece of flying; typically a ship will turn into the wind to allow an aircraft to land nose into the wind. The aircraft had to deal with the ship's forward motion as it rolled and pitched in the heavy swell, and its own sideward motion to keep up with the ship. Furthermore, the loading door was on the starboard side of the aircraft which was right at the back of the flight deck, so to board her, we had to run under the rotors at the front, which dip down when slowed.

Once we were aboard, the Wessex it lifted off and flew low and fast across the Task Force ships until it climbed steeply, then rapidly descended onto the lumbering grey ammunition ship. We were met by one of the naval air mechanics who serviced the Wessex onboard. I was amongst many who were accommodated in the for'ard superstructure in 02H officers' smokeroom. Shortly after we arrived, one of the senior rates came round and handed out paper and pens. He instructed everyone to write their personal account of what had happened the previous day. When we'd finished, the statements were collected as part of the official enquiry and report[6]. After that, every man was instructed to write a thirty word telegram home. As I sat with paper and pen, all I could think was, 'what do you write?'

That evening as we sat in the bar, one of the ship's company put his head into his hands and started weeping. Others followed. I was one of them. The shock was hitting now, and with it came anger, and outrage. This had only just started and it was clearly a long way from over. How many more attacks would we face? How many of us in this room would never see England or our families again? Added to that was the grief, that in addition to Basher Briggs, another 19 of the ship's company were 'missing,

---

[6] These reports were subsequently 'lost' by the MoD for many years and have only been 'relocated' in the last few years, and released under The Freedom of Information Act.

presumed killed'. Our shipmates, our friends, every one of them somebody's husband, or father, or son, or brother and we knew for certain that they were all dead; no one could have survived that explosion and inferno. Every one of them with a circle of relatives and friends, all of whom would now be facing a lifetime with a void, an emptiness. I was racked with dreadful mental torture, and a sense of soul-destroying helplessness. I wanted to kill every single Argentinian I could.

In the ensuing days, we busied ourselves helping the *Resource* ships company with re-supplying the remaining Task Force ships. We were so pissed off at not being able to hit back and give the Argie bastards a bloody nose. On a personal level, I was consumed with a hideous fury at what they had done to us, to the ship, to me. Then as I calmed down a little, I realised what a selfish idiot I was being. At least I was still alive. Then official confirmation was issued that our twenty shipmates listed as 'missing, presumed killed' were now confirmed as 'killed in action'. Again I thought of them, of their families, and of course couldn't help thinking, what if *their* grief had been my family's grief? The sense of loss and emptiness was overwhelming, and further fuelled my anger. I was to carry that anger for many years to come.

I knew that most of my classmates from seamanship and radar training school were somewhere in the Task Force. On the *Invincible* there was Mark and George who had spotted the inbound Etendards, plus two good mates Buster Brown and Steve Mulcahy and five others, who had drawn the *Invincible* as alphabetically their names came before mine. More classmates were on *Coventry* and *Cardiff* en route from the Armilla patrol, *Exeter* en route from the West Indies, and *Ardent, Active, Andromeda, Bristol* and *Hermes*. Most of these ships had the same radar and weapon fit as *Sheffield*. I understand it was some days before Steve and Buster *Invincible* dared to look at the list of people who had been killed, to see if my name was there. The average age of those in my class, now at war, was nineteen.

To begin with, those of us from *Sheffield* were told we were to be dispersed to other ships around the Task Force that we were qualified to work on. That meant the same engine fit for the stokers, the same weapons systems for the maintainers and operators. Most of us wanted to stay in the Task Force. I asked one of the senior rates to ask the Gunnery Officer if I could be transferred to one of the other ships immediately. The request was declined. I was told all *Sheffield's* men had to stay together until the decision as to how and where we could be distributed was taken.

A number of G Squadron 22nd SAS were billeted aboard *Resource*. During the day, they wandered around in grey pussers[7] overalls and white plimsolls. The only experience any of us had of the SAS was of the spectacular storming of the Iranian embassy in Princes Gate, London, two years earlier. The assault, broadcast live on international television, was a resounding success. To us, the SAS seemed like mythical supermen.

Because the *Resource* was effectively a merchant ship, the junior rates had a bar onboard. One night I was in the bar with some of the ships company. Two of the *Resource* crew sat at the bar in dresses and make up – in the middle of a war zone! In the Merchant Navy homosexuality was not outlawed as it was in the Royal Navy. They referred to everyone as 'she,' even the Captain. One of them offered to buy me a drink and I politely declined. The other *Sheffields* and SAS troopers watched me becoming more and more uncomfortable in the face of the propositions put forward by these two openly homosexual RFA men. One of them kept on at me, and eventually sauntered over and asked me if I was sure I didn't want to join 'the Happy Club'. I shoved him away, and he fell backwards breaking a couple of glasses. His partner dismounted from his bar stool and squared up to me, but I wasn't bothered. I had so much pent up anger and aggression, I was happy to take the pair of them on, irrespective of the result.

Not all SAS men are hulking, muscle bound psychotics. They mostly look average, they blend in. They are tall, short, big, skinny but what they have in common is, they are all very fit. One of them watching the shenanigans thought the joke had gone far enough. He walked over to the bar.

"OK, that's enough, leave the kid alone," he warned the two men.

They turned their attention to him.

"Well aren't you a big boy then," they mocked.

"Just shut the fuck up and leave the kid alone OK?"

They carried on, so the trooper belted the first one clean across the floor, after which, the other one scarpered. I walked across to the one lying prone on the floor, blood oozing from his nose.

"Let that be a fucking lesson to you, wanker," I spat, then I turned to where the SAS troop were sitting, drinking orange juice. "Thanks mate," I said to Roger, the bloke with the fists.

---

[7] Naval

"Any time kid," he said, laughing. "They were beginning to piss me off."

Many of these men were tragically lost in a helicopter crash before the end of the war.

Each time an air raid was detected the RFAs went to Emergency Stations, as opposed to Action Stations. The SAS and some of our gunnery teams from *Sheffield* were manning GPMGs on the upper deck. Charlie Adamson the Chief Gunnery Instructor was appointed MGD(V) aboard *Resource*. Given that she was a high value unit, *Resource* was in the centre of the screen of ships, near the carriers. You could sit and watch out of the porthole as the enemy aircraft attacked the screen, and see the black puffs of smoke as the frigates and destroyers spat back their defiance.

A number of the *Resource* ship's company did nothing when Emergency Stations was piped. It appeared to me that they didn't seem concerned. When I asked why, one of them said, "come with me". We went below into the ammunition hold. It was big, and although dimly lit, you could see it was laden with every type of weapon and munitions you could think of. Huge racks of shells and missiles, and hundreds of thousands of rounds of 7.62mm ammunition, with their dry, brassy smell. I expected to be able to detect the cordite but I couldn't. Just as well, you only smell the cordite inside ammunition once it has been fired!

"If this thing gets hit," the man said to me as I looked around, "there won't be a ship or a Task Force left, or possibly any of the islands. So why worry?"

He had a point. It would have made one hell of a bang.

Officially of Age

Shortly after midnight on 9th May *Yarmouth* came alongside *Sheffield*, intending to make her ready for towing to South Georgia. The swell was greater than expected and as she came astern, she collided with *Sheffield* and pushed in the starboard bulkhead of her operations room door. The boarding party from *Yarmouth* boarded *Sheffield*, and a tow was secured to her fo'c'sle, after which *Yarmouth's* helicopter transferred the men back to their own ship.

The weather worsened and the swell picked up even more. An attempt was made to secure a large tarpaulin over the hole in the ship's side, but it wasn't successful. As weather conditions worsened, *Sheffield* started to take on water and list to starboard.

10th May

My 18th birthday. In the early hours of the morning, the Yarmouth's CO, Commander Tony Morton, and his First Lt, Lt Cdr Plummer, were called to the quarterdeck. Captain Salt was already there. *Sheffield* had been listing ten degrees to starboard for an hour or so, and then she heeled over onto her starboard side and shipped tons of seawater through the hole made by the Exocet entry. She soon slipped beneath the waves to her final resting place. All those present had tears in their eyes.

The Gunnery Officer of *Sheffield,* Lt Cdr Bates, was the senior officer present aboard *Resource*. He gathered all of us together in the mess and made the following announcement: "*This morning whilst under tow from Yarmouth, Sheffield was listing ten degrees to starboard. At 07:00 hours nothing could be done to save her and, witnessed by Captain Salt, she rolled over on her starboard side and sank. So Sheffield is no more. Oh yes, and happy 18th birthday Seaman Lawton.*"

I hardly even heard his last remark as I was in tears by then. HMS *Sheffield* went down in position 53° 04's, 56° 56'w, the first Royal Navy ship to be sunk in action for nearly forty years.

That night in the bar, Leading Seaman Bob Mullen made sure everyone knew it was my birthday. Sailors are all supposed to drink rum, but I couldn't hold it and was soon pissed out of my brains and taking the mick out of the SAS, calling them all 'wankers' and 'poofters', and threatening to 'fill them in'. They just laughed at me. They didn't even find it necessary to give me a token slap.

The following evening as I finished eating, a number of the troopers returned from having spent a few days on an intelligence gathering mission on East Falkland. They tramped straight down the dining hall for something hot to eat, just as serving time was drawing to a close. They were soaked, they were freezing, they were starving and they looked menacing. One of them asked the Chief Cook, an obnoxious Jock, if he could rustle them something up. His reply was quite straight forward. "No. Scran's finished."

Without a word, one of the men vaulted the counter and put a large knife to the Chief Cook's throat. Whether he had been carrying it, or picked it up off the galley bench I didn't see, but it had the necessary effect.

The galley range was immediately flashed up again.

A couple of days later the Chief Cook, who was also the Bar Manager, was trying to close the bar. He went over to where some of our ship's company were drinking with the SAS. "Come on you *Sheffield* wankers, drink up and fuck off. And as for you lot…" he indicated towards the SAS men, "I dinnae give a fuck who ye are, or who ye think ye are…"

He didn't get to finish what he was saying, as one of the troopers sent him crashing across the bar.

Next morning, I bumped into the two crew who had invited me to join the 'Happy Club'. They immediately apologised, shook hands and said they hadn't realised they were being offensive, and that obviously, after what had just happened, everyone must be a bit edgy. I accepted the apology, although I remained wary and sceptical of the men. They asked if I liked reading and when I confirmed I did, told me I should get some books from the library, as it was right next to my accommodation. "You could just walk straight in and help yourself and no one would mind." Maybe they were OK after all, I thought.

I opened the door to the library and found it in total darkness. I flicked the light switch on. There were maps and charts of the islands and southern Argentina all over the walls. I stepped inside and realised there were weapons and ammunition and all sorts of kit everywhere. On the floor I saw the famed, sand coloured winged dagger beret, bearing the 'Who Dares Wins' motto and badge. I bent down to pick it up not to nick it, just to look and hold something so infamous. Just as my fingers closed on it, I saw, from beneath a blanket, an eye watching me. Not blinking, just watching. I stood up and backed towards the door, flicked the light off and slowly and quietly closed the door behind me as I left.

I heard laughing behind me. It was the two members of the Happy Club.

"You could have got yourself a bigger fucking in there than we could have given you if those lunatics had caught you," they laughed. I found myself wishing for another brawl in the bar, so that I would have the opportunity to plant at least one of them.

The order was issued that the surviving ship's company would now not be divided amongst the Task Force but we would remain aboard the RFAs until we could be returned to the UK. The following night *Resource* conducted a night RAS with *Coventry*. I thought of my old classmate 'Spider' Webb and actually envied him, still being in on the action. After the RAS, I went and saw the Gunnery Officer Lt Cdr Bates again and asked if I could join one of the other warships. Again, my request was denied. Unusually, the following day a daylight RAS was held with *Invincible*. I had never seen aircraft recovering during a RAS before. That must take some skill, I thought. My divisional officer was on the bridge with the Gunnery Officer. I approached the two officers and said, "Sir, most of my class from last year are on *Invincible* and…"

The Gunnery Officer exploded. "No Lawton. Fucking no! You are *not* going to *Invincible, Coventry* or any other fucking ship unless you are ordered to! Now get off the bridge."

The day before we were due to leave *Resource*, there was a big piss up in the bar. The *Resource* ship's company had been raising money for the Royal National Lifeboat Institution and had threatened to shave off the bushy ginger beard of one of the *Sheffields* for funds. He said if they raised a certain amount, they could shave half of it off. The SAS troopers went round the bar press-ganging money out of everyone until the required amount had been reached. One of them then produced a scalpel-like instrument from somewhere and preceded to dry shave half the beard off. The night ended up with a sing song and the old favourite *The Music Man*. After many renditions of the various songs people could actually play, Chris Kent stood up and said he could play it for the SAS. Everyone joined in, expecting him to take the chorus with "stab, stab, stab", or "kill, kill, kill" or something of that ilk. Instead, he let forth with (including hand motions), "wank, wank, wank".

He had to be clinically suicidal, but that was Chris for you. Most people took cover as two of the troopers gave him the hiding of a lifetime.

MV British Esk and Ascension Island

The time came to leave RFA *Resource* and begin the journey back north to Ascension Island. The only ship heading that way was the requisitioned BP tanker, mv. *British Esk*. I was pissed off to be leaving the Task Force. I even asked if I could be allowed to stay on *Resource*, but Captain Salt's order was final. We came down here as a ship's company and we would go home as a ship's company.

The massive Sea King clattered onto the deck of the RFA and we clambered aboard. It was fully laden when it lifted off for the BP tanker. Suddenly, one of the crew appeared and mouthed the words 'air raid warning red' to everyone in the back. The chopper dived towards the sea in a stomach churning drop. The aircrewman was scanning the skies, he drew back the cocking lever on the big door-mounted machine gun, and the sea looked awfully close. My unbidden thought was, 'fuck no! Not now. We've been so close and come so far, don't let it end now.' I closed my eyes in the faint hope that if I didn't see something coming – like a 30mm cannon shell for instance – it wouldn't actually hit me. Suddenly a grey mass appeared and the aircraft climbed steeply, banked over, and settled down hard on the aircraft harrier *Hermes*.

The air raid over, the Sea King launched without warning and climbed into the murky skies, heading away from the heaving deck of the aircraft carrier. She came to the hover and the aircrewman gave the thumbs up to the first man. He fitted him into the winch strop and the man descended from view. This was repeated numerous times until it was my turn. I was not looking forward to this. The aircrewman shouted instructions into my ear which were totally inaudible, then the strop was secured under my arms, the toggle pulled down, and the winch lifted me from the door of the helicopter and out over the tumultuous South Atlantic ocean. The wind was howling, the rain was driving, and it was freezing. Below I could make out the long green tank deck of the *British Esk*. I looked back up at the helicopter, keeping my arms fixed firmly by my sides. As I looked down again, the ship's side suddenly appeared riding up a wave, and towering above me. Then the ship plunged into the trough and the bow disappeared in a frenzy of spray. The Sea King moved slightly to starboard over the area where the *Esk's* main deck had appeared. With a tremendous impact, the deck of the tanker came up underneath me, lifting me so that the winch cable became slack. The two men on deck wrestled furiously to get me out of the strop as the tanker started to drop away again down the trough of a wave. Just as the winch wire was becoming taught again, the strop slipped over my head and I half stumbled and was half dragged aft to the accommodation block of the tanker. I was already soaked to the skin, and absolutely frozen.

Once all the *Sheffield* ships company were accounted for on the *Esk*, she turned northwards, escorted to the edge of the TEZ by a warship. From there until Ascension she was on her own, we were on our own. Because there were reports of a hostile submarine in the area, we were told to keep our lifejackets and survival suits with us, just in case. Although attack was unlikely, it could not be discounted.

When *Esk* was one day out of Ascension Island, a Chinook arrived carrying some members of the Naval Family Services Department. There was also a fresh uniform of working denims and new ID cards, stamped 'HMS Sheffield Survivor'. So that was it, we were officially survivors from conflict. I felt fairly bad about it. The Navy had been in touch with our banks and obtained cheque books and other essential documentation for us. Each division held their final divisional meeting, and the divisions and departments were effectively disbanded upon completion.

Ascension was warm and sunny and seemed a million miles away from the cold and hostilities of the South Atlantic. The remainder of the journey home was to be by RAF VC10.

The flights home were not until the evening and we were allowed to kill time as we wished. André Lahiff and I went to the beach for a while, and then watched the Phantoms landing and taking off. Although the place was barren and volcanic, there were a couple of inviting sandy beaches but neither of us was in the mood. We hardly said a word all day, both lost in our own thoughts, mine of my family and our imminent return home, plus all those others, my friends still fighting in the South Atlantic. I hoped and prayed they would all return, and not share our fate although somehow I doubted all of them would make it. I was right.

The ship's company had already found the bar. By the time evening came, some of them, namely Scouse Morrison and Andy Myers, had had quite enough to drink. Somebody had upset Andy 'The Gorilla' Myers, and a space cleared around him as he became aggressive. The regulating staff on the island tried to intervene, which only made the situation worse. The First Lt arrived and tried to calm Myers down and also threatened to return him to Detention Quarters[8], which did not bother him in the slightest. Eventually though, things settled down. The Jimmy gave us an update of what had been happening 'down south.' He said the frigate *Ardent,* and our sister ship *Coventry* had both been bombed and sent to the bottom with a similar loss of life to that of our own ship. I had friends on both. I despaired.

The ship's company were taken to the airport. Scouse Morrison was far too pissed to be let near the plane, and the RAF loadmasters refused to let him on. The VC10 lifted off (minus Scouse), stopped to refuel in Dakar and arrived at RAF Brize Norton in Oxfordshire the following day. Flying home – what an inglorious way for sailors to return. We should have sailed.

Our war was over.

---

[8] Royal Navy prison

CHAPTER 9

This Was My Finest Hour

Summer 1982

On July 16th we had a memorial service in St Anne's church in the dockyard. I went down with Toni, and Mum and Dad. Nick Borritt the craggy faced Gunnery Instructor read the Roll of Honour. There was a child nearby sobbing with its mother. As the list of names was read out, it started wailing, "I want my daddy, I want my daddy."

I've never forgotten it. Nor can I forget the widows, the parents without sons, the other kids who would never see their dads again. It horrified me that there was nothing I could do to help them, to stem their tears. It was clear their sense of loss was overwhelming, their grief insurmountable, yet as I watched, my only thought was, 'there but for the grace of God, go I'. It was the only way I knew how to deal with it.

For the first few months after the war, mainly the summer of 1982, I'm told I was a nightmare, far more difficult than any 'normal' eighteen year old sailor. Most of the summer disappeared into an alcoholic blur, interspersed with bouts of fighting, aggression and violence. I wanted a release, I needed to vent on someone, anyone, I didn't care who, or why.

One night I was out drinking in the bar in the local holiday park, where tourists from Bedford and Wolverhampton would come to spend a week in a caravan or chalet in the summer. There was a kid called Damian in there who I didn't like. He was about the same age as me and it was the first time I'd seen him since I'd been home. He came up to me at the bar.

"Sorry to hear about what happened," he said. I shrugged and turned away. "Can't have been very pleasant," he continued.

I kept my back to him.

"Fuck off, twat." I said.

"There's no need to be like that," he said. "I'm sorry for what happened to you. An Exocet wasn't it?"

I turned round and punched him square in the face. He hit the deck.

"Fuck off, wanker," I said.

A crowd of people descended on me and dragged me outside.

After a moment or two, the Bar Manager appeared.

"You're not welcome here anymore," he said. "We don't need your sort in here. You're barred. And don't bother coming back or I'll get Beano to fill you in." He glared at me. "You think you're some kind of hard man do you? Let's see how you go against him. Now piss off." Beano was the local boxing champion. I knew of him because he'd been at my school, and I'd seen him throw a few trouble makers out of the chalet park before. I went off for more booze, not even marginally pacified by my unprovoked assault on Damian.

One night, a friend Jonesy and I, went to a party in North Walsham, a market town about fifteen miles away. Jonesy had just passed out of his army basic training at the infantry Junior Leaders Battalion in Shornecliffe, and we were on a drink-a-thon. He and I had been mates since we were eight years old; he'd just missed the war, though he subsequently reached the rank of Regimental Sergeant Major before being commissioned. He is now a Major and has more than made up for it.

At the party there was an environmentalist tree-hugging, peace-loving, do-gooder. Someone told her I'd just come home from the South Atlantic so she unloaded her opinion on me calling me a murderer, and a few other choice things. If it had been a bloke I'd have decked him but I managed to retain an ounce of decency, and stopped short of hitting a woman. Instead, "Piss off, you fat spotty fucking lesbian," came out of my mouth.

One of the blokes with her told me to watch my mouth or he would 'do' me. I looked at Jonesy and he raised his eyebrows at me quizically. I smiled and nodded. Jonesy tore down the hallway towards the living room, where the peace lover and her protector stood. He grabbed the doorframe and launched himself headlong at the protector, and delivered the most perfect flying head butt I'd ever seen. The bloke didn't know what had hit him. He was unconscious before he hit the floor. Jonesy and I pissed ourselves laughing and got into the drink.

One weekend we were having a party at my parent's house. It had started off in The Greyhound, our local pub, and everyone adjourned across the road to our house. The party was in full swing when a bloke called Mike made a lewd suggestion to one of Mum's friends. We didn't really know him that well, he had only just moved to the village, he wasn't specifically invited but tagged along with everyone else.

Mum's friend was mortally offended and a bit of a scene started. My dad came over to see what was happening, and when he was told what Mike had said, he grabbed hold of him and threw him out of the house. I saw the tail end of the action and rushed over to see if I could 'help'. I was still like a coiled spring. Toni and two other friends restrained me, but I was seriously pissed off at missing out on all the fun, so I poured more booze down my throat until my legs turned to rubber again, and I passed out.

The following week I was in the Pleasure Boat Inn down at Hickling Broad. My family and I had lived there for a while in 1972. The place was full, and I was pissed by the time we arrived. My sister Toni is older than me and usually she could control me, but not that night. Mike, the man Dad had kicked out of the house spotted me too. He walked towards me, apparently to offer to buy me a drink and apologise for the incident in the house, but I just lost it and went for him. Toni and another of our friends, John, grabbed hold of me and battled to keep me inside the pub as Mike ran out. I had one of them hanging on each arm, but I still managed to get out of the door. I was on fire with rage – the fact that the incident was long over, and had been dealt with, meant nothing. I was determined Mike was going to pay again. John was doing his best to get his arms round my neck, while Toni was trying to pin my arms to my side. But I fought them all the way, swinging wildly, determined to land one on Mike, who wanted nothing other than a quiet life. The more he backed off, the more enraged I became. Toni was terrified that this time, her stupid brother was really going to do some damage to someone. Eventually someone else waded in, and I was pinned down by sheer weight.

"Fucking lunatic," I heard someone say. "He should be locked up!"

Two weeks later I came home for the weekend. On a Friday between 4:30pm and 6:30pm, half price railcard tickets held by students and members of the armed forces couldn't be used out of Liverpool Street station because of the affluent city business suits trying to get home. This was a source of perpetual annoyance.

I had no intention of waiting another couple of hours, so I got on the train and went straight to the bar. There was a Royal Marine already there. He was still in his army trousers and olive green pullover with the shoulder flash announcing 'Royal Marines Commando'. He looked like a typical Marine, broad across the shoulders, hands like shovels, a crew cut and moustache.

He was buying a six-pack. I nodded to him. He nodded back. We retired to a corner, did the introductions and got stuck into the beer; Mick the Marine had clearly already had a few. The train lurched out of Liverpool Street and swayed across the tracks, clanking and clunking its way onto the rail heading north-east through East Anglia up to Norfolk.

I had recently been on a 'dance to France', a cheap overnight ferry trip to Le Havre. I'd come back laden with spirits and wine which were thrown in with the price of the ticket, and now, I had the wine and some gin in my bag.

A few of the business suits were in the bar, buying their end-of-week treat and talking about banks and stocks and deals and stuff that the bootneck and I knew nothing about. We minded our own business and whiled away the time chatting about our respective services. We talked a bit about the South Atlantic; I was in no real mood to go into it, neither was he.

"Excuse me." We turned around. A man in an immaculate pinstripe suit stood by the table.

"Were you in the Falklands?" he asked, a cut-glass accent.

Mick said very simply, "Yes."

"Can I buy you a drink?" the suit asked.

Mick gave the same simplistic answer, adding "please" as an afterthought. As the man turned to order at the bar, Mick said, "You better make it two. We both were."

The suit came back with two miniature bottles of Scotch, and placed them on the table. I hated Scotch.

"Do you know how proud it made us to be British, watching what you did?" he said. "We have showed… no not 'we', *you, you* have showed what it means to be British again. You have put the 'Great' back into Britain and it is something I personally will never forget. Cheers."

We clinked miniature bottles and skulled them. It was horrible and burned my throat.

The bloke must have been about fifty or so; certainly old enough to remember the Second World War, and Korea, Suez and all the other shit that had happened in the country in the past few decades.

Amongst the throngs of people in the buffet car were a couple of women

64

in their late twenties. Both dressed in smart suits carrying brief cases. I was in the standard weekend attire for sailors at the time – Fred Perry T-shirt with ship's crest over the left breast, jeans, white socks, and loafers.

I turned to Mick and said, "I don't fancy yours much."

"It seems to escape you that I am a Royal Marine," he said. "If it is female and breathing, it is fine. Whereas you are in the Navy and in your case it doesn't even have to be female."

We laughed like hell and the sound echoed around the carriage over the top of the subdued business speak. Everyone looked over but nothing was said. A couple more drinks arrived on the table. There was no introduction, just a nod. I nodded back.

An hour or so later, we had cleared suburbia and a lot of the suits had disembarked for their 2.4 kids and semi-detached weekends in Chelmsford and Colchester. The bar carriage was still half-full including the donor of the first Scotch.

"Tickets please," came the cry as the guard walked through the carriage. He stopped at Mick and me. He looked at Mick's ticket. Like me, Mick had used his half-price railcard. The guard slowly raised his eyes at him. "Your ticket's not valid on this train," he said.

"So what does that mean?" asked Mick, knowing full well the answer was to pay the balance, or get off at the next station and wait until the cheap trains arrive in a couple of hours.

The guard did not disappoint him. "Well what's it to be then?" he asked, when he'd explained.

"Fuck off," growled Mick.

The carriage was suddenly silent, the conversation stilled.

"What did you say?" snapped the guard.

The pinstripe intervened. "I think he told you to feck awf," he said, in all seriousness.

Mick and I pissed ourselves laughing, but we were the only ones.

The guard was furious. "I'll deal with you in a minute," he said to the suit, then he rounded on Mick. "Look mate, I don't care who you are, where you've been, or what you've done. The rules are the rules and either you pay up, or you get off."

Mick glanced sideways at me and I could tell he was pissed out of his brains. I was sure he was going to club the guard, and as far as I was concerned, rules or no rules, on just this one occasion, the guard would do better to exercise a bit of common sense and leave it.

The tension built and built, then came a woman's voice.

"You fucking little Hitler."

I looked up. One of the two women in the power suits was standing in the middle of the carriage, hair tied up, thin rimmed glasses, hands on hips. She towered over the guard even without heels, and she looked impressive. I felt my jaw drop, and as she took a step towards the guard, I remember thinking 'I'm gonna get myself a city business chick!'

"You call *that* a uniform?" she said to the nonplussed guard. "You're a disgrace. Look at it. It's filthy, and crumpled. Did you sleep in it?"

I was too stunned to laugh.

The guard took a step backwards, reddening. "Look madam, er…. the rules are… the rules. His ticket isn't valid."

"Valid, my arse," the woman snapped at him. "I'll pay the fucking money and then when I haul you and British Rail before the court of public opinion in every national newspaper on Monday, you can make your excuses to a grateful nation then."

I looked at Mick – his jaw was gaping too.

"You should be saluting these chaps, not persecuting them," the pinstripe chipped in.

"Here here," chorused his two colleagues.

That was the signal for the floodgates of verbal abuse to open, and the guard stood opening and closing his mouth like a goldfish, without making a sound. The great British public verbally harassed him into retreat, and he backed out of the carriage to a chorus of jeers and laughter.

I looked at Mick, and he gazed back at me, as amazed as I was. This was great; it confirmed that we were a law unto ourselves. In fact we were above the law, we could do whatever we liked and get away with it. Nothing could touch us.

Mick stood up, swaying slightly, though it was hard to tell whether it was the drink or the train. "Thanks for that, mate," he said to the nearest bloke.

"No, thank you," the man said, and that mantra was repeated all the way down the carriage – the thanks, the shaking of hands, the back-patting. Mick or any other Commando could probably have robbed a bank and got away with it if they'd been wearing a Royal Marines green beret. When he reached the woman who had sent the guard scuttling for cover, Mick stood in front of her with his arms folded. Eventually, she stepped forward and put her arms around his neck, and he unfolded his arms and threw them around her waist. Then he lifted her several inches from the floor.

When he put her down, she stepped back a pace. "Thank you," she said. "You're a hero."

As I watched, she then reached into her bag, took out a tissue, and put it up to his face. Then I realised, he was crying, Mick, the hard drinking, hard talking, hard fighting Commando – was crying. The commuters were all watching. Some turned and looked at me quizzically. I just looked back, I didn't know what else to do.

After a moment or two, the woman hugged Mick again and kissed him on the cheek. He pulled his shoulders back, held his head up, then turned to walk back. Everyone in his path had the sense to look away as he made his way back to his seat. As he sat down opposite me, I made sure I was staring out of the window. Then within seconds, a can of beer cracked open and was slid in front of me.

"Cheers," Mick said, holding up his own can.

As we drew into a station Mick's rescuer approached. "I'm getting off here," she said. "Don't forget. I mean it."

He turned his attention to her. "So do I."

She squeezed his shoulder then disappeared through the door.

I looked at him and raised my eyebrows and watched as a slow grin spread across his face.

"This mean green sex machine is gonna get him some good lovin' next weekend," he laughed.

"You reckon?"

He fished around in his pocket and pulled out a business card. I hadn't seen that little transaction.

"Next weekend," he said. "She's got a gaff up the West End, and yours truly is invited to stay."

He was grinning like the cat that got the cream.

"What about her mate, did you put a word in for me?"

"Sorry Jack," he said, laughing like an idiot. "Forgot to ask!"

The bastard!

The train pulled in at another hundred year old village station, most on this line looked like something straight out of 'The Railway Children'. I think most of the British Rail staff were as old as the buildings. A group of teenage school kids in smart uniforms got on the train and they looked at Mick's uniform as they walked past. Two girls and two boys, the girls were definitely sisters, one aged 11 or 12, the other nearer 15 or 16. They had wandered past a couple of times, the younger one skipping, still revelling in the impending freedom of the weekend's excitement that you have, when still caught in the wonderful innocence that pre-teen childhood is. She smiled a genuine smile, maybe remembering mum and dad's lessons that 'if ever in danger someone in uniform can be trusted'. They went past us again and stopped a little bit further up the carriage, whilst the younger one whispered in the elder's ear. Her sister responded but the younger girl shook her head and pushed the older girl towards us. They walked up to the table, the young girl half-hidden behind her elder sibling. They were both very fair haired but had deep brown eyes; I thought how unusual it looked.

"Excuse me," they said to Mick. "Are you a soldier?" The younger girl was blushing, the redness of her cheeks accentuating her milky white complexion.

No greater insult could ever be offered to a Royal Marine. His brow furrowed. I kicked him under the table. "They're only kids remember."

He thought for a moment before he answered. "No," he said finally. "I am a Royal Marine, they are better than soldiers."

I rolled my eyes skywards and sighed heavily.

"Were you in the war?"

"Yes I was."

The older girl held a paper and pen forward. "Can we have your autograph please?"

Mick took the paper and pen and scrawled his best moniker on it. He passed it to the younger girl, who beamed us a huge smile. Clearly this encounter was going to be worth swapping a few bubblegums for in the school playground on Monday. She took it, thanked him and skipped off.

"Thanks" said the older girl.

"You're welcome" slurred Mick.

"No, not just thanks for the autograph, but … for … everything, y'know – everything – that you did – all of you." She put her head down and didn't look whilst she spoke that part, it seemed difficult for her and I wondered why. She shifted uncomfortably on her feet. "Every morning in assembly we said prayers for your safe return – all of you, everybody down there. When the news had been on of ships sinking and people being killed in the battles, we prayed for those men, their souls and their families. I'm not religious, not many of us are or really believe in God, but if our assembly prayers helped bring you home safely, then I'm grateful that our school – me and my friends did what little we could."

I had a lump in my throat and I could feel tears welling up in my eyes. I couldn't speak but I just nodded an acknowledgement. Mick squeezed the girls hand and then we both turned and stared out of the window, neither wanting to look at the other. A few minutes passed. He looked at me.

"Are you surprised they asked me for my autograph then?" he slurred.

"No," I slurred back. "I'm just surprised a Royal Marine can write."

"Twat."

"Thanks."

Mick and I cracked the gin. I knew it was a mistake. By the time we got to Mick's stop, we were both wrecked. We burbled a good bye and promised to catch up again sometime, and Mick lurched off the train. He missed the step down and crashed onto the platform. I could hear him swearing. As the train pulled out of the station I watched him zig-zagging his way to the exit.

I continued to slurp the gin with the tonics we'd got from the bar until I was totally cabbaged and fell asleep on the train. One of the station staff was shaking me, we had slid quietly into Norwich, and the train was empty. I staggered off the carriage onto the platform and instead of ringing my dad to come and pick me up as I had arranged with him and mum, I decided to get the train to Great Yarmouth half an hour away. To this day, I have no idea why. I slumped down into a seat and fell asleep. It was 6:30pm.

When I regained consciousness, the train was empty, in darkness and I was freezing. I had no idea where I was. Somehow I managed to get off the train; I was confused and had no idea why I was standing next to a large sign saying 'Great Yarmouth'. I tried and failed to work out how I'd got there – eventually I spotted a taxi rank and staggered across to it. As I fell into one of the cabs, I slurred to the driver to take me to Hickling, some sixteen miles away.

"You got any money, mate?" he asked.

"'Course I 'ave. Just drive."

"Don't get stroppy with me," he said.

I didn't care. I was warm and comfortable so I settled down to sleep. I had a vague notion of someone asking if I had money, but it was too much effort to focus, so I gave up.

When I woke up, I found myself in a strange car. There was an old red brick building in front of me. I peered at it through the windscreen but there wasn't a flicker of recognition. I opened the car door and got out into the freezing night. Above the door, illuminated by a light, there was a sign: 'Police Station.' Fuck, I was in the shit – again. Just at that moment, the door opened and the cabbie and a young copper came out, the cab driver pointing at me. "That's him."

I didn't know what I'd done but it was obviously wrong, so I turned and ran. Instead of running down the driveway which sloped down to the road, I ran up onto the lawn which was level with the top of the driveway. At the end of the lawn where it met the pavement was a drop of about three feet. I was looking over my shoulder at the two men in pursuit and didn't see the drop. I ran straight off the end of it and crashed onto the pavement.

The copper and the cabbie ran down the driveway and out onto the pavement. I was already on my feet when I saw them and dashed straight out across the main carriageway of the trunk road that linked Norwich to the ferry port of Great Yarmouth. How I was not hit by a truck I will never know. The two men gave chase down the other side of the road catching glimpses of me in passing headlights until I disappeared down a ditch. They eventually gave up and returned to the police station, where the sergeant, Jed Stone, a friend of my dad's, was waiting for them.

"So where is he?" he asked.

"He did a runner," said the young copper sheepishly, when he got his breath back.

"A runner? I thought you said he was comatose and you couldn't even wake him up." He looked at the taxi driver, who shrugged.

"Have you called his old man yet?"

Sgt Stone had recognised me from a pack of photographs in my suitcase.

'No I was waiting till you two clowns brought him in.'

A few moments later, he made the call.

"Hello Jed, don't tell me – you've got my son," sighed Dad.

"No I haven't," Jed told him, "but I'd bloody well like to get my hands on him. He was last seen running down the carriageway of the A47 towards Norwich."

Jed briefed Dad and added that they had my Naval suitcase at the police station.

"Ok," Dad said. "I'll come and get it." It was midnight.

When I woke up, dawn was approaching, but I was shivering with cold, and I ached all over. I looked around me; wherever I was, it stank! I sat up, and added a splitting headache to my problems. I found myself on a cold concrete floor, there was a porcelain wash basin in front of me, and dingy cream walls around me, covered in graffiti. I grabbed the basin and hauled myself up, instantly a wave of nausea hit me, and I vomited. My head felt like it would burst. When I finished wretching, I opened my eyes to try to get some sense of where I was. A urinal trough. A toilet cubicle. A wash basin. I'd spent the night on the floor of a filthy public toilet.

I closed my eyes and tried to piece together the events of the previous evening. I could recall snippets but not much. The train, getting on the piss with the bootneck, the passengers telling the guard to piss off, a vague memory of a taxi but the rest was a blank. And to cap it all, my bag was missing; it must have been nicked, I didn't even know where I was. I staggered outside into the light, and took in the surroundings. There were two pubs almost adjacent with just a car park between them – The Kings Head, and the Queens Head. Acle. I was in Acle. That was the only place with those two pubs next to each other. How the hell did I get here?

I found a telephone box and felt around in my pockets for some change to call Mum and Dad. I had none, so I made a reverse charge call.

"Where are you?" said Dad, a sigh in his voice.

"The phone box in Acle, near the pub."

"Wait there."

The phone went down.

Half an hour later, Dad arrived; we drove almost all the way home in silence. Just before we reached the village, Dad asked, "So what happened?"

I told the truth. "I can't remember. I got a bit pissed, someone nicked my case off the train."

"Your mother's been worried sick all night."

I looked out of the window and just thought 'shit, shit, shit. I fucked up again. Why couldn't I learn my lesson?' We walked into the house; my Naval suitcase was laid on the living room floor.

"So your case got nicked did it?" Dad said. "What's that then?"

I hung my head in shame.

"Do you want to know what happened?" he went on.

Jesus, this sounded bad even by my standards.

He then recounted everything that Jed Stone and the taxi driver had told him when he went to collect my suitcase from the police station. He

71

had searched for me all over, as all dads would. Eventually he gave up and came home. I started to snigger.

"Funny! You think this is bloody funny do you?" he yelled. He was enraged, angry in a way I'd rarely seen before. I just shook my head like a stupid school kid.

"Do you have anything to say to your mother?"

Sorry hardly seemed adequate. No words seemed adequate.

"What'll happen now?" I asked.

"Tonight," he said, "I will take you to Caister police station where Jed will be. As will the taxi driver. You will pay him the £15 fare you owe him from last night plus whatever it costs him to get to Caister nick to collect it."

"But I was going out to town tonight with Andy."

I realised it was a stupid thing to say when I was halfway through saying it, but somehow, that didn't stop the words from spilling out of my mouth.

The look Mum gave me was response enough.

"Sorry," I said.

She shook her head and walked out.

"Whether or not you get done for fare evasion is down to Jed and the cab driver," Dad said. "Because I was a copper you'll probably get off with it, but that is only cos Jed owes me a favour. Now sort your bloody self out young man!"

He walked out, leaving me alone. Alone, that is, but for the incriminating suitcase, the monumental hangover, and the regret.

One afternoon I went to the town a couple of miles away where I'd gone to school. I went on the piss with one of my mates but the pubs closed at 2:30pm. He went home but I went next door to the off licence and decided I would be a bit more refined today. Instead of sitting on a park bench drinking beer from cans, I would sit on a park bench and skull a bottle of wine. The mother of one of the kids I'd been to school with saw me staggering down the road, swigging from the bottle and phoned my mum, who duly arrived to pick me up. I was like an old wino – only 50 years too early. I went home and crawled into bed. When I woke up, the bed was soaking – I'd pissed myself in my sleep.

CHAPTER 10

Losing It

I came home again for a couple of weeks leave. It consisted of little more than getting pissed, being obnoxious to people and alienating anyone who wanted to help. I'd replay the events of the South Atlantic and get angrier and angrier and look for a release. That came only with alcohol and whatever subsequent events were fuelled by the drinking sessions.

"Can you hear that?" Dad said. "It's your mother crying… because of you. You're an animal. You're a bloody moron."

I turned and walked out of the house, to the inevitable location – the pub. I rang my mate Andy and told him I needed to stay at his house for a while. He came and picked me up and we went to his place in a village four miles away. His mum and dad had a massive house, and I got camped up in the spare room. I didn't tell anyone where I'd gone. Although Mum and Dad were despairing at my drinking and behaviour, they were still expecting me home at closing time, but of course I didn't appear. And when I didn't come home all night, that caused them even more distress. They guessed where I was though, and Dad came round on his way to work the next morning. He walked into the room and just sat on the bed, then asked me with such sincerity, "Why are you here son?" The word 'son' stung me, it speared me to know I could hurt someone who cared about me and loved me so much.

As he sat staring at me, waiting for an answer, a tear ran down his face. I'd never seen my dad cry before. Next thing, he leaned over and hugged me tighter than I could ever remember. I didn't know it was possible to drown on dry land, but drowning I was – in the depths of my own despair. All I could say was that I was sorry and I would come home later the same day. I did so and made a really conscious effort to calm down.

Despite my best efforts though, I had learned a new emotion which was holding me back. I had learned how to hate, and it was remarkably easy. I hated the Argentinians, the place, the people, the politicians, the pilots who had flown against us. I hated the British politicians who fucked it all up, those in the British Task Force that had let us down. I hated everything – the situation, the war, and now I know – I hated myself.

One afternoon I'd had a good lunchtime session and really fancied a drop more to drink. The pubs were closed in the afternoon and there was no off licence in the village. So I came up with the most logical solution – I would simply drive to the next village, about three miles away, and go to the off licence there. The fact that I had drunk about ten pints and was probably four times over the legal limit was irrelevant.

All went according to plan until I lost control of the car. It mounted the pavement and headed straight for a group of six kids on bikes, who thank heavens, managed to scatter. I then tore through a hedge, and a fence, and came to rest in a field. When he saw what I'd done, my dad was incandescent with rage, and my sister's boyfriend said he would give me the hiding of a lifetime. He was restrained only by my sister and the other RAF guys who shared the house. It was in the road where they lived.

My mother had written to Commander Bootherstone, the CO of HMS *Arrow* to thank him for picking me up, after the abandonment of *Sheffield*. She also wrote to Major-General Jeremy Moore, the CO of the British land forces. Both of them had stated how proud they were of the young men under their command. Maj-Gen Moore said he had 'never been so proud, and if anyone complains about the youth of today, they should have been down here beside me, and seen the youth of today, those gutsy teenagers fighting like Trojans. Young lads with the hearts of lions, then let them complain about those same youths of today'.

When I read those replies, I wondered if I could include myself in the leagues of the men they were proud of. Not with my current behaviour I couldn't. I was ashamed at the heartache I'd brought my mother and father. My dad was an ex-Merchant Navy Officer, had been a policeman on Hull docks when it was the biggest deep sea trawling port in the world. He was no soft touch, but I had reduced him to tears.

My parents would have been justified in shutting the door on me, but they didn't. They carried on supporting me no matter how many times I disappointed them. Throughout that period, no matter how many times I embarrassed my sister in front of her friends with my appalling behaviour, she also gave me nothing but unflinching support and forgiveness. She hosted a party at Mum and Dad's house. Jonesy and I were inevitably pissed. We both stripped off and placed a beer glass at the end of the garden path. We then waddled up the path as fast as possible clenching a 10 pence piece between our arse cheeks. The objective of the 'game' was to run over the top of the glass and attempt to 'bomb' the coin into it. We invited Toni's friends to join in. They politely declined. It got to the stage when if she invited her friends round for a party or barbeque they'd ask, "Is your brother home on leave?" They'd clearly seen or heard enough of my behaviour.

Arrested (Again)

On 9th November 1982 I joined HMS *Nottingham*, the newest Type 42 destroyer the Navy had and also *Sheffield's* sister ship. I joined exactly the same day, lived in the same mess, was given the same part of ship to work on, the same watch – it was all uncannily and unnervingly similar. Not long before Christmas some of the lads in the mess had been out into Portsmouth for the night. I was drinking with Andy 'Sky' Larkin, another ex-*Sheffield*. After a suitably heavy drinking session in some of Portsmouth's finest hostelries, the evening culminated in Joanna's Disco on Southsea Esplanade. A few more pints in here just managed to push us over the edge of social comprehension. About 2am the disco closed and we all left. There was a fracas outside and I was arrested. It was no great meleé and I went quietly into the van. Upon arrival at the police station I was frogmarched inside, still in handcuffs. There was a sergeant on duty and a young woman copper behind the desk; there was a copper either side of me.

'What have we got here?' asked the sergeant. He had a face that had weathered a lot of storms and was wearing medal ribbons of a conflict long past on his police tunic.

"What's your name?"

"Lawton, Adam."

"How do I spell that?"

"A – D – A – M."

"I know very well how to spell Adam," snapped the sergeant, his patience clearly being tried.

"Well why did you ask then?"

A copper hit me in the ribs and I sank to my knees.

75

"Don't be a fucking smartarse in here," he said.

They dragged me to my feet and one of them took out my wallet from my back pocket and opened it. My Royal Navy ID card stared back at them.

"He's a matelot," said the copper.

"What a surprise," the sergeant said. "Call HMS *Nelson* and get them to send a patrol van round to pick him up. They can deal with him. Throw him in the cells till they arrive."

The copper grabbed hold of my arm and started pulling me towards the cells, but I resisted.

"Why are you getting the Navy to pick me up? Can't you deal with me yourselves? What's up with you, are you a queer, I bet that's it – you don't like girls do you?"

"Shut up, you fuckin' twat," the copper said.

"Ah, I've hit a soft spot haven't I," I said. "Is it the same soft spot that your mate touches when he does you with his truncheon?"

The cell door swung open with a squeal that told me the hinges needed oiling. I was flung on the floor and one of the coppers knelt on my back and removed the cuffs. Then I heard the door slam shut. As soon as I heard the key turn in the lock, I started mouthing off again.

"Now I can fight back, you lot piss off! You fuckin' chickens, come in here and have a go if you think you can."

There was someone singing, badly, in a cell further down. Another was generating the unmistakable sounds of its occupant vomiting.

"Shut the fuck up you lot," shouted one of the coppers.

"Piss off you queer," I yelled back.

The policewoman appeared at the window in the cell door.

"Look, why don't you just sit down quietly, you're not helping anyone being like this. Patrol are coming to get you, but they're tied up at the moment so it's going to be a couple of hours. Obviously we're going to tell them what you've been like."

"Show us your tits love."

The window slammed shut. It opened again a second later.

"Oi! Big mouth! Just keep fuckin' quiet OK, we've got enough to deal with without a twat like you. Understand?"

"Queer," was all I said in response.

I heard the cell door being unlocked. This meant that Naval Patrol had arrived to take me back to the barracks in HMS *Nelson*. The door swung open and the two coppers were stood there grinning, each of them was holding a telephone book. I froze. I had heard infamous stories of blokes in the cells getting a 'telephone booking' but I thought they were an urban myth. The only thing to do was assume the foetal position. I curled up tightly and wrapped my hands around my head.

Bruising is caused by the fracturing of blood vessels below the skin after a blow. When it is a sharp or pointed instrument delivering the blow, the bruising is worse. Telephone books are large and flat so they don't cause much bruising. Useful for inflicting untraceable pain on someone.

"Not such a brave big mouth now are you?" one of the coppers said, as he and his mate rained down blow after blow.

I was pleading with them to stop, but the thuds kept coming.

"For Christ's sake leave him alone, he's only a kid." The policewoman was standing at the door. Either the coppers were bored or knackered, but whatever, the 'telephone booking' ceased.

As the second copper left the cell, I muttered, "And let that be a lesson to you." One of them made to come back in but the WPC grabbed his arm. She pushed him out, then bent down and picked up a blanket which she draped over me. I was sobbing. The pain was excruciating.

I must have eventually drifted off to sleep because I was awoken by the cell door unlocking. It swung open and two RN Patrol members were stood there in full uniforms, white belts and gaiters.

"Aha, Able Seaman Lawton... again. What a surprise."

I recognised the Leading Regulator. He had been in HMS *Dryad* at the same time as me and dealt with a fracas there. He was also on duty when I'd been picked up the previous week. It was a relief to see them; at least I knew I wasn't going to get a monumental kicking even if I was going to get in the shit. They escorted me outside, where a blue Sherpa van with the wording Royal Naval Provost on the side was waiting. It was fitted with blue flashing lights like a police vehicle and there was cage wire on the windows. I climbed in the back; it stank of sick and disinfectant. We arrived at HMS *Nelson*, home of the RN Provost Marshal for Portsmouth.

I was taken in front of the duty Regulating Petty Officer (RPO). He was a fat bastard. The Leading Regulator read out my name, rate, and number, and gave a summary of what the police had told him. The 'telephone booking' was conspicuous by its absence. I wasn't asked to say anything.

I was still pissed and swaying a bit. "Stand to attention. Stand still, you fuckin' scrote," screamed the RPO.

I was doing my best and had decided that to antagonise anyone else in authority that night would be clinically insane. The RPO simply said, "cells".

"Left turn, left wheel, quick march! Left, right, left, right."

I was marched away supposedly in step with the Leading Reg' and his colleague, but it was more of a synchronised shamble. The cell was like most cells, a bed with a one inch thick mattress, a blanket and a small barred window. The Leading Regulator took my shoes and belt. I lay down on the mattress and pulled the blanket over me, but I couldn't sleep. About half an hour later the door was unlocked and swung open. The RPO was there.

"On your feet, geddup, stand up!" he screamed. I don't think he could talk without screaming. I sat up on the edge of the bunk, he grabbed me by the hair and hauled me to my feet, then he marched back to the cell door and stepped out. A Lieutenant entered the cell and the RPO followed him in. "Stand to attention when an officer enters the room," he screamed.

"Thank you RPO, that will be all" the Lieutenant said, in a calm, quiet manner.

"Sir, regulations state…"

"Yes RPO. I am aware of what regulations state. That will be all."

The RPO withdrew.

"As you were, Able Seaman Lawton," said the officer. I relaxed.

"Sit down."

I sat down on the bunk, immediately suspicious.

"What are you doing here, Lawton?"

"I was brought here by patrol sir."

"Why?"

"I don't know sir."

"Don't you? I think you do. You were in the South Atlantic this year weren't you? On *Sheffield* I believe."

"Yes sir."

"Wait here." He turned and left the cell. The Leading Regulator appeared a few seconds later. "Come with me," he said. I followed the Leading Reg; he opened the door of an office.

"Wait in here, sit down, be quiet."

"Yes Leading Reg."

The Lieutenant entered, I made to stand, but he said, "at ease," and I relaxed again. He had a file of papers and a couple of books; one looked like the Incident Log. He studied the documents and looked at me over the top of the Incident Log.

"Able Seaman Lawton, you came second out of thirty in your part II Seamanship class and third in your Radar class, that's not bad. You completed training and left HMS *Dryad* with six weeks accelerated advancement for promotion to Able Seaman. You had a promising career. What has happened to you?"

I was about to answer, and say "I don't know sir" when I stopped, I hesitated and I thought. I actually thought, and probably for the first time I reflected on what had happened and the path my life seemed to be taking. Could I be teetering on a precipice of my life being wasted – ruined? I was given another chance to live back in May, I could so easily have been amongst the casualties, to waste that chance would be an insult to all those who had that chance taken from them. I felt abandoned, let-down by the system, but I didn't want to say so or complain for fear of being seen as someone who lacked moral fibre. I had lost interest in the Navy, I thought it had lost interest in me. I just felt that no one cared, that no one gave a shit. However, there had been 30,000 people in the South Atlantic, some had it worse than me, some better, but had they gone around blaming everyone and everything else for whatever wasn't going right now? I realised that irrespective of the Navy, the system, the authorities or anything else, the responsibility for my actions lay with me. And I had really, really fucked up.

"Well" repeated the Lieutenant, "what has happened to you?"

I stuck with my originally intended answer "I don't know sir."

"How many times have you been picked up by patrol in the last four weeks?"

"I don't know sir."

"Why not?"

"I've never really thought sir."

"A very good point, Lawton," the Lieutenant said, still in that same controlled voice.

He put the documents down on the table and leaned back in his chair. He just looked at me; I didn't know whether I was supposed to say anything or try to explain so I just kept quiet. Then he leaned forward rested his forearms on the table, put his hands together and interlocked his fingers. He seemed to be studying me very closely without staring. It made me feel really uncomfortable, probably deliberately. I was suddenly nervous, almost scared of him.

"What have you thought about? And before you answer, saying 'I don't know sir' is not an acceptable response."

"I don't really have a response sir."

"Well at least you're honest," he said. "You are hardly covering yourself in glory are you? This is the third time you've been here in four weeks. Now on those two previous occasions, you were lucky. Although the doctor was satisfied that you had been drinking, you were not certified as medically drunk at the time. So basically you managed to get off with it. Do you know what QRRN's are?"

"Yes sir."

"What are they then?"

'They are the Queens Regulations for the Royal Navy sir."

"Correct. Are you aware of the penalties under Queens Regulations for returning to a Naval establishment drunk?"

I looked up at him. "But I had no intention of returning drunk sir. I was going to stay ashore until I sobered up but it was patrol that brought me back, so aren't they the ones who contravened the regulations by deliberately bringing me back when they know I shouldn't be here."

He looked at me, the corners of his mouthed twitched as he stifled a smile at my creative attempt to circumvent justice and Naval discipline. Then the smile disappeared. He ignored my technicality and with the same unnerving calm, simply repeated the question.

"Able Seaman Lawton, Are you aware of the penalties under Queens Regulations for returning to a Naval establishment drunk?"

I got the hint.

"Yes sir."

"I'm satisfied that if I wake the duty medic now, in your current state, you will be certified as drunk, would you agree?"

"Probably sir, yes."

He leaned forward in his chair and visibly relaxed. I wondered if he was trying to lull me into a false sense of security. He folded his arms and picked up the Incident Log and documents again.

"Is there any reason why I shouldn't do this Lawton?"

I was trying to think cohesively. There must have been a reason why he wasn't following standard protocol of waking the medic, having me certified as drunk and getting me in the shit again. Naval discipline is not flexible, those with rank and authority do not cut any slack or leeway to their subordinates and risk contravening regulations themselves. In front of me was an extremely decent Naval officer, an extremely decent man. A man willing to place compassion and understanding before the Naval Discipline Act and its consequential penalties.

I took a chance. "If you don't drop me in the rattle sir, I will sort myself out and won't get picked up by patrol again."

He beamed at me like a school teacher pleased that one of his class had finally grasped algebra.

"Excellent, Lawton. Now, how did you get those marks on your arms?" The smile disappeared.

"What marks?" I said.

"Those large red tomato-like blotches. I understand you were arrested by the police – correct?"

"Yes sir."

"Did they do that to you?"

"No sir," I lied.

"I don't believe you," he said. "If I investigate those marks and the circumstances of your arrest, it will mean waking the duty doctor, then in the course of examining you, he will certify you drunk and we have just agreed we will avoid that. Show me your back."

I unbuttoned my shirt and turned round, pulling my shirt tails up.

"That looks like a painful lesson you are not going to forget in a hurry."

"Yes sir." I said.

"Do you know what your problem is AB Lawton?" He looked extremely serious.

"Enlighten me sir."

"Exactly that," he said. "Your mouth. Or more accurately your inability to keep it shut and/or not make smart comments to people, like that sarcastic remark to me then. That's what lands you in it, you cannot help yourself. Looking at the information of your last two arrests it's a recurring problem. Do you agree?"

"No sir," I said. "That's not true."

He fixed me with a piercing stare. He was trying to help me, but I appeared not to be getting it. His tone changed slightly, it was the first time it had. He was serious, there was menace in his voice, he was getting his point across. He leant across the desk towards me, I leant backwards. "Well Lawton, it's a fact and it's one I suggest you address quickly and thoroughly. If you persist with this course of action what do you think will happen?"

He didn't wait for a reply. He stood up and walked to the back of the office, then he walked behind me speaking as he went. To sit there and have to face the front whilst being addressed from behind gave me a feeling of total helplessness. It was really unpleasant.

"Let me answer that for you. You will be awarded 'Second Class Punishment'. Do you know what a month of Second Class is like?"

"A major pain I would imagine sir."

"That's correct. After Second Class you could go to Detention Quarters. Do you know what a spell in DQs would be like?"

"I've heard it's not too bad if you don't mind PT sir?"

"Do you like PT Lawton?"

"No sir, I hate it."

"Then you wouldn't want a spell in DQs would you?"

"No sir."

"After that, the only option then is Colchester Military Corrective Training Centre. Have you heard about 'Colly,' Lawton?"

"Yes sir. It's the military prison where they send all the really bad and mad bastards."

"That's correct. There are some fairly unpleasant characters in there, and they are in for some fairly unpleasant activities. On completion of their sentences, most will be dishonourably discharged their service with disgrace. They'll be lucky if they can get a job again." He sat down again and looked directly at me. "How does that course of action sound?"

"Not very attractive sir."

"No I didn't think it would. You will stay here tonight and tomorrow morning you will be released with no further action. Is that clear?"

"Yes sir."

"Do you have anything to say?"

He reached for the telephone and picked up the handset.

"Yes sir, could I have a cup of tea please?"

He put the phone back down without dialling and looked at me incredulously.

"Is that all?"

I got the hint.

"No sir, thank you sir. I won't let you down sir."

The Lieutenant picked up the phone and summoned the Leading Regulator to escort me back to the cell.

The Leading Regulator opened the cell at 6am the following morning. He beckoned me to go with him, and I followed him down the hall. He opened a cupboard full of cleaning gear. There was no need to say anything, I knew the routine by now – you scrub your own cell out. I grabbed the mop, bucket and long handled scrubber, filled the bucket up with hot water and threw in a load of detergent. Half an hour later the cell was spotless. He returned with my belt and shoes. Once I put them on he held the door open for me to exit the cell. I followed him to the front desk. The fat RPO was there.

"If it was my decision I'd have thrown the book at you, you fucking little scrote. You're not worthy of being in this man's Navy!"

"Thank you RPO," I said, smirking at him.

The RPO's eyes narrowed. "Lawton, if you ever cross my path again, never mind my sword, so help me God, you'll be sorry you were ever born. Now get out of my sight."

"Right turn! Right wheel, quick march! Left, right, left, right."

The Leading Reg took me outside. As we walked towards the patrol van, he said, "You were lucky. You *are* lucky, but just remember, your luck eventually runs out. On any other night, you would probably be seriously in the rattle now."

"I know Leading Reg," I said. "I won't be back again."

And I meant it.

As I re-assimilated back into the Naval way of life in late '82 I tidied up my act, sorted myself out and kept out of trouble. I kept off the drink and by early 1983 things had returned pretty much to pre-war normality.

I can't remember if I thought that sort of behaviour was acceptable then, or if I even realised how destructive I was being. Reflecting back on it now, it is not something I am proud of but I simply couldn't help it.

On my return to the UK, throughout all this time, and despite all these incidents not one single individual Naval Officer, doctor, psychologist or counsellor approached me and so much as asked:

"Are you OK?"

"Do you want to talk about it?"

"Can we help?"

It was expected that we would carry on in good old British 'stiff upper lip' style. So carry on we did. We carried on wrecking people's lives, our own or others, it didn't really matter. I didn't realise then, but now I think that I was pissed off with the British Government, not for my being sent to war in the Falklands or for anything to do with my responsibilities as a seaman in the Royal Navy but for ignoring us when we got back. What happened to me was as a result of my accepting the Queens shilling and 'signing on the dotted line'. When you join the services, the reality is that you may be called on to fight and if necessary to die. I never imagined when I joined at the age of sixteen that within a year we'd be at war but I accepted it without question and with hindsight, without regret. I do believe however that if a Government is going to send its people to war (be they seventeen or thirty seven years old) it has a moral duty to look after them and help them get over the trauma of those events on their return.

CHAPTER 11

Seeking Closure

Easter, April 2001

Nineteen Years Later

The unpleasant memories of 82/83 had gone away, 'it' had been long forgotten, or so I thought. In 1995, I emigrated to Brisbane, Australia. I had a good job, had built a new house and was driving a brand new 4 x 4 Frontera; life was good. About 1998/99, for no apparent reason, memories of the war had begun to replay themselves in my head. The mix of emotions I'd experienced in 1982 had started to resurface, having been dormant for well over a decade. The sights, the sounds, the smells, even the smoke, all were haunting me, and I have to say, it scared me.

In April 2001 I went to New Zealand for a week. My sister Toni, brother-in-law Paul and their daughter Molly, who was three, had flown out for a few weeks to stay with friends. I decided to pop over to see them while they were in the area, taking my daughter Lucy, then six, with me. Not only would it be good to catch up with Toni, but also, it would give the two cousins a week together.

We stayed with Pete, one of Toni and Paul's friends whom they had met while travelling in Vietnam. He ran a dairy farm about half an hour's drive from Whangarei, on the far north east of the North Island. The whole area was quite remote, with the odd house or farm dotted around every few miles. The farmhouse was about a five minute drive back from the road, down a track, and was set amidst fields and meadows. I remember the house had a wide verandah at the back that looked on to a vista of green, rolling hills.

At this latitude it was quite cool, unlike the tropical climes of Brisbane, with the much deeper greens of the temperate climate, similar to England.

You could sit on the verandah and absorb the total silence. The peace was beautiful; I hadn't heard the sound of true silence for as long as I could remember.

Nothing had changed much between Toni and me since I'd last seen her in 1999. In fact nothing had changed much between us since we'd been toddlers; we've always been unusually close.

One night, all four of us had a few beers over dinner and Paul and Pete ambled off to bed. Toni and I sat up drinking a crate of Heineken; it was the only booze left in the house.

The conversation started as a bit of a catch-up, what had been happening since we'd last seen each other. We covered the usual stuff – jobs, kids etc. The night before we left Brisbane my latest girlfriend had kicked off a massive public scene in a packed outdoor restaurant, so that was the end of that. We had a bit of a laugh about it then we talked about the children, Lucy and Molly, and how they got on. They had spent a few weeks together in 1999 when we last holidayed in the UK but hadn't seen each other since. Since her mother and I divorced, Lucy had been living two weeks with me and two weeks with her mother; it seemed to suit her well.

Toni and I perched on a couple of stools as the mountain of empty beer cans and cigarette ends grew around us. At some point in the evening, I mentioned the South Atlantic. Toni asked if it had been troubling me, although she already knew the answer. It was the first time I'd mentioned the subject to her in a long time. It had hardly been mentioned at all in '82, which is when it should have been hung out to dry. It was all too painful then, and it became a taboo subject in our family's house, and my life. If the truth be known, no one knew how to deal with or address the subject.

We sat up all night and sank the entire crate of beer between us, and I had a download of what had happened over the previous couple of years. I told Toni how the events of 1982 kept coming back to me and as we talked, I made a decision to return to the South Atlantic. I thought of requesting a meeting with the two Argentinian fighter pilots who had flown the Exocet carrying Super Etendards. I asked Toni what she thought, and as always, she was totally supportive. I made my decision. Whatever it took, I would somehow find the men who sank *Sheffield*, and I would meet them in Argentina.

I believed what I needed was to return to the South Atlantic, to go to *Sheffield*'s memorial, to lay my wreath, and to say my goodbyes. I also felt I wanted to spend time with the Falklands people who were now living their chosen lives because of the sacrifice of my shipmates.

When I returned to Australia, I contacted Leading Seaman Bob Mullen. He had been the Leading Seaman in charge of 3Q Starboard mess where I was billeted when I first joined *Sheffield*. He had recently featured in an Exocet documentary in which the two Argentinian pilots were also interviewed. Bob put me in touch with Dominic Streatfield-James, a BBC researcher who was also an ex-Naval officer. He had been a Sub-Lieutenant on the destroyer *Gloucester* during the Gulf war in 1990-1991.

His interest in *Sheffield* arose because he'd heard that seconds before the Exocet hit, a pipe was made – "*AAWO op's room AAWO.*" The Principal Warfare Officer (PWO) realised something was wrong and made the broadcast over the ships tannoy/PA system to summon the AAWO back to the operations room to defend the ship. This made Dominic wonder why the AAWO wouldn't be at his defence watch position, manning the air plot as two hostile aircraft approached on attack profile. Thus, he began asking questions, and the documentary, an investigation into the loss of *Sheffield*, came into being.

Those still serving in the Royal Navy were prevented from appearing on the programme by the Ministry of Defence. The MoD maintained that there was never a cover up, yet they had 'lost' all our statements, refused to release any findings from the board of enquiry and made excuses for Lt Cdr Batho. Nobody was ever brought to account for the loss of *Sheffield*, even after the Task Force Commander, Rear Admiral Woodward expressed his 'surprise' that courts martial were not convened.

Lt Cdr Batho went on to be promoted twice more and given his own command. One of my shipmates from *Invincible* sailed under him aboard HMS *York* and said he was the most despised CO that any of the ship's company ever had the misfortune to sail under.

I contacted Dominic and explained who I was and what I wanted to do. He told me that one of the best people to talk to was a journalist and researcher named Nick Tozer in Argentina. I got in touch with Nick in Buenos Aires and told him what I was after. He said it would take a bit of arranging as the two pilots still required clearance from the Argentinian defence department to meet anyone. Nick though, was a bit of an international 'fixer' who arranged meetings like this. I was originally told he would charge me for his services, and I was well pissed off, but in the event, that didn't happen.

After I had returned to Australia, I felt much better. The talk with my sister had been extremely cathartic, but unfortunately my respite didn't last long. The dreams came back first, then the daydreaming – the sights, the sounds, the smells and even the taste of that acrid black smoke.

I tracked down a couple more members of the ship's company, with the help of the internet. One had been a Stoker in one of the engine rooms where the missile had entered. He had been badly burned, and had rocketed to unfortunate worldwide fame as he was filmed being raced across the flight deck of *Hermes* by medics who were wearing full anti flash and battle dress, he was wearing nothing but the rags that remained of his overalls with his hands swathed in bandages. The TV company that filmed the incident had sold the footage many times over all around the world, yet not one person had ever contacted him to ask how he felt about it being re-shown. He told me he rang the TV company to ask if they would make a financial contribution to help with his own return to the islands, where me might lay his own ghosts to rest. They refused.

I spoke to one of the lads who had been in the same mess as me. In late '82 he had joined HMS *Manchester* when she was brand new, just as I had joined *Nottingham*. There were a lot of ex-*Sheffields* and *Coventrys* on *Manchester*. When I was on *Nottingham* there were many occasions when she tied up alongside us. Although they were both brand new, *Manchester* was one of the Batch II Type 42s and was 'stretched' by about forty feet at the bow. There were also quite a few ex-*Coventrys* on *Nottingham* but only myself and Andy 'Sky' Larkin, the baby gunner were from the *Sheffield* Operations dept. Both being eighteen and from the same previous ship, we went ashore a lot together in 82/83.

I asked after certain members of the ships company. The stories were ugly and brutal. One man's eldest son left home as soon as he was old enough. The man himself told me, "he couldn't stand living with me, my eldest daughter went too. All the kids have been scared at one time or another, even my wife has. We haven't had one day's fun in our nineteen year marriage".

He was attending regular treatment sessions with 'Combat Stress', an organisation which deals with Post Traumatic Stress Disorder acquired in conflict. He told me he was attending with half a dozen other members of the ships company. Some, still only in their 40's, retired from work on 'Total Permanent Disability' pensions.

I thought about my intentions to return to the islands, and re-considered the meeting with the two pilots. I questioned whether I should be doing it, what my motives were. Listening to this information though, I knew very well what they were. If I didn't make an effort to deal with the problems that were plaguing me, then this would be my future too – my kids deserting me; my nearest and dearest terrified of me and group therapy while retired as permanently mentally disabled before I was even middle aged.

Through my searching, I had also located a couple of ex-Radar Plotters. Firstly I rang Chris Kent. I remembered Chris for leading the RPs in the New Years Eve 81/82 Sods Opera[9] when they did the brilliant take-off of The Village People doing 'YMCA'. He was the bloke mincing across the stage in stockings and suspenders. It had been over eighteen years since I'd seen or spoken to him, but he remembered me as the drunk, skinny eighteen year old who threatened to fill in half of the SAS. I also recalled him for the courage or stupidity of the 'wank, wank, wank' verse of the music man song to the SAS onboard RFA Resource in '82. He'd also stood up for me when the mess bully picked on me a second time, the first week I joined the ship. I told him how I was feeling, and some of the things I did and how it was affecting me. Chris said he had kept in touch with a lot of the lads and saw Bob Mullen regularly. He'd also seen a number of the blokes affected by the events.

"Are you drinking a lot?" was the first question he asked.

"No," I said, "I've never been a great drinker, not since 82/83 anyway. It doesn't affect me that way." I'd always been into fitness training and the drink played havoc with it; I'd rather train than drink. I told him of my plan to visit Argentina and meet the pilots. I asked him what he thought.

"Do what you have to do," he said. "It's your life, live it the way you need to." He warned me that it might not please everyone, but nevertheless, he wished me all the best, and told me to call him any time if I felt the need to talk about it again. We said we'd share a beer in Pompey when I was there for the 2002 reunion.

Sometime later I called Bob Mullen again to get Captain Salt's number. I told Bob of my intention, and he too, was totally supportive. He echoed Chris Kent's sentiments. "Do what you have to do."

I wanted to speak to Captain Salt to get his approval. We'd both been

---

[9] Shipboard entertainment, taking the form of spontaneous sing-alongs.

out of the Navy for many years, but good Captains keep their men's respect. When I rang him and introduced myself, he sounded as if he'd only heard from me yesterday. I think the only words I'd ever spoken to him before were, "aye aye sir". Now, he even insisted I call him Sam, which I just wasn't comfortable with. The message was the same – "If that's the way you have to deal with it, then do it, but let me caution you about involving journalists. They may not be as upfront as you are about their reasons for wanting to help you." We spoke a little more about the events themselves, about what happened afterwards and how the media reported it. I agreed the details of those conversations would remain confidential, and they do.

When the anniversary of the sinking came round in May of that year, I was particularly troubled. As usual I went and sat in a church and cried. It was affecting me very badly that year. My work was suffering, I wasn't sleeping, I wasn't training well at the gym, I wasn't eating properly. I found out later that some of the people at work had 'noticed' and thought that something was wrong, or that I 'was carrying some kind of burden with me'.

Although I was certain that the way for me to come to terms with all this lay in the South Atlantic rather than on some shrink's couch, I wanted to find a way of dealing with it until I could go. I went to a counselor from the Vietnam Veterans Counselling Service in Brisbane. She wanted me to start seeing a psychiatrist and having group therapy. I flatly refused, and she couldn't understand why. She pointed out that if I saw a person qualified in the treatment of these conditions, I could be officially diagnosed with Post Traumatic Stress Disorder, and this would enable myself and the person treating me to develop a full treatment plan and timetable.

She meant well and it was great in theory but I hated the thought of being diagnosed with an official mental disorder, or with some kind of psychiatric condition. What if a prospective (or current) employer found out? I couldn't believe it wouldn't affect my future career chances. Also, I had already been through one custody battle with my ex-wife over our daughter, Lucy. The last thing I wanted was someone alleging I was a screwed-up war veteran and then having to disprove it.

In fact, the following year that's exactly what did happen. Just weeks before I left for the Falkland Islands, my ex-wife's lawyer stood up in court and told the bench I was suffering severe mental problems from the effects of the war, and was in no way fit to be a parent to my daughter. Some of her family presented written statements to the court saying they had witnessed me swearing at Lucy, threatening to kick her and leaving her, at just five or six years old, alone in the house while I went out drinking all night. My ex-wife won the case. If my planned departure for the South Atlantic hadn't been imminent, I declared I would kill both her and her lawyer with my bare hands, for fabricating and presenting that shit.

May and June faded, as did the memories, but I was determined that next year I would sort it out. By Christmas, most of my trip to the Islands and to Argentina was arranged and I felt fine again. I felt almost as though the trip was no longer necessary. Needless to say, I was pissed off with this because I knew it would change at some point and there would be nothing I could do to control it.

I contacted a travel agent in Stanley and arranged an itinerary for a three-week stay in the islands, with accommodation and excursions to all the places I wanted to visit. I was shocked to discover that the cost of that three-week stay was more than the price of my round the world ticket. Through Denzil Connick, the secretary of the South Atlantic Medal Association (SAMA82), I got in touch with Terry Peck. Terry had been the Chief of Police at the time of the invasion, and had escaped and lived rough in the islands until he linked up with 3 Commando Brigade. He had fought with 3 Para on Mount Longdon, and was now the representative of the Association on the islands.

He emailed me to say he didn't mind the travel agents charging the fat American tourists extortionate prices, but didn't like to see the lads of '82 fleeced like that. He told me he would send me a revised itinerary. As good as his word, the following week a new itinerary came through. It was covered with phrases like 'pick up by Terry' and 'free'. The only things I paid for were my bed and board in the actual lodging houses, and the excursions. I didn't hold any grudges against the travel agent though, as I hadn't told them about why I was coming, or my connection with SAMA82.

Terry put me in touch with some of the islanders, who were to host me for overnight stays and excursions. Some of them emailed me with phrases like – 'things have definitely changed for the better since 1982, and that is thanks to you and all the others who came here, and we will never ever forget that'.

I believed that was what I needed to find out about if I was ever going to return to my normal self.

CHAPTER 12

Return to the South Atlantic

Saturday 30th March 2002

After twelve very long, cold and uncomfortable hours spent on the floor of Santiago airport, I checked in for the Mount Pleasant flight, wondering how many of my fellow passengers were making the journey for similar reasons to me. The destination was listed only as Mount Pleasant. The Falkland Islands was not mentioned, perhaps to save antagonizing the Chileans neighbours. I got talking to a German ornithologist and wildlife photographer who was interested in my reasons for going to what he described as 'the ends of the earth'. I told him I was going on holiday. I was too tired to get into the question and answer session that always follows when you tell people you took part in the events of 1982.

We passed through into the departure lounge and I looked around for anyone looking like an obvious military person. There were a few candidates but none I could have immediately fingered as matelot, squaddie or bootneck. Another elderly couple asked me my reasons for going; I stuck with the same story. They told me their son had paid for them to go on a unique holiday, something completely out of the ordinary. They were certainly in for that. I was satisfied that there was no one with any obvious military connections, although I would have been surprised if there were no military people onboard at all.

I was nervous as I took my seat, but it was a totally different kind of nervousness to that I'd experienced in 1982. Flying never normally bothers me but this time it did, so I sat next to a Chilean couple who spoke no English, which meant peace, quiet and reflection.

We took off for Punta Arenas, via Puerta Montt in early morning mist. During the journey south we transited over the Patagonian Andes. To give all passengers a decent chance at getting good views of the magnificent scenery below, the pilot started rolling the aircraft a considerable number of degrees onto one side for a few minutes and then back onto the opposite side. I wondered what it would have looked like to any other aircraft, a passenger 737 rolling from side to side. They would probably have thought the 'plane was in difficulties. I had managed to acquire the Chilean man's newspaper and was practicing my Spanish reading. There in the middle pages was a picture of General Mario Menendez, the Argentinian military commander during the 1982 war, who had finally surrendered to Major-General Jeremy Moore. The whole article was about the conflict and there were numerous other, now familiar photographs. I asked one of the hostesses who spoke English if they would translate it for me. It would be interesting to get the South American perspective of the twenty year anniversary.

It didn't say much that I didn't expect. The Argentinians believe that we seized the Islands from them in 1833; therefore they were the liberators simply repossessing what is rightfully theirs. Then it talked about some of the tactics and logistical issues they had faced which contributed to their downfall and defeat. I think the defeat of the Argentinian forces in 1982 was about more than just logistical difficulties but I'm not an expert and don't consider myself qualified to comment.

The scenery was breathtaking. There were rivers which didn't appear to be moving, then I realised, it was because they were ice. They weren't flat but it was as if the river had been freeze framed. It reminded me of when I saw a frozen waterfall in Norway. There were rugged mountain peaks bathed in snow and as the sun broke through the early morning mist and fog, the reflection turned the white of the peaks a mixture of purple and blue. I remembered the film 'Alive!' A Chilean rugby team's plane had crashed in this sort of terrain. Some of the survivors had eaten the dead and a couple of hardy souls had trekked across the Andes to find civilisation and rescue. They must have been quite something to accomplish what they did.

We finally arrived at Punta Arenas. The flying times of my journeys were getting shorter, yet they seemed to be taking longer as we neared the Falkland Islands. We were herded off the aircraft, processed through passport control because we were leaving Chile and then herded back through security. Each time, I had to take off my boots, which was a pain. The departure lounge was on the other side of a flimsy partition from arrivals. It seemed a long-winded procedure to achieve very little, but rules are rules.

On the journey to Punta I had struck up a conversation with a (unbeknown to me) Senior Naval Intelligence Officer from British Forces Falkland Islands (BFFI). In the ensuing conversation about Naval postings and drafts I found he had held a number of Operations Officer roles and commanded a Type 42 Destroyer which staggered me because he simply did not look old enough, or senior enough. (Although Commander Alan West, the Captain of the Type 21 Frigate HMS *Ardent,* which was sunk in Falkland Sound, was, having celebrated his thirty fourth birthday on the way south, the then youngest sea-going CO afloat.) He was justifiably awarded the Distinguished Service Cross for *Ardent's* participation and sacrifice. When the office on the plane told me he was 40 and a Commander it all seemed perfectly feasible but I was still a bit pissed off. He was older than me and looked half my age.

He told how he and his wife had been posted to the islands for a year and enjoyed it so much he had requested an extension to the appointment, which had been granted. I didn't know how a year-long posting to the islands was looked at in military circles. Was it a bonus or a potential marriage wrecker?

The things they had enjoyed most were the quality of life, which everything revolved around. Not being stuck on trains or sitting in traffic jams, and sure there was a price to pay for it, but they believed it was well worth it. I asked about the chance of getting a day at sea on the on-station warship, and explained that I had written to C-in-C Fleet, Admiral Sir Alan West (the then Captain of the previously mentioned HMS *Ardent*) asking about this. He had replied saying he could promise me nothing from London, but had passed my details on to the In-Theatre Operations Officer. The Commander and I exchanged phone numbers, and he said he would see what he could do.

CHAPTER 13

Punta Arenas to The Falkland Islands

As the aircraft sat on the runway, the young air stewardess's first mistake was to welcome everybody aboard the flight to 'Las Malvinas'. She hadn't finished speaking when an angry woman behind me shouted, "The name of the place is the FALKLAND ISLANDS!"

As we climbed above Tierra Del Fuego the pilot announced that our flight time was 1 hour 40 minutes, longer than I had imagined. I felt I was so close but it is five hundred and seven nautical miles from Punta to Mount Pleasant.

I tried to imagine what it was like for the pilots of *Armada Argentina* and *Fuérza Aerea Argentina* (the Argentinian equivalent of the Royal Navy's Fleet Air Arm and the Royal Air Force), setting out fully-armed to attack the British and to defend what they saw as part of their homeland. Most of them were Roman Catholics. Did they pray en route? Did they have their Rosary Beads with them and photos of their wives and children? We know some of them did from those who were captured after ejecting, and those found dead in the wreckage of their aircraft.

The journey passed uneventfully, save for the butterflies I felt. I was starting to feel physically sick now and was glad I hadn't touched a drink in a couple of days.

As the 737 descended through the cloud it bumped and rocked and for the first time in my life I was nervous coming into land at an airport. My mouth was dry, my palms were sweating, and my pulse was racing. I found myself thinking about songs with 'Return' in their title. The one that stuck with me was 'Return to Innocence' by Enigma. My heart was pounding now, and I was covered in goose pimples.

We cleared the lower cloud base and there was my first glimpse of the islands. The whole scene was scattered with patches of water, not quite lakes but bigger than gravel pits or large ponds. In amongst these were 'rock runs'. They looked just like rivers running down a mountain but they were all solid large rocks. I wasn't sure whether to just look and take it all in, or to take photographs. I settled for the latter and rattled off a few frames.

The military complex of Mount Pleasant looked small compared with its surroundings. One long runway big enough to accommodate the resident Tornadoes, the bi-weekly Tri-Star and any other aircraft the RAF wanted.

The aircraft circled around the south end of Mount Pleasant and banked steeply to port to face westwards into the wind. I was praying for the pilot not to screw this one up, not that there was any reason why he should, but I just wanted to be on the ground. The tension increased as did the noise and vibration as the flaps slid back and down, the plane leveled off, squared itself with the runway and with the gentlest of touches made it safely into Mount Pleasant Airport, the Falkland Islands. The stewardess hedged her bets this time by just welcoming us to 'Mount Pleasant'. I was here – at last.

It was a massive feeling of relief as I descended the stairway onto the tarmac. I looked around at the rugged and rocky surrounding hills which hadn't changed in a million years and at the still quite pristine buildings and roadways, which were populated with the occasional disinterested-looking servicemen.

It was a basic military airbase with added customs and baggage retrieval. The Customs Officer was a Royal Marine veteran who had settled in the Falklands. I came through and recognised my host Terry Peck and his wife Eli from the photographs I had seen. Terry shook hands with me warmly and firmly and in a broad West Country drawl welcomed me to the islands. We made our way out to a four wheel drive jeep, and I loaded my bags into it, and we set off for Stanley. We chatted about the journey and the route I had taken from Australia, and Terry started up a running commentary about the landscape. Not long after we started off, he pointed out Briggs Road in the military complex, named after Petty Officer David Briggs DSM (Posthumous), the Petty Officer Stoker lost in *Sheffield*.

As we drove from Mount Pleasant to Stanley, a distance of some 35 miles, I realised that all the roads in the MPA complex were sealed and tarmacked. Beyond the complex though, on the stretch into Stanley, the road was unsealed and stoned. With the heaving South Atlantic on our right, and the mountains on our left, the first major landmark we passed was Mount Challenger, a very long steep sided outcrop. This was followed by Mount Harriett and Mount William, taken by 42 Commando Royal Marines and the Gurkhas respectively. They looked like dinosaurs buried up to their shoulders by the earth, with only their backs sticking out, topped by stone Stegosaurus fins. When I had lived in Hull, one of my regular fitness training partners was an ex-Royal Marine who had been on Mt Harriett. Above his fireplace, he had a painting of his company going into the night attack; I had often wondered what it looked like – this was it. Terry stopped and let me take photographs when I wanted to. We passed a sign warning of a minefield on the other side of the fence. There would be plenty more of these in the next couple of weeks.

We drove into Stanley past a road sign that told me it was twinned with Whitby, not far from my own origins in Hull. Whitby was also the birthplace of Captain James Cook who discovered Australia, where I live now. We passed buildings that were glaringly new, like the Cable and Wireless building and the school with an appallingly bright blue roof that contrasted well with the old Government House, the scene of so much action twenty years before. The Governor's residence had a big glass conservatory along the front. It looked to me like an over-sized greenhouse. I wondered how the tomatoes were coming along.

We turned along the sea front road and stopped where I got my first glimpse of the 1982 Liberation Memorial outside the Secretariat where the surrender was signed. The wind had whipped up and was now howling down the harbour from the mountains. It was freezing and cut into my face and ears. I'd last experienced this sort of weather on an oil rig in the North Sea in about 1993.

Terry introduced me to a couple who had just pulled up. Tony and Ailsa Heathman ran the farm at Estancia House, and I would be staying with them the next day.

Arriving at Shackleton Drive, the first thing I noticed was the smell of the burning peat fires. I unloaded all my gear with Terry whilst Eli cooked supper. Terry and I sat down for a quiet beer and talked about the events of twenty years ago, before I took a much needed long hot shower, shampoo and shave. It's amazing how those three small things can make you feel like a million dollars when you've been deprived of them for a few days. Eli served up a sumptuous meal. The best scran I'd had in days. I started to laugh at the thought of the rubbish I'd eaten en route through Tahiti, Easter Island, on planes and in airports, then to be presented with roast lamb with all the trimmings – it was heaven. To have it washed down with a beer or two was just perfect.

After the meal, the tiredness hit. I was knackered and I slept soundly for more than twelve hours, which was something I hadn't done since I was about two years old. It was also the first decent sleep since the night before I departed Australia on the previous Tuesday.

CHAPTER 14

Welcome to The Falkland Islands

Sunday dawned in a first class fashion – a cup of tea in bed, bloody ripper mate! And rare! The only time this happened was when I returned to the UK once every few years to stay with Mum and Dad, or when I could get a decent girlfriend (and they have been few and far between). A minor thing, but a bonus way to kick off the day.

After a magnificent breakfast courtesy of Eli, Terry and I went through the books, photos and stories of the events that had brought us together. Never before had I been made to feel so welcome and offered such a home away from home. If this was a sign of the hospitality and understanding to come from the islands and the islanders then I had made the right decision to return here.

I walked up to Stanley Services to see a girl I had struck up an e-mail exchange with. I presented her with one of the little cuddly cling-on koalas I had brought as a 'thank you' for all the people who had helped, and were going to help me with transport, accommodation and the like. In return she gave me a big map of the islands to help me find my way around.

Stanley is the smallest and most remote capital city in the world. It feels like a British village, with red telephone boxes and letter boxes. It must be the only capital city with a cathedral, that is not actually a 'city'. The whole place is built on a north facing slope overlooking the harbour, and catches the daytime sun throughout the year.

I started the day with what would become a habit now, loading my gear into the wagon for the move to my next hosts. I got rid of all non-essentials for this week and stowed them in the corner of Terry's spare room. Terry and I took a drive into Stanley past the 'Globe' pub and along Ross Road, made famous by footage of Argentinian tracked vehicles after the invasion.

Whilst wandering around the main store I was introduced to Gavin and Deirdre, a couple from Fox Bay on West Falkland and their daughter

Rachel. Their little girl looked to be the same age as my own daughter Lucy. I showed Rachel the photo I carry in my wallet of Lucy cuddling a koala at one of the nearby wildlife parks in Brisbane. I asked her if she knew what the animal was. She shook her head shyly. Then I produced one of the little cuddly koalas from my jacket pocket and handed it to her. She was fascinated and had obviously never seen one before, but living here, that was hardly surprising. She whispered a thank you and ran back to her mum. The family asked if I would be visiting the west and I told them I did have a couple of days in Port Howard. They invited me to stay if I was in West Falkland. The hospitality and 'open house' of the Falklanders is legendary but I was still surprised at how true it was.

I wandered across the road to the gift shop to locate a couple of postcards to send to the very few people I had promised one to, then once I'd finished we set off for the Heathman's and Estancia House. We took the same road along the harbour front as we had done the previous afternoon. It seemed different though, the day before I hadn't even noticed the Upland Goose Hotel. I'd been trying to take in so much, but I was dog tired, so I don't think I'd really seen anything. Now though, the colours looked brighter, sharper, no doubt my senses returning to normal after a good night's sleep.

We passed Mount Harriett again and I was awestruck at the rock formations of the mountain. How someone had managed to get up there and fight on it was a whole other question, and one I was determined to answer by climbing to the top for myself when I got back to Stanley in a week or so. After passing Harriett and just before reaching Mount Challenger, we turned right onto the Mount Kent road. We crested the top and I saw the long spiny vertebrae of Goat Ridge and just north of that, the impressive twin peaks of Two Sisters.

Mount Kent is the second highest mountain of East Falkland and now home to the RAF radar station. Near the foot of Kent we pulled off the road at the sight of the wreckage of two Argentinian helicopters, a Puma and a Chinook which were shot down by Sea Harriers. I can't remember whether Terry said he had witnessed the incident or had had it recounted to him. Either way, for all its carnage, it had been a spectacular sight. The choppers had been full of troops and the Harriers on Combat Air Patrol came upon them by chance. The two Harriers had streaked over the mountain top, screamed across the terrain looking like they were no more than ten feet from the ground and engaged the choppers with 30mm Aden

Cannon. Of course, they never stood a chance and crashed to the ground in flames.

All that remained in the wreckage were the rotor blades. Terry said that was pretty much all that had remained immediately after the incident as a reminder of the last few moments of an awful lot of men. I wondered what had been going through the minds of the pilots in the helicopters. The ones in the back probably wouldn't have known what hit them, maybe the pilots wouldn't have either, depending upon how observant they were and how much time they had to react. I put the thoughts out of my mind.

Nearby was a large rock run. I looked in awe at the vicious looking stone run zigzagging down the mountain and I picked up a piece of rock, which was surprisingly light for its size. I was expecting it to be almost as heavy as granite, but when I tapped it on the ground, it fractured in half to reveal a bright pink inside. Contrasted against the grey exterior, it reminded me of a freshly caught salmon cut in half. I had a couple of mates who were geologists, from some work I'd done in the mining industry. I wondered what they would make of it.

We arrived at Estancia and had tea and cakes. It was a good job I had a lot of walking, mountain climbing and physical exertion of one form or another planned, because if I was going to be fed like this every time I went to someone's house, I'd be a right fat knacker within three weeks. I thought the Islanders must do lots of walking and similar activities because if this is the lifestyle, why weren't they all enormous?

We talked again about 1982. It was what I had in common with everyone there and I wanted to hear it from the point of view of the civilians and Islanders.

Hearing them talk reminded me of a holiday I'd had on Guernsey when I was about twelve. There I had heard from some of the locals who had lived through the only part of the British Isles to come under Nazi occupation during WWII. In the Falklands, as in Guernsey, the women talked about how they had told the occupiers exactly what they thought of them and exactly what they could do. Maybe an occupying army is less likely to shoot a mother than the man of the house.

Terry and Eli left to go back to Stanley, leaving me in the capable hands of Tony and Ailsa Heathman. They were clearly outdoor people, with fresh complexions from so much clean air. They had lived at Estancia since 1980 and in May/June 1982, had hosted six hundred men from the 3rd Battalion the Parachute Regiment in their garden and shearing shed, just as their daughter Nyree, had her first birthday. They still kept in touch with some people from 3 Para, including two of my friends in Brisbane, Stephen (Oz) Straughan and his wife Caroline. Steve had been in 3 Para and fought on Mount Longdon, Caroline had then been married to another Paratrooper, Mark Dodsworth, who had sadly been killed on the mountain. I had seen Steve and Caroline just prior to departing and they had said to pass on their regards.

I tried to ask a few intelligent questions about the amount of land the farm owned and numbers of sheep etc, but all I know about farming comes from going to my uncle's farm on the Yorkshire Wolds for my summer holidays when I was a kid, getting in the way and pissing everyone off until I got sent home again. The difference here was that the place was full of dogs. Masses of them, a dozen or more. Obviously, with a lot of sheep, they would be needed.

After a long sleep and a couple of marathon meals, I wanted a walk to clear my head, so I headed off west across the estuary and walked along the southern edge of an inlet that led up to Estancia Brook. It tapered to a pointed headland with Sparrow Rincon on my left and Paso Grande Creek beyond. Eventually I was left with water on both sides of me and I sat and marveled at the scenery.

Where the tide hadn't gone out, the sea was a stunning deep blue. It contrasted with the pale sandy shores and the backdrop of the drab green of Mount Estancia and Mount Vernet, making the Estancia settlement minute by comparison.

Looking in one direction I could have been in the Yorkshire Dales, in another the Lake District, the Derbyshire Peak District, or the highlands and islands of Scotland. A cloudless sky reflected on the sea. It was quiet and eerily still, and I felt as though I could have screamed out at hundreds of decibels and no-one would have heard me. So I did. And they didn't. It felt great.

This was the first time I'd come across vertical slabs of rock. All I know about the earth's crust is from science lessons when I was about thirteen, or from watching the odd National Geographic broadcast about volcanoes. It appeared that all the layers of rock, which were anywhere from one inch to six inches in thickness, had been turned through ninety degrees and were sticking out of the ground. I had never seen anything like it before and assumed it was to do with layers of rock or plates inside the earth's crust pushing together against one another, the weakest one giving way and being pushed up.

I found the remnants of an old machine gun nest made from bits of pallet and corrugated tin that someone had carted from Christ knows where. (Or why, there was nothing there to guard?) I climbed up the bank into it to assess the view and to try to second-guess what its previous owner's intentions or orders would have been.

I turned around and came back down the bank on the north side. The tide was out, leaving miles and miles of mud flats, not too dissimilar from sights I'd seen on the Norfolk coast where I grew up.

It couldn't have looked more peaceful and I felt a pang of resentment at whichever stupid fuckers were responsible for screwing this up in the first place, whether it was one hundred per cent Galtieri and his cronies, or Thatcher and her Government. That was a thought I hadn't really paid much heed to before but it was a question I was going to be asking of the Islanders – did you know or think invasion was a possibility? Did you try to warn London? Did they listen? Why had the war happened? Had the British appeased Galtieri in the way that Neville Chamberlain pandered to Hitler?

I sat down then and asked myself some questions, saying them out loud. Why was I here? What was I doing? What did I hope to achieve?

I was glad there was no one listening as I started on the answers. I had come here to rid myself of everything associated with the events of 1982, with twenty years of guilt, of anger, of frustration and the inability to do anything about what had happened. As I sat having this conversation with myself, something I'd never done before, I did actually wonder if I might be going mad(der). So I felt guilty, about what? About surviving when others didn't, about not being able to save *Sheffield*, and if we had been able to, perhaps saving other ships from the same fate, and other sailors too. About not shooting down the attacking aircraft that had hit us. About not doing my best, not trying hard enough to save the ship, or some of the men. Could I have done more?

Why did I feel so angry? The anger was for similar reasons. I felt anger too at chance, for dealing so many bad cards on that day. If one of a number of factors had been removed from the equation, then I know the outcome would have been different. Would we have survived the next few weeks of war? I would never know.

And my frustration? I was frustrated at not getting a fair crack of the whip. I have heard that war is the ultimate test of a man's character and courage. I'd had my only chance to prove myself – but did I fail? We'd been welcomed home as heroes. Heroes for what? There's nothing big or proud about being sunk.

As I sat there, further thoughts crept in – When my daughter Lucy looks at the photos of my ships and medals, and when we march together on Anzac Day, or Remembrance Day, and she asks, "Why, Daddy?" What answers do I give her? I have none.

I also thought about my own mortality. How had the nearness to death, my own and that of my shipmates, and of course the loss of my ship, affected me? How would I ever make sense of such senseless waste and loss? How would I ever live with the memories? Would the guilt wear off or would I simply sidestep it, bury it, knowing it had no place in my life? Some people had never given such things a second thought. What happened had been almost a non-event to them. Why couldn't it be like that for me?

I hoped that at some point, either the answers would come, or the questions would simply fade away.

Trekking across the estuary, I saw ahead of me a long white trail that looked like chalk fragments. When I got closer it turned out to be hundreds of yards of sheep's skulls and bones. This was where you threw the carcass once you've finished with it. I walked along the length of the sheep's graveyard, the bones picked clean, almost pure white.

When I got back I explored the yard at Estancia House. There was a complete whale skeleton about twelve feet long, and next to it, a single whale vertebra, twice the size of the ones in the full skeleton. That must have been one massive whale.

There were old army trucks, left where they were last used in 1982. I let my imagination run riot as to what I could have built here with a cutting torch and welding set.

I felt relieved and refreshed at the physical and mental cleansing. Tony Heathman insisted on taking me on a run across the fields on the other side of his land, west towards Bluff Cove Peak, where Brigade HQ had been situated. Back in Brisbane I owned a Vauxhall Frontera 4x4 but this was my first real experience of 'true 4-wheel driving' Falklands style. We parked up and took a walk up the hill encountering a couple of well-constructed sangars, or lookout posts. Their architects should have been making a living in Yorkshire building stone walls. Not only were they still standing, but they were sturdy and windproof. As I perched on the rim of one, I noticed that next to me was a belt of 7.62mm ammunition from a General Purpose Machine Gun which is a big heavy Rambo style machine-gun fired from a bipod. Not too far from a large crater, was a piece of parachute strap with the heavy metal ring from the back end of a bomb still attached to it.

A few feet away lay the fusing mechanism and tail fins of the offending 500lb parachute retarded bomb, with the remaining parachute straps and cords attached to it. It had been one of a number which had been dropped in an attempt to kill the British Field Commanders, but it landed at the wrong time and didn't harm anyone.

Further up the hill toward Bluff Cove Peak was another crater surrounded by sangars and old jerry cans, which had what appeared to be both bullet and shrapnel holes torn raggedly through the centre of them. I wondered how men could survive such massively traumatic injuries. I thought of what it was like inside the 'Red and Green Life Machine' at Ajax Bay at the height of battles, then my thoughts took me to the casualties I had seen being casevac'd from *Sheffield*; the burns, the shrapnel wounds. I shuddered and turned towards the bottom of the hill.

Further down the gully was where the 105mm battery had been. It was still easy to see the position of each gun, marked as they were by stacks of empty and rusty ammunition boxes, black plastic charge containers, sandbags, pallets, bits of camouflage netting, and other debris. The sun was very low in the western sky now, and the peace, quiet and beauty of East Falkland in the shade of Mount Kent was eerie. The mountains, wind, and peat bogs all made by nature, accompanied by military hardware and the junk of war strewn around. The place had seen so much bloodshed in such a short space of time, while before '82, the only deaths would have been from natural causes.

As we arrived back, the sun was slipping beyond the hills of San Carlos. The gold hue faded, leaving pink and purple strips of light cloud over the farm. Other than that, the sky was still clear. Hopefully it would be a fine day tomorrow.

Tony got us back to Estancia House just in time for everyone's favourite meal, '365'. That's what they call mutton in the Falklands because they eat it every day of the year.

Over the meal we talked about the events of the month of May, twenty years ago. I wasn't surprised to find that everyone's memories were as vivid as mine; they are not the kind of things you forget.

I listened to accounts of the initial invasion and occupation through to when the Argentinians arrived at Estancia Farm. Ailsa said that around the time of their daughter's first birthday, some Argentinian soldiers had arrived at the house looking for food and/or supplies, but had been sent on their way. Shortly after, one of their officers came down to 'rectify the situation' only to be told by Ailsa, in that broad West Country twang that is native to the islanders, "You're not getting anything from me. Now fuck off!" She then slammed the door in his face.

Upon arrival of the 3rd Battalion, the Parachute Regiment, one of the rooms inside Estancia House was turned into a casualty station, mainly for Paras with trench foot. The remainder of the Paras were taking it in turns to sleep in the shed outside. When he told the story, my mate Oz went into great detail, always laughing, about how they would look forward to coming back from patrol because they knew they'd get 'a night in the sheds.' Under the circumstances, the filthy stinking shearing sheds were five star luxury compared with sleeping in a water-logged hole in the ground, covered by a poncho.

The Heathmans asked about Caroline Straughan and how she was doing. They had hosted her on her own pilgrimage some years ago and also talked of another girl who had been there with her and suffered in the same way. Unfortunately, to the best of our collective knowledge she had not managed to 'hold it together' and no-one knew what had become of her.

They talked about how much had changed since the war and it was clear that they were very grateful to the men and women of the Task Force who had come to liberate them. Tony produced a photo album of the attack on the two helicopters I had seen on the way there, showing great palls of smoke rising over the ridge. He was also a great fan of the 'Royle Family' on TV and we laughed a lot about that.

Ailsa told me that Captain (now Rear Admiral Retired) Christopher 'Kit' Layman DSO MVO RN was staying at Port Howard Lodge on West Falkland. He was the Captain of HMS *Argonaut* in 1982 and had lost two ship's company in bombing attacks on 21st May. He had also been my Captain on HMS *Invincible* in 1985 and left there to take up the post of Commander British Forces Falkland Islands (CBiFFi) in 1986. The brother of one the men lost in *Argonaut* lived on Macleay Island just off the coast of Brisbane. I had been to a few Naval piss-ups with him and I'd thought of him and his family, as my flight from Brisbane took off and passed over his island.

Ailsa rang Admiral Layman and they chatted like old friends, which of course by now they were. I spoke to him and although I didn't expect him to remember me, when I relayed a story of the sketch I took part in at a

Sods Opera, he remembered me and the other AB, Brum Hansford, who had performed the 'Everybody needs somebody to love' scene from the movie *The Blues Brothers*.

"Yes, I remember it well, the star turn it was," he said. The day after the performance on the *Invincible*, I was on watch on the bridge. Capt Layman had said to the bridge staff that it was "damned well executed", which I presumed was Naval Captain talk for 'shit hot'.

I was told that Admiral Layman visited the Islands almost every year on fishing trips and I tried to re-arrange my itinerary to get a day's fishing with him, but it was not to be. He left Port Howard the day before I arrived from Sealion Island, and had departed Stanley for the UK before I arrived back in town. I had enormous respect for Captain Layman, an excellent Naval Officer and Captain, who saw that his officers and men who were competent, were promoted or recognised, not because they sucked up to him or laughed at his jokes, but because they were good at their jobs. He thoroughly deserved the rank and success he achieved.

On the evening of Sunday 1st April the local radio station re-broadcast all the original taped programmes, broadcasts, and speeches made by Sir Rex Hunt. It was a minute by minute account of the approach of the Argentinian invasion force and was real edge of the seat stuff. It went into great detail about the movements of the Argentinians towards the islands, and what the civilian population should do, and gave regular updates on the massively outnumbered Royal Marine garrison which was doing its utmost to prolong the inevitable fall of Government House.

In the midst of the two-decade old broadcasts, a speech was relayed from a modern day Argentinian politician. It is probably one of the most sensible things I have ever heard a politician (irrespective of nationality) say. His words were "*Until such time as we can offer the Islanders at least what they already have, but realistically substantially more than that, then they are absolutely not going to bother even talking to us.*"

Exactly. Who would look for another job with a lower salary? Nobody.

At the moment the Falklanders are very well off in terms of development, investment, and prosperity. They have nothing to gain by taking any form of governance, assistance or input from Buenos Aires.

There is significant money to be made from the fishing around the islands. They could be worth a lot to Argentina but they couldn't solve that country's problems. Argentina is a large country with a population of twenty million. The money generated by 2000 Falkland Islanders would not even make a dent in its mountain of debt.

It's also important we remember the cost of the conservation and wildlife programmes, which preserve creatures such as sea lions and sea elephants in their natural habitats.

Would the Argentinians bother to do this? Let's face it, they didn't even bother trying to save the future human generations so I wouldn't hold out too much hope for the animals if things went really pear-shaped again.

CHAPTER 15

Mount Estancia

I decided I would climb Mount Estancia. I wanted to try and gauge what 3 Para had achieved by climbing those formidable mountains and then managing to fight their way up others and re-take them. It was of course different as I was doing it in broad daylight, I was carrying just cameras, and I only had the wind to cope with, nothing compared with what the squaddies of 1982 had against them.

It was less than fifteen hundred feet high so it was hardly a mountain but to someone who hadn't done any hill walking in many years (or in fact at all), it looked rather imposing. I knew I couldn't take all day because Ailsa had to run me to Douglas and then get herself back. I also didn't know how I would fair with the weather; if I didn't wrap up well enough, the wind and cold would bring me down in no time. If I took too much clothing and started to sweat, I'd have to take it off and carry it, together with the cameras and other accessories I wanted to take. In the end, I decided I was better too hot than too cold, so I decided to wrap up.

It was a good job I wasn't in a fashion parade. The trousers I'd selected as the mainstay for the three week hike around the Islands were a baggy pair of stone-washed jeans that were gathered at the ankles, with side pockets big enough for all my maps and other paraphernalia. I'd bought them in the States almost ten years ago, when they were trendy. They had been in a box in my garage ever since and only saved from extinction by this upcoming trip. I hoped it didn't rain; denim was a bastard if it got wet and if these got soaked, they'd weigh a ton and probably chafe like hell. Having thought I'd had a big enough whinge to myself about what could possibly go wrong I left the house and headed off across the fields to cross the creek and start up the mountain.

As I got nearer to the bottom of the creek bed, it seemed that for every step I took down, the mountain top went up by two and as I stood on the edge of the river crossing, it looked far higher than I'd imagined.

I knew that to get up and down in the time I'd allocated, I had better think positive. Plenty of others had done it under far harsher conditions. OK, so fifteen years ago when I was a Navy Field Gunner I could probably have run up it with a rucksack, but that was when I was a lad of twenty two.

I crossed the estuary through freezing, ankle deep water. Well at least my feet were awake. Struggling up the first part of the hill made me feel every day of my thirty seven years, and pissed off that I hadn't come fifteen years earlier, when I could have done it as a hobby. As I neared the top of the first section, level with the main road, I got an acutely painful earache. It felt as though I was going too high in an un-pressurised aircraft or diving too deep without clearing my ears. Irrespective of the fact that I could clear my ears perfectly, the earache would not go away and the higher I climbed, the worse it got. There was nothing else for it but to find some shelter from the wind and produce the hip flask given to me by one of my best mates when I got married. The flask had sat in the bottom drawer of my writing bureau gathering dust for the past seven years but I knew it would come in useful one day. I'm not a whisky drinker but I'd brought it because I thought I might need it as cold weather repellant, and also in case I found myself simply 'needing a drink.' I pulled a good swig on the neat Scotch, which had no effect on the earache whatsoever, but which felt bloody marvelous. I wondered if it would dehydrate me and I was not carrying any other water with me. The journey was short and the conditions didn't look as if constant rehydration was going to be the biggest of my worries. I did not however, want to learn fell walking and mountain climbing the hard way.

I couldn't work out why the earache had come on. It couldn't be from the altitude because I had driven along the road yesterday with no ill effects. I could only put it down to the wind speed and pressure affecting my eardrums. In spite of it, I was determined not to stop.

A couple more stints of onwards and upwards saw me puffing like a carthorse, and the stops got longer as the walks got shorter. I could see the crest of Mount Estancia and I was determined to crack on. As I ascended, the earache disappeared as suddenly as it had come. When I was almost at the crest I put on a burst of speed, only to find it was a false crest and the real summit lay some one hundred yards beyond. When I reached it, I was again disappointed to find that this too was a false summit. Although I thought the next peak was definitely the top, having been let down twice, I resigned myself to an upwards trudge until I simply ran out of 'up'.

My thoughts drifted back to the years after I'd left the Navy when I was searching for some sort of physical challenge. An ex-Royal Marine friend of mine had told me that there was a Territorial SAS unit in Leeds. I rang the CO of 'B' Squadron 23rd SAS, to ask about the requirements for joining. I'd kept up my level of fitness from the Field Gun Crew reasonably well; I trained every day, and was a qualified aerobics teacher and weight lifting instructor. I played rugby for the local pub and had a physically demanding job on an oil and gas drilling rig. However, when I was told that running was the core of the physical fitness requirement I immediately lost interest. Carrying ridiculously large rucksacks didn't bother me, but I knew that either the running would bore me stupid, or I'd lack the correct mental attitude to go the distance. I binned the idea and stuck to teaching aerobics to girls in leotards.

Lost in my thoughts, I tripped over a rock, gashing my knee and bringing me back to reality. I didn't have anything to wrap round my leg to stop the bleeding. I did though, have my Swiss army knife tied to a lanyard. I took the knife off and tied the lanyard round my jeans at the level of the wound so it pressed the jeans into the bleeding. It would have to do. I pressed on.

The wind speed was phenomenal. It was blowing up the mountain and from the north-west. I sheltered behind a rock wall for a while, then continued on. Every time there was a break in the wall and the wind roared through, it inflated my jacket to Michelin man size and carried on blowing me up the mountain. I tried a few times to turn into the wind and take photos down the hill and over the valley but it was impossible, I couldn't keep the camera steady. The wind speed increased as I closed on the summit and my jacket began to blow like a spinnaker sail.

Looking around at the actual terrain of the mountain I could not imagine how the first patrol had managed to reach the top. There were clumps of grass all over the place, big enough to hide a group of men or a machine gun, and large lumps of rock that would have easy for the enemy to use. The rock wall was big enough to stand up behind and its undulating crests made natural battlements. During the day, an advancing enemy could be seen for miles, and during the night, there could have been no excuse for not holding them back. The place was like a natural fortress, and this was one of the smaller hills that there had not seen any fighting.

At long last I reached the summit and sat down to recover from the wheezing, I sounded like a bronchial Old Man Steptoe on forty fags a day. Once rested, I spent a few minutes walking along the rocky crests and the ridgeline to a small pile of stones marking the highest point of the mountain, which is approximately one thousand feet. All those false crests had been worth it, at this final peak of stones there were three hundred and sixty degree views. Back down the mountain, Estancia House looked like a tiny speck on a map, (as opposed to twenty years ago when it would have been a spic on the map! I laughed at my own joke.). On a clear day like this, the view went on for miles, up to Teal Inlet and Douglas in the North West, to Bluff Cove Peak and Mount Kent in the south, with the battlefields of Two Sisters, Goat Ridge and Mount Harriett. In the far distance too hazy to see properly, was Stanley itself. Out across Mount Vernet in the east was Berkeley Sound and the open South Atlantic Ocean.

I hadn't been able to do much physical training at all for the past two years because of injuries I'd sustained on the rugby field and the oil rigs, so I was proud of myself for getting to the top. I felt like a mountaineer. My legs and lungs had wanted to give up halfway up the mountain, but I had forced myself to carry on and I'd made it.

Before I set out on this journey, this pilgrimage, I knew I'd experience lots of emotions, as I did in 1982 and had done ever since. This however, was not a time for quiet reflection, for sorrow or for grieving. It was a time for feeling good to be alive and grateful that I was here when others weren't.

I rattled off some panoramic photos and started the more leisurely stroll back down the mountain. I thought this would be much quicker but I soon realised that if I went fast I would arrive at the bottom of the mountain with two broken ankles. The terrain was full of pot holes, just big enough for your foot to fit in and trip you up. Even when the side of the mountain evened out a bit, I couldn't pick up the pace much as the jarring on my knees and back was playing up like hell. I stopped to examine the gash across my leg which I'd sustained on the way up. It had dried up and my jeans had stuck nicely into the cut and dried blood. I tried to pull it out, all I achieved was pulling the scab off and it started bleeding again. I tied the lanyard back on around my jeans and pressed on downwards.

When I finally reached the estuary, I found the tide had come in, which meant either that I would be walking all the way round, or be wading through what was now waist deep freezing water. I was really pissed off with myself for not noticing this when I was half way down the mountain and altering my course then. I had been onboard RFA Resource with the SAS for a few weeks in 1982, and I'd thought then that I might have a crack at it. It was a good job I didn't bother; I was quite obviously useless at all the things you have to be good at to be in the Special Forces.

Fortunately, the trek wasn't as bad as I first thought and as I followed the river creek around for a few hundred yards, I found a section where it was narrow enough to jump with only one foot copping a drowning. I followed the fence line westwards back towards Estancia, by which time my lungs were burning in a way I'd not experienced since I played rugby in Yorkshire on a freezing and snowy weekend some ten or twelve years previously.

When I got back to the house I was truly knackered and soaking wet. I peeled off my wet and muddy boots and trousers in the outside porch. Standing there in my boxer shorts, thick woolly sweatshirts and 'Benny hat', I must have been quite a sight for the attractive young girl who opened the door.

"Hello, who are you?" she said, looking down at my bone white legs.

"Err, Adam," I said. "I'm staying with your mum and dad."

"OK, want a cuppa?" She stood back to let me in.

I gratefully accepted a brew from Tony and Ailsa's daughter Nyree. We chatted about her impending secondment to an agricultural college in Australia, very near to where my mate from the *Invincible* lived now. All the time she was talking, I couldn't help noticing, she had beautiful eyes.

I finished my tea and got ready to leave for my next stay. With my gear packed I loaded it into the Landover and went to find Tony to bid him farewell. When I found him, he asked me to see if there was any dog food in the shed and I obliged. Finding no tins of Pal or Pedigree Chum, I told him 'no' and he laughed. I was confused. He disappeared for a couple of minutes and re-appeared brandishing a double barreled 12 bore shotgun. I was desperately trying to establish a link between dog food and a shotgun when the double report of the shotgun barrels answered the question. Two low flying upland geese had just become dog food and Tony had completed the day's shopping requirements.

"Always shoot them in pairs," he said, "they mate for life."

It seemed kind in a brutal sort of way. I bade him farewell as he went off to fix fences, sort out the farm and no doubt assassinate more local wildlife. What a truly great character he was. I was grateful that he'd had the opportunity to live exactly the way he chose.

Ailsa and I set off for my next bed for the night in Douglas via Teal Inlet. She told me all about the roads, the rivers, the farms, the people, the supply capabilities and how it had all changed since 1982. Prior to the war, when there were no roads in 'camp' it took hours to get anywhere. She pointed out the sight where Top Malo House used to be. Thinking of it being used by Argentinian Forces, the Paras had put paid to it and it had never been rebuilt. We stopped at Teal Inlet and there were actually some trees, real trees in this most barren of landscapes.

I had brought a bagful of poppies with me, which, thinking ahead to this trip, I'd obtained the previous Remembrance Day at home in Brisbane. I laid my first ones here by entwining the wire stems to some flowers already there at the beautiful silver cross. This was the memorial to the men who had been temporarily interred there before removal to their final resting places. The twenty nine names inscribed on the plaque showed that the majority of the men were Paratroopers and Royal Marines, with a few Royal Engineers who had been attached to them. The area chosen for this was certainly peaceful and looked out towards Port Salvador and the northern inlet which grants access to the sound. I hoped that all the other memorials I intended to visit would be as good.

We carried on North West to Douglas passing one old farmer, who Ailsa told me spends half a day driving to Stanley on his tractor to pick up supplies and then the remainder of the day driving back with the goods. We stopped and I got out to take some photos. I tried to imagine what 3 Para and 45 Commando would have felt when they looked at the miles of boggy terrain ahead of them, flanked by mountains on one side and the waters of Port Salvador on the other. It couldn't have been inspiring.

It was about now it dawned on me why I never seemed to get the time right. This is because Stanley and the camp have a one hour time difference. I had always thought it ludicrous that back home, the states of Queensland and New South Wales have a latitudinal (horizontal) border and a one hour time difference running down the centre of a street in the border town of Tweed Heads. This means at closing time, you simply cross the road and drink for another hour. The shops, offices, and so forth all open and close at different times depending upon which side of the street they're on. It costs businesses millions of dollars a year.

Here in Stanley, the reason given for the difference is that those working in Stanley needed an extra hour to cut peat and do their gardens etc, whilst the people in camp did this during the day.

CHAPTER 16

Teal Inlet and Douglas

We turned up the long peninsula named Rincon Del Moro which runs next to Douglas Creek and into the northern end of Port Salvador. I saw a few houses scattered in the distance, and the settlement of Douglas which was our destination. Passing Hope Cottage, which was the usual accommodation for people visiting the area, we made our way up to the home of a couple named Rhoda and Arthur who were to be my hosts for the night. Arthur reminded me very much of the chief farmhand from my uncle's farm when I was a kid. A tough, outdoors type, always smiling with hands as hard as leather but like all Falklanders a fresh rosy complexion. Rhoda made me think of some of my earliest memories of my nanas, always ready with a warm house and a brew of tea. Some people have décor and contents that make a house seem like a home. It was Rhoda herself who made the house a home.

I had seen my first wind turbine in the Islands at Estancia and I thought that maybe it was a one-off. When I arrived at Douglas, it seemed everyone had one, just like satellite dishes in the early nineties. No sooner was I in the door, even before I unloaded my kit, the tea and sponge cakes were on the table and stupendous they looked too. I was going to be fat by the time I saw my family in the UK or my mates back in Australia. I didn't care.

With the hospitality and niceties out of the way, Arthur said he would run me down to the end of the peninsula called The Moro. Although he had moved to the Islands from his native Scotland, he was now a typical islander, hardy and weather beaten. We took his old Land Rover and headed over the hills. I was by now getting the hang of the unusual fixing mechanism for securing the gates in the fences. My first experience had been with Tony Heathman and I'd thought I'd need a degree in engineering to suss it out. Now, no sooner had we cleared the settlement than Arthur lit up the fag he'd been dying for. "Not alood tae smoke. She doesnae know." I produced the hip flask again, still almost full with good neat scotch and Arthur accepted gratefully.

The Land Rover bumped and scraped along, exacerbating the back ache brought on by this morning's trip up Mt Vernet. Sheep, cows and assorted birdlife watched as we passed within a couple of yards of them. We stopped a few times so I could take photographs of the natural surroundings, the most natural of anywhere in the world.

On the left was King's Creek and beyond that, King's Ridge and King's Hill, the barren landscape repulsing visitors. We reached the end of the peninsula and directly across from us was the point of land which separates Pitaluga Bay from Plaza Creek. With the flat, barren terrain and no landmarks, it was difficult to judge how far away it was. It could have been a couple of miles or a thousand yards.

I wanted to walk back but when we reached the end of the jetty I realised that it was more than five miles, and I'd never complete it before dark. I decided to leave the tabbing and yomping to the insane; doing it in the dark, I'd almost certainly fall into a hole and break my ankle or be trampled by cows.

I spent some time getting close-up photos of rock shags and other sea birds; this place was an ornithologist's dream. The birds were even tame. In the shed by the jetty were the remains of a Mercedes-Benz 4-wheel drive which had been brought to the Islands and abandoned here by the Argentinians. It didn't look like anyone had tried to do much with it in the last twenty years. As it was getting late in the day I headed off back towards Douglas with Arthur. About three miles out from the settlement, I decided I would walk the rest of the way back. Arthur stopped to let me out and I headed on down to the coastline to follow the creek inland so as not to lose my bearings if it got dark. I knew that eventually, I would come to the houses as long as I stuck to this.

Following the cliffs around the headland I took in the scenery and watched as a large bird of prey repeatedly swooped gracefully down at the water. On one of its forays, it climbed skyward with a fish wriggling in its talons. I wondered if there were ospreys in this part of the world and made a mental note to look at Arthur's bird book when I got back to the settlement.

As I walked, I happened upon the old sea-plane terminal, a corrugated shed affair. There were two long wooden walkways hinged in the middle, with cartwheels at each end, which would be pushed out into the water near the 'plane for the passengers to alight. So this was Douglas International terminal! I'd heard stories that the Argies tried to fly the old seaplane. It careered along Stanley harbour but never got off the water.

I took a short cut across one part of the estuary towards a disused 'killing shed' and half way across, found myself shin deep in stinking mud and slime. Putrid though it was, I decided it was quicker to keep going than turn round and walk all the way round. The wind had picked up quite a bit, and rather than try and walk directly into it, which I found was absolutely knackering, I turned diagonally for the point of the creek that jutted out in to the river and followed the cliffs along for a while. I knew that further down I could then cut straight back in to where the house would be.

As I walked, I found myself in a small depression, completely sheltered from the wind. With the setting sun shining on this little green oasis, it was actually quite warm, either that or the whisky was taking effect. I sat down to have a breather and lay back looking up at the sky. The only sounds were the wind, my own breathing, and every now and again, the screech of an eagle. I drifted off to sleep. I awoke feeling really cosy, like being in a warm tent with rain beating down outside.

The sun had set when I arrived back in Douglas. I deposited my filthy jeans and stinking boots outside the house, then hosed the boots off. I was surprised at how quickly it actually became dark. I thought of the most dangerous times of the day in 1982. It had always seemed to be dawn and dusk when we went to action stations in readiness for the incoming air raids. Both our sister ship HMS *Coventry*, and the m.v. *Atlantic Conveyor* had been lost in dusk raids, with the latter being one of the biggest single logistical setbacks of the war for the British.

Tea time came. The obligatory mutton 'roast 365' with everything, which we also had when I arrived at midday, but I was finding that after a bit of physical activity, polishing off the mammoth portions allocated to me was not a problem.

I asked Rhoda about the wildlife and birds around the place, and looked through some bird books. She told me about some very rare birds of prey called Striated Caracara, known locally as 'Johnny Rook'. They are total kleptomaniacs and when tourists leave cameras and photographic gear on the ground, the birds try to nick them. I wasn't quite sure how much of this was true and how much was a wind-up but I made a point of remembering to be careful around the birds whenever I saw them.

I settled in for an evening watching the telly, the only viewing available being that of British Forces Broadcasting Service. No-one in the islands even had a TV before 1982, so there was something else that had improved, I supposed. The beer kept on coming from a grateful Arthur, who had enthusiastically helped me neck my entire flask of scotch on our jaunt down the peninsula. At the neighbour's house was a section of Paratroopers from the Resident Infantry Company (RIC) who had asked that I go over for a beer with them. Never being a man to turn down a social invitation from military people, I happily obliged, hoping there might have been at least one old hand who would have known my mate Steve from 3 Para. Arthur and I wandered over and I was supplied with a hot toddy and a beer. The young Paras introduced themselves. I didn't need to ask whether any of them had been here in '82. Some of them looked as if they hadn't even been born then.

The senior man was a corporal and the section commander and also an Australian. At twenty eight he would have barely remembered the war, especially overseas. I asked what they had been doing since they joined up and heard stories of Northern Ireland and other overseas postings and exercises, some glamorous and some 'absolutely fuckin' shithouse'. It was good to see some things didn't change. There was one rosy-cheeked youth who I swear didn't even shave. I asked him how old he was. Mustering the bravado he was issued with at Aldershot when collecting his maroon beret, he puffed out his chest, cleared his throat, lowered his voice by a couple of octaves and growled "seventeen".

"Seventeen! Bloody seventeen! Do we send our seventeen year olds here now?" I asked. I shook my head and wondered why a country would send such a boy to do a man's job. I saw the look in his eye when I questioned his age, and almost regretted my words. I never doubted for one minute that if the chips were down, like the other seventeen year olds who came here twenty years before him, he would do as they had done with the same degree of professionalism and courage. The traditions of the Parachute Regiment were what they lived by. Wealth or fame couldn't buy a place in the Parachute Regiment. It was earned through blood, sweat and tears. Only the dedicated made the grade. The pass rate of the Paratrooper recruit course is very low simply because the standards are so high. It was a bit like the Field Gun Crew but the Field Gun Competition was just a tri-annual event and only for a few months of the year. This was their existence. I was glad I'd never had to fight a Para or Marine or anyone else who wore a coveted beret.

At that moment it was a good feeling to be British, though I questioned what kind of government would send its sixteen and seventeen year olds into active combat zones to sort out the messes it had created. On the other hand, is a man any more a man the day he turns eighteen, or nineteen, or twenty two? Is he any more prepared to cope with battle whatever his age? The fact is of course, we all accepted the Queen's shilling, we all chose the military life which included letting idiot politicians screw up and then sorting the messes out for them, whilst they revelled in the glory of 'their' victories. If you volunteer for something, you give up the right to bitch about the process and the outcome.

I was miles away, lost in thought, when Arthur drained his hot toddy and reminded me, 'but you were seventeen when you came here'. He was right, I looked at the lad again and wondered if his mother and father worried like my parents and hundreds of other parents had. Of course they did, they wouldn't be parents if they didn't. I was a parent myself and I worried about all sorts of things. A feeling of dread washed over me when I thought about Lucy joining the services. I knew I would be proud to see her in her uniform and attend her passing out parade with all the other old codgers, but if she was called on to go into action? It just didn't bear thinking about what conflict would be like by the time she was old enough to serve. I just prayed that she stuck with her dreams of being an artist, dancer or vet.

My thoughts drifted back to my teenage years and I remembered my carefree attitudes, and found myself wondering whether young men like me, who came here and were forced to grow up so quickly, and so harshly, were actually robbed of their innocence. Did what we had learned and done here make us stronger people? I drained the beer and the hot toddy; I was well away by the time we left.

Arthur and I made good our escape but on the way back to his house, he collected more beer from the garage. I knew it was a bad idea, but I was past the point of caring. I slumped down in front of the telly again and chatted to Arthur about his many years in the islands working out at Cape Dolphin, and how he had arrived here from Scotland. Eventually I stumbled off to bed and now being in my third bed in three days, was impressed to find that yet another mattress was ultra comfy. Even if I hadn't had a skinful I would have been asleep in seconds.

CHAPTER 17

20th Anniversary of Invasion and Occupation

2nd April 2002

Normally I am an early riser at home but in the Falklands I found I was sleeping until at least 8am. Whether it was a combination of it being dark until then, me being jetlagged still, and having extremely comfy beds to kip in, I didn't know. What I did know was it was bloody wonderful not to wake up at 5am.

What a difference between the 2nd April 2002, and the morning of 2nd April 1982! By this time twenty years ago, the resistance of the Royal Marine garrison had ceased and they had been ordered to surrender by the then Governor, Sir Rex Hunt. And Stanley had fallen into Argentinian hands.

Now though, we sat around in the living room, such a typical Falklander homestead, so warm and cosy, so 'British'. Arthur and Rhoda reminisced about their experiences of the occupation when the Argentinians had arrived at Douglas.

The night before the occupying forces arrived had been the Queen's birthday celebration, and Arthur got particularly well oiled. In the two weeks preceding this, the settlement had been over flown a number of times by a Pucara and other aircraft and the population of the settlement had gone outside to watch. Unbeknown to them at the time, the pilots were actually counting how many people were resident at the settlement. When the soldiers arrived, the majority of people were rounded up; however Arthur was still in bed with the mother and father of all hangovers. The Argentinians kept questioning the residents – "Uno hombre, uno hombre?" (One man, one man?) They entered his house and forcibly removed Arthur from his bed at gunpoint.

As well as the young conscript soldiers, there were also some hardline

Special Forces, or Buzo Tactico present. At one point, a member of the Buzo Tactico had leveled his rifle and made it ready at one of the residents. The man's young daughter walked in front of the Argentinian soldier. "You're not going to shoot my daddy are you?" she said.

Whatever the intention of the soldier had been, the innocent bravery of that little girl defused the situation. He lowered his rifle.

After lots of funny anecdotes which made light of what was obviously a terrifying situation, I was privileged to qualify for a lift to Port San Carlos in Arthur's new Mitsubishi *Pajero*, a considerable improvement on the ramshackle Landover in which we had bounced our way down to Rincon Del Moro. The weather was typically Falkland, grey and overcast, with low cloud cover, drizzle and mist.

I wondered what the young Argentinian conscripts would have imagined when they arrived here, especially those from the north of the country where the weather is tropical. It is written somewhere that some of them were told they were going to the south of mainland Argentina to fight Chile over a piece of Tierra Del Fuego. All I could see was mile upon mile of moorland, peat bog and granite-like rock, with a few sheep farming settlements scattered across thousands of square miles of open ground. I knew why I was here, but just imagine not knowing. I can believe that Argentinian morale was pretty low, and the vast majority were probably sitting in wet trenches thinking, 'OK, so now we've got it. What the hell do we do with it?'

The drive to San Carlos took almost exactly the same route that 45 Commando, Royal Marines had taken in '82, except in the opposite direction. The settlement of Port San Carlos appeared. It looked like a couple of houses, which is what it was.

Port San Carlos

When we arrived at the home of Jenny and Tony Anderson in Port San Carlos, we went through the ritual of tea and home-made Falkland biscuits before Arthur and Rhoda left to get back to Douglas. I sat and chatted with Jenny and Tony about themselves, and their family's history in the islands. Like all Falkland housewives Jenny fussed over making sure I was OK with my tea and biscuits, and not going hungry or cold. Tony was a big burly character, I thought he could probably lift a couple of sheep. Then they showed me to my room in a massive thirteen bedroomed house. It used to be a cook house (single man's accommodation) and it reminded me of my uncle's farm houses in the Yorkshire Wolds.

Jenny and Tony were born and bred Islanders. They were residents of Goose Green at the time of the invasion, although they said that the Argentinians had not actually arrived there until around the 21st April (just before South Georgia was re-taken). They had pretty much been left alone apart from having their weapons confiscated until the morning of the first British air attacks on 1st May. It was then that they and the remaining one hundred and thirteen residents of the settlement between the ages of four months and eighty nine years were herded up, and imprisoned in a small community centre.

Jenny said that at first, conditions weren't bad, although there were only two toilets (one for each gender). That changed as the British bombing attacks by Harriers intensified and the Task Force drew closer to the Islands. Then, the more aggressive Argentinians, who were probably Special Forces, extended their hardline attitude toward their unarmed civilian hostages.

It was only my fourth day on the islands and I was asking myself the question, 'had the sacrifice been worth the result?' How could I ever be in a position to answer? The only people who can are the two hundred and fifty five families of the servicemen who gave their lives, or the relatives of the three Falklander civilians killed. Is the loss of a son, father, husband, brother, ever 'worth it'? I was lucky enough to live through it, therefore it would be easy enough for me to say 'yes', and I don't doubt that all of the islanders would say the sacrifice was worth it. It was their freedom and their way of life that was preserved.

The hospitality I'd received and the carefree way of life I'd seen made me think it was worth it. Jenny and Tony then told me about Captain Alfredo Astiz who was wanted for the alleged torture and murder of two nuns, amongst others, and I found myself thinking, 'yes, this was definitely worth it'. In the end there are some things worth fighting for. If they have to be fought for, the chances are that someone has to die for them, that is the way it is, and the way it will always be.

I know there are people who lost loved ones who would seriously question whether the sacrifice was worth the freedom of these islanders. I think I can understand why they would feel that way but I also ask myself, would it be right to leave Britons in a British dependency under that kind of threat? Where would it have stopped? Would Gibraltar have been next?

I badly needed some fresh air and I set out for an afternoon's exploring. Port San Carlos River appeared to be an object of interest to the red faced Turkey Vultures around the killing shed. Hopefully it was the smell of blood and not the thought of some of my fresh meat that was attracting them. I knew from my ornithology days that vultures did not attack living things. They're scavengers, waiting until their prey is dead, and that was something I had no intention of being for another forty years or more.

I set off eastwards along the north bank of the San Carlos River. No sooner had I cleared the end of the shed when I came across the first sangars constructed by men of 42 Commando, Royal Marines. The amount of corrugated tin and wood and pieces of broken up pallet that had been used to build these lookouts, made me think the only way they could have done it was to tear down some of the sheds which had stood in the settlement at the time.

The north bank of the river provided excellent ground for digging in and for watching attacking aircraft coming in from San Carlos Water and up from the centre of East Falkland on a north west course. It was a virtual shooting gallery, forcing the aircraft to fly low and take on the camouflage of the hills. After walking for a while, I came to the memorial for three Royal Marines aircrew of 3 Commando Brigade Air Squadron who had been shot down on 21st May.

I had been told many years ago that one of the men had been floating in the water in his lifejacket when the Argentinians had opened fire on him. I looked down to the wide open river that the memorial overlooks and hoped that it wasn't true. The memorial to the men looks North West up the San Carlos River and into the sound, with West Falkland in the distance. It was a beautiful spot for a memorial, a more peaceful spot you could not wish for.

I continued along until I reached the promontory called The Knob. I turned and looked back toward Port San Carlos, the entrance to the river with the sound, Fanning Head and the entrance to San Carlos water all in view.

I walked to the top of the hill, which was quite a hike by the time I got up there, but it was well worth the effort for the view. Westwards, I looked down into the sound, north towards Cape Dolphin and round to Douglas where I had just come from. Eastwards over the land mass of the major part of the island and south over San Carlos Water, (nicknamed Bomb Alley after the bombing attacks by the Argentinian Skyhawks and Mirages) and then down towards Grantham Sound. I headed back along the top of the ridgeline looking down at the terrain leading into the river, as smooth as a billiard table with sudden small granite peaks jutting out at bizarre angles next to sand bunkers. There were hundreds of sangars left, untouched since they were abandoned twenty years ago. Making my way back through various sheep pens and dog runs and other associated farmyard enclosures, I knew by the smell wafting from the cookhouse that I would be just in time for another gargantuan calorific intake.

I hadn't had this much fresh air for a long time. Once again we got stuck into mutton and vegetables. I felt myself slipping into an afternoon nap but I didn't want to waste any of my time here. I wanted to use every precious minute by seeing and doing different things as I was only ever going to get this one chance.

I asked Tony what his plans were for the afternoon. "Fixing some fences," he said and "slaughtering some sheep."

I asked how they did it here. I was offered the chance to help, but refused, not because I was in any way squeamish, but I wanted to do other things. Tony told me that once he'd taken everything useful off the carcass, he threw the remains down on the beach where they would be picked clean in half an hour by the vultures. It reminded me of a Nepalese mountain funeral ceremony known as a 'Sky Burial'. The (human) body is laid out on a mountain and the vultures devour the carcass.

I wandered over to where the executions were about to begin. Did the sheep really look worried? Their bleating had certainly risen in tempo. Some were becoming hysterical; they must be able to sense that their time is nearly up. I wonder if they think like humans do when they're involved in a crowd crush or similar situation. Do they actually wonder if this is 'it'? They were already shorn. Did they associate getting shorn with getting killed, like when you go to the electric chair?

I set off around the headland towards the entrance to San Carlos river and Falkland Sound. That trek would take me up towards Fanning Island, Sand Bay and Green Beach. There were vultures everywhere, watching me. I checked my pocket to make sure I had my knife. There were also plenty of rocks and stones to use as ammunition. I was surrounded by sheep carcasses, mostly picked clean but some of the birds were still stabbing at a couple of the more recently deceased.

Slippery rocks and sheep carcasses formed the shoreline. As I reached the top of the first hill, it started to rain, and though most of the mist kept a reasonable distance, it was too overcast to get the colours of the land.

When I was halfway down the shoreline towards Green Beach, it began to rain in real South Atlantic style. I had left my rain proof poncho in the house and I resigned myself to getting wet through. But then I came across an indentation in the cliffs, where a load of corrugated iron sheets had been thrown down onto the stony shoreline, some laying flat and some resting at angles against the cliff face. I dragged a couple more down and made a shelter from the rain; the first sangar constructed in Port San Carlos since 1982! Once I had re-fastened my jacket and trouser zips, pulled my hat down over my ears and used my camera bag for a pillow, it was warm and cozy. I lay listening to the rain beating down on my makeshift roof. It was just like listening to the torrential downpours on the old and leaky tin roof of the wooden colonial house I lived in when I first moved to Australia. I curled up in the foetal position, tucked my hands between my legs to try to keep them warm, and drifted off to sleep.

I woke with a start to a hideous clanging noise, sprang up, and smashed my head on the underside of the corrugated iron 'roof'. Then I regained my senses and started to laugh. Between the sheets of the tin above me, I could see the bald face of a huge Turkey Vulture, surrounded by lots of his friends. But, I was outnumbered, and worried. I reached down and gathered up a few rocks, got my knife out and dragged a large lump of wood into the sangar as further defence. I chucked a few rocks to get rid of the audience. A sharp smack on the roof got rid of the ringleader and as I inched my way out of the sangar, the vultures shambled off in search of easier prey.

Back on my feet, I continued up the shoreline towards the mouth of the river but eventually ran out of shore. It was impossible to walk round this part of the cliffs, the water was too deep (and icy cold), the cliffs were too steep, and the rocks were too slippery, so I headed back to the shelter. Scrambling up there was a bit of a feat itself, I must have dragged down half a ton of dirt and I was caked in it by this time. And my boots felt like they weighed half a hundredweight.

I made it to the top and carried on into the dipping sun towards Green Beach. I walked right up to the peninsula of the rocks and turned round to look at the beach from the angle the Paras and Marines would have seen it as they approached. The scenery was probably the last thing on the minds of the men in those landing crafts, and I wondered how many of them were thinking it might be the last thing they ever saw. Oz Straughan, who had come ashore here with 3 Para, later told me they were expecting a reception like in the movie *The Longest Day*, about the Normandy landings. What they got when they came ashore here was waist deep, freezing water. Their feet did not dry out again.

Getting as far round as Fanning Island, I gained great views down Port San Carlos River, San Carlos Water and south west down the sound. Twenty years before, the peace of these waterways had been shattered by the scream of jet engines, the whoosh and roar of anti-aircraft missiles and the constant chatter and rattle of heavy machine gun fire. I wondered what the wildlife had made of it and how much of that had been killed. By sheer coincidence, I found what resembled a 30mm cannon shell on the beach, not something I would relish being on the receiving end of.

As I stood there on the headland, the skies cleared, the sun came out and the seabirds overhead wheeled and soared, their cries carrying for miles across the still reflective waters.

The surface of the entire expanse of water was unbroken by boats or anything else. Light waves lapped at the water's edge, and the icy South Atlantic water seeping into my boots reminding me of the inhospitability of the latitudes. In these waters hypothermia soon sets in.

I headed back towards Port San Carlos settlement, walking along the grassy embankment at the top, which in 1982, had been commissioned as an open air Royal Naval Air Station called HMS *Sheathbill*. It was named after a snowy white bird which resembled a pigeon but is actually of the Seagull family and whose diet consists almost entirely of penguin shit! The place had been used as a forward operating base for Harriers to land, re-fuel and re-arm giving them more time on Combat Air Patrol (CAP) instead of returning to the carriers, 150 miles to the east.

There had been tension between the sailors of the ships on the gunline and landing areas that were being attacked day in and day out, and the sailors in the relative safety of *Hermes* and *Invincible*. A joke went around that the *Hermes* and *Invincible* ships' companies should get the South Africa medal because they were closer to Africa than the fighting. The sailors in destroyers and the frigates had a point; the carriers were stationed well out of harm's way but that was because they were high value units. If one or both of them had been lost, with our Sea Harrier air cover, then we might as well have packed up and gone home.

There was a huge groove cut out of the hillside, and it looked almost as though it was where an aircraft could have hit the ground but I couldn't remember any reports of aircraft coming down in the area.

When I eventually reached the cook house, my legs were aching. I had covered more miles in the last two days than I'd covered in the last two years.

We whiled away the evening with Tony and Jenny talking about the island's past, how and where they had farmed, our respective children, and what we thought the future held for the islands. At one point, Argentina had been one of the richest nations in the world. It then steadily declined until it was only one of the richest in South America. In 1982 the rate of inflation was something ridiculous and the military junta did what all dictatorships do when they need a diversion from their own disastrous policies. They kicked off a war to divert the public's attention. They had gone some way to recovery after the 1982 military junta. Politically things hadn't permanently improved that much. In the few weeks before my departure from Australia, I had watched the Argentinian media closely. There had been a number of different heads of government in a very short space of time. People had lost their life savings and some of the population could not even afford to buy food. There were mass civil protests and riots and the country was almost on the verge of civil war. Why would Argentina run the economy of the Falklands any more efficiently than its own?

I eventually found my way through the maze of rooms to my bed and thanks to a combination of fresh air and unaccustomed exercise, I crashed out immediately. I was finding it more and more difficult to get up in the mornings.

Before moving next door, I wanted to get the obligatory photo of my hosts. Tony insisted on wearing his West Ham baseball cap. West Ham seemed to be the favourite team in the islands, they could have formed a supporter's club down there.

I was moving next door to 'the POD', a guesthouse run by Patrick and Pat. Yes, two Ps in a pod! They were a great couple, Patrick was a native islander and Pat had moved down a couple of years after the conflict.

There were also two RAF personnel, Steve and Colin, on weekend Rest & Recuperation (R&R), who were staying in the self-catering accommodation and were going to accompany us on the tour around Fanning Head. Colin had had too much beer the night before and was not up to the rough ride in the pick-up. He had opted to stay in bed. He left me and the remaining airman, Steve, to take the trip to the rookery of

Rockhopper penguins. Once we had left the settlement there were no roads, and not even tracks. There were just fields to drive across, serious four-wheel driving, bogs and peat, the land as the Lord commissioned it, one wrong turn and you'd be here forever. As we bounced over the terrain, the young airman Steve asked me why I was there. I simply said, "… came here once before." He didn't push it; he'd only have been a kid during the war.

Every now and again I jumped out to open and close the home-made gates attached to the home-made flimsy fences which divided the islands into various landholdings. I could hardly see the point of the fences, they held back nothing, they were mere token efforts. As I stood thinking about them, Patrick thrashed the pick-up through in a whirling flurry of mudslide. Approaching the peak behind Fanning Head we took a sharp left (although it didn't appear to be around anything in particular) and started ascending an incline that must have to have been at least forty five degrees, if not more.

I was convinced the pick-up would give up and either stall, refuse to go any further, start sliding backwards, or do anything other than what its driver intended it to do. I would have sworn the only things that could have made it up there would have been tracked vehicles or mountain goats, but we made it to the top and the view from there was panoramic. It took in the entire area of the British amphibious landings in 1982, the attack courses and escape routes of the Argentinian aircraft, and also where the Sea Harriers would wait to pounce and ambush them, either on their way in, or on their way out of 'Bomb Alley'.

Below us was Fanning Island, a horseshoe shaped piece of land tucked into the shore, making the back wall of the almost complete square protecting Green Beach. The sun shone on the tranquil waters of Falkland Sound, now the resting place of a number of men of both nationalities. Once again I found myself trying to work out why someone would want to destroy such peaceful and beautiful islands.

We made our way round to the seaward side of Fanning Head, which in the early hours of the morning of the 21st May, had received countless 4.5 inch high explosive shells from the guided missile destroyer, HMS *Antrim*. Hours later *Antrim* was hit by a bomb (which failed to explode) and was riddled with cannon fire, causing a number of casualties.

A fierce fire fight had also taken place here between the Argentinians, who had been dug in for a few weeks, and the British Special Forces, who had come ashore to eliminate any of the enemy threatening the landing beaches. The tracer rounds of the fire fight had been visible to the soldiers and sailors aboard the convoy of ships making its way stealthily into San Carlos. For some of those men it was a sign of what would come their way.

We parked the pick-up some distance from what I would describe as a black and white mass. We continued on foot through the rough terrain, watching every step so as not to break an ankle.

En route to the penguin colony we came across bits of the aircraft belonging to Teniente Ricardo Lucero, who ejected when his plane was shot down over the sound. He was subjected to unfortunate and almost worldwide fame because a news camera crew was on hand as he was rescued from the water. A Royal Marine stood over him with a rifle at his head, shouting to the first aid team, "Well come and get the fucking spic bastard then!" In the background the Naval first aid team can be seen running over towards them. When Lucero was told he was onboard HMS *Fearless,* he at first refused to believe it, he was convinced she had been sunk. After being treated aboard *Fearless,* he was transferred to the British hospital ship SS *Uganda* and subsequently repatriated to Argentina. Apparently his dislodged kneecap, which was damaged on ejection, mended fully.

We approached the Rockhoppers as slowly and quietly as we could, although I now understand that we could have arrived with a massed brass band of the Household Cavalry playing with flags flying, and the bushy eye-browed little critters would not have cared less. They are by nature very tame. It would have been quite easy to pick one up; they are not the gainliest of creatures on land.

The weather wasn't very cold but there was a strong wind blowing and the penguins sat huddled together against it. They looked almost unreal, with their bright red eyes, big peroxide bushy brows, and seriously gelled back 'bad hair day' hair, and bad attitude. In fact they did look just like a crowd of teenagers.

Because they are so easy to catch, one year in the 1800's, almost 600,000 of them were exterminated and boiled for their oil. One penguin equals approximately one pint of oil. I wondered how they got up the cliff face, a great deal of which was muddy, then the question was answered for me, as one penguin did precisely what his name suggests. He dug his claws in, and hopped up, simple as that.

From there, we drove round the northern tip of Fanning past Pebble

Beach and Race Point which brought us to Surf Bay. The scenery was again magnificent and we came across two other breeds of penguin common to the area, the Gentoo and the Magellanic. The Gentoo is easily recognisable by the wide white stripe extending across the top of its head. They are also the fastest of the penguins when swimming underwater reaching 36km/h. The Magellanics are the closest thing to a striped penguin. They have white stomachs but there are two black stripes between the head and the breast and have a white stripe around the head. These birds were much more nervous and as we tried to close on them to photograph them they would break into their best penguin waddle.

The sand on the beaches was pure white, although covered in thick seaweed and kelp. Sometimes it was hard to distinguish the water's edge, with its foamy white surf. It contrasted starkly with the black and white of the penguins, and their bright orange feet.

Patrick was a mine of information about the land, the wildlife, the history and anything else you could possibly be interested in. We climbed a hill to the top of the penguin rookery, and every now and again would see a penguin bob up out of its burrow and have a quick recce to see where we were. They looked like the fairground games that have targets bobbing up and down, designed to be shot.

We continued onto Poloma Sand Beach in Middle Bay, then walked along some of the cliffs and bays. Bright green grass appeared, carpeting the long lines of jagged rock sloping down into the sea spray.

We crested another rise to see the surf rolling lazily into a bay as wide as Scarborough. The sky was bright blue, the sea flanked by tough yellow clumps of grass on one side and those moonscape rocks on the other. Patrick's pick-up descended the hillside, stopping for us to get pictures of a Crested Caracara, which sat surveying its domain, clearly confident that it was both feared and revered.

At the bottom of Poloma Hill our pick-up became amphibious as we drove straight across a massive pond. Patrick didn't bat an eyelid, he did it regularly. At the other side we found Black Faced Ground Tyrants, inquisitive little birds about the size of sparrows, with the hovering abilities of humming birds. They flew right up to the pick-up windows and hovered there, looking in at us. Sadly though, the little buggers wouldn't stay still long enough for us to get a decent photograph of them.

Now en route to home, we stopped at Findlay Rocks, where there was an old SAS sangar built into the rocks. Apparently some of the Argentinian spotters had been camped close enough for the SAS men to hear them talking yet they had not seen or heard the British Special Forces soldiers. Some spotters! They were introduced to the British by HMS *Antrim*'s 4.5 inch gun. It was round about this time I realised how much my backside hurt from bouncing around during the excursion. Every mile of driving here was different. I was used to roads. Here driving meant mountains and valleys, pools and streams, peat bogs and beaches.

Back at the POD we had a brew while I sorted through Patrick and Pat's collection of books and videos on the islands, their dependencies, the wildlife and the birds.

Being a bit of an underwater enthusiast, I settled on a couple of diving videos made by the local diver Dave Eynon who had originally been a diver on the North Sea oil rigs where I had once worked. I contacted Dave who runs South Atlantic Marine Services, to see if I could arrange a dive in my last week in Stanley. The water is five degrees – I tried to work out whether I *really* wanted to do it or whether I just wanted to be able to say, 'Been there, done that, got the t-shirt'.

After the evening meal washed down by the obligatory beers, we all retired to the bar to talk about their lives and past times here, and their views on the future. Patrick was very funny about his work for the British Ministry of Defence in London during the 1982 conflict.

He had been in New Zealand, sheep shearing, when the invasion happened on Friday April 2nd. By the Sunday morning, he was knocking on the door of the MoD in Whitehall.

The door was opened by a young, snotty-nosed public servant. Patrick presented himself as a native islander, volunteering his services to go down with the first batch of troops to act as a guide. The poh-faced youth gave a condescending response. "And what makes you think we're sending any troops down?"

A pissed-off Patrick replied, "well you'd fucking well better be!"

He was invited in, and despite his insistence that he would be most use as a guide to the troops, the MoD refused to listen. In the event, he spent the duration of the war in a critical role, drawing, detailing, and correcting maps and charts for use by the military Task Force during the amphibious invasion and subsequent land battles. I hope he got the South Atlantic Medal, as did the rest of us, for his part.

He recalled one incident where he was woken in the very early hours of the morning by a telephone call from a young officer who was planning some of the logistics for the operation. The officer informed Patrick that he had loaded three hundred pairs of skis into a container for shipping to the South Atlantic.

"Skis?" Patrick said. "The best thing you can do with them is unload them, then fill the space with food and ammunition. Skis are of no use whatsoever."

The young officer became agitated and informed Patrick that he was an expert in Arctic warfare and a graduate of the Arctic warfare school. Patrick asked him how many times he had been to the Falklands.

"Er… none," came the faltering reply.

At this point, Patrick told him to shut up and start fucking listening. When he returned to the Islands after the conflict was over, he asked one of the military logistics men if any skis had arrived in a container. "Yes," he was told. "They're still there, unpacked and unused. What twat sent them?"

CHAPTER 18

San Carlos Water

We picked up Steve and the remaining RAF bloke who'd been too pissed to come out the previous day and set off for Blue Beach, San Carlos, the site of the British landings. The first half of the journey was pretty easy going; however it soon degenerated into rough track which must have caused a lot of snapped axles and broken differentials.

My spine took a hammering to the point where my coccyx started hurting. We crested the top of the Verde Mountain range which looked down onto San Carlos Water, Blue Beach, Bonners Bay, and the few homes in the settlement. The colours of the landscape here, and the water, had amazing clarity. It was like God himself had taken his paintbrush and applied it to San Carlos Water.

We viewed the path the attacking aircraft took, swooping low across East Falkland down onto the beaches of San Carlos. Just visible in the distance was the buoy tendered to the wreck of HMS *Antelope*, the Type 21 Frigate, sister ship of *Arrow* – our own saviour. *Antelope* was made famous by the horrific explosion of her magazines that turned night into day, and was captured on camera. The picture now adorns the cover of numerous books and magazines on the Falklands war. She lies in shallow water just a few hundred yards from Ajax Bay, where the British Field Hospital had been set up and where 45 Commando, Royal Marines had come ashore on Red Beach.

We drove down into the settlement and passed the now abandoned Blue Beach Lodge. I was disappointed to see such an historic building in such disrepair. We made our way on up to the landing beach and the site of the British military cemetery which is the final resting place of a number of men lost in the conflict. There is a whole collection of plaques inscribed with the name of every British serviceman lost in 1982.

I stood in the cemetery just a few yards back from the shoreline in San

Carlos. The sky was a brilliant blue and overhead gulls and terns soared effortlessly and silently. The small but immaculately kept yard was surrounded by a sandstone wall hewn from the rock of Fox Bay. There were only a dozen or so plots in the yard, most of the sixty five men killed in the land battles having been returned to the UK to be buried in their home towns or villages, or regimental graveyards. Another one hundred and seventy five have no grave but the sea.

I wandered along the plaques, reading and recognising the familiar names. The wind had dropped and the writings stood out in an eerie sunlit silence. *He gave his life, that others may live in freedom.* Another, *Never forgotten, always in our hearts.*

Until now, I had been OK, but reflecting on the loss of these valiant young men, just a year or so older than me, became too much, and I started to cry, quietly at first, but soon, with twenty years of sorrow pouring out, I was racked by heaving uncontrollable sobs. I buried my face in my hands, overwhelmed by thoughts of these young men whose lives had been so cruelly taken. I had never known such grief, or such emotion.

Patrick and the two RAF men turned and left the cemetery, leaving me alone in my grief. They no doubt felt it was for the best, but the truth is, if ever I had needed a friend or a reassuring hug from someone, anyone, it was then.

I sat with my back pressed against the cemetery wall and asked myself whether I had the strength to go through with this. Could I confront and defeat the thoughts that had haunted me for two decades, for more than half my life? Or was this, where it had all begun, the beginning of a breakdown? I had two and a half weeks left in the islands and then I was going to meet the Argentinian pilots. I was washed out. I didn't know if I could do it.

I pulled myself together and as I turned to leave the cemetery through the metal gates, I pulled the poppies I had brought with me from inside my jacket. There was a small Union Flag on a long stem next to a cross pushed into the soft soil. I knelt and entwined the poppy stalks so that the cross, the flag, and the red flowers all became one. I read through the Visitors' book and left an entry of my own before replacing the book in the waterproof box by the gate. Then I left the cemetery without looking back.

I stood gazing over the waters of San Carlos; not only the cemetery was home to those who had given their lives here. Many were committed to the sea in traditional sailors' burials. Others had simply gone down with their ships as they sank. This was their final, unmarked resting place. The memorial to them stated, 'For those who gave their lives and who have no grave but the sea.' Nameless and unremembered at the bottom of Falkland Sound were also a number of Argentinian pilots we had shot down, who were too low, or too badly injured to eject.

As many others before me had, I was here witnessing the true futility of war. It had happened, but quite why it had was escaping me, and in some ways, it always will. I had thought I was beginning to understand that some things are worth fighting for and need to be fought for but suddenly I wasn't sure. I felt like a pendulum swinging backwards and forwards between the understanding of the need for the war, versus the perennial pain and suffering it brings.

I wandered down to the beach and into the icy water and stood at the point where the men of 40 Commando, Royal Marines poured out onto their first dry land in over seven weeks, the South Atlantic sea seeping into my boots and my jeans. How could this serene and beautiful setting have seen such violence?

High on the hill on the western side of the bay is the memorial to *Antelope* and her sister ship *Ardent*, the point overlooking the final resting place of both ships and the twenty three men killed aboard them. I thought of *Ardent* and some of the men I knew on her. Only months before the conflict, three of my classmates had joined her as their first ship. I saw Trev Hawkes in HMS *Dryad* just after the war. *Dryad* had been our training school, and we were both returned to wait for our next ships. Ross Saxty from York, had been in my 'Basics of Radar' class, then we split up and were trained on different computerised systems. I knew he had made it home, but never heard of him again. 'Budgie' Burgess was a gunner I met during my short spell in the gunnery school HMS *Cambridge*. I later served with him on HMS *Nottingham*. One of *Ardent's* gunners, Bagsy 'Scouse' Baker I served on *Invincible* with was a Portsmouth field gunner who years later spent a couple of days with me in the Devonport Field Gun HQ whilst he was waiting to join a ship. We only talked about the conflict once, neither of us wishing to dwell on it. *Ardent* had been devastated in rocket and bomb attacks, she had lost a bigger percentage of her ships' company than any other ship. In her final moments, members of her ships' company were witnessed firing machine guns up into the bellies of the aircraft that had dropped the bombs which a split second later, were to take their lives. The bravery and devotion to duty of the Royal Navy sailor did not flinch, even in the final seconds of the inevitable, nor had it for centuries. I then found myself thinking about Richard Dunkerly from my school back in Stalham. Our sisters were in the same class. He was killed in action aboard *Ardent*.

Directly ahead of me, San Carlos Water opened out into Falkland Sound. It was here that *Argonaut*, commanded by Captain Kit Layman, had been hit by two bombs. Matt Stuart, who had been in training at the same time as me, was killed. It was his eighteenth birthday. He was eleven days younger than me. The other Able Seaman lost was Iain Boldy. He had been married for just three months. Both Matt and Iain were committed to the sea in traditional sailors' burials in the Sound, from *Canberra*.

I bent down and dipped my hand into the freezing water to pick up a couple of shiny pebbles and slip them into a small plastic money envelope. I pulled out a sticker from the sheet of A4 address labels I was carrying, and wrote on the label where they came from. I had done this at Green Beach and I planned to do it at all the major sites, after which I would take them to the Falklands Chapel at Pangbourne College in Berkshire and put them with all the other stones and rocks being collected. The idea was that rocks or stones from the home towns and villages of all UK personnel killed in action would be collected, then used to build a cairn of remembrance.

Looking at the mirror-like reflection of San Carlos, with only the whispers of wind through the grass for company, I knew that there was no more peaceful a resting place on earth than this, and I decided that when my time came, I wanted my ashes scattered here.

I turned and walked out of the water onto the sand, looking back at the settlement, the whole placed seemed asleep, dormant. There is a small cottage a few hundred yards from the edge of the bay. Patrick and the RAF guys were stood nearby, one of them beckoned me over. "Time for tea and biccies," he said. We were hosted for tea and biscuits by Ben and Hazel, the sister of Rhoda with whom I had stayed at Douglas. Their quaint Falkland cottage overlooked the whole of the water into which the amphibious assault force had steamed almost twenty years previously.

The inside of the cottage was painted an alarming canary yellow. I wondered if they were fans of Norwich City, then wondered if they had even heard of Norwich! After tea, we made our way out into the cool breeze of Blue Beach. Its Union flag was flying at half mast in honour of the recently deceased Queen Mother. I wandered past the dilapidated Blue Beach Hotel and Lodge wondering how much the Falkland Island Development Corporation would take for it. How much would have to be invested to make the place liveable, hospitable, and usable again and fit for guests? I knew it would be more than I made in a couple of years. And even then, always supposing I could afford it, how long would it take to get a return on the investment? Given its history and surroundings, I was sure the potential was there, for someone with the right vision.

Even the famous old jetty was still standing, where half the army and loads of heavy equipment had come ashore after the beach-head had been secured. Why had it fallen into this state of disuse and disrepair? Maybe there simply weren't that many visitors to this area to justify it, although that seemed strange. I imagined Blue Beach would have been one of the most visited places.

We took in Blue Beach museum which contained hundreds of artefacts from the war, including a beret and belt belonging to a young Paratrooper killed on Mount Longdon, and numerous weapons, newspapers and letters from 1982. It was good to know that these things could remain in such a place, open to the public, un-manned, and without danger of being stolen or defaced, unlike any other museum in the world.

I got back to where the truck was parked and marvelled at how the jetty had stood up to so much heavyweight abuse twenty years ago. Patrick told me that prior to the war, it had born untold carriage loads of pressed wool backwards and forwards over it, and they were heavier than anything which had crossed it during the war.

We piled back into the pick-up and headed for the Sussex Mountains following the route that 2 Para had taken on their way to Goose Green, I looked up – it was a beautiful clear day. We drove south and passed the highest peak on the islands, Mt Usborne at some 2,312 feet high. It stood proudly and magnificently above the rolling green heather and yellow gorse. A few hundred feet below its summit lay wisps of cloud, scattered like fairy clocks in an English summer meadow.

Our route was easier now, on a track which was a motorway by Falkland standards, but which in '82 the Paras had kept clear of for fear of ambush. We passed the turn-off for Goose Green and picked up the road for Mount Pleasant.

We drove into the military complex and I noticed many road names with military significance, again passing Briggs Road, which I had noticed when I arrived. We arrived at the Administration Block, and before going on their way, the two RAF blokes shook my hand. "I hope you find what you're looking for, and you get what you want from this trip," Steve said. He clearly meant it, I was touched.

Patrick had to wait for his next three guests who were going to the POD for some R & R and guided tours, much the same as we had done. He said we'd be here for a while so I decided to have a look around.

In the reception area of the main block I stood reading various military notices and standing orders. They all came flooding back. I smiled at the dress rules and regulations which dictated what you would wear and when you would get out of bed.

There was a notice for male personnel about haircuts and the wearing of sideburns, and where they should be trimmed to, different for all three services. As I strolled around, two RAF aircrew officers came out in flying suits, both with the standard issue air force moustache.

They stopped and stared at me. I stared back. One of them looked me up and down as if I was something he wanted to scrape off his shoe. I turned my back to him. Admittedly you probably don't get too many people in military bases with goatee beards, shaven heads with bright yellow bandanas, and clothes in the state mine were in, but tough! I was on a trekking holiday; I was bound to get dirty.

One of them came up behind me. "Who are you?"

I turned. "Hello. I'm Adam," I said, sticking out my hand. "Who are you?"

The Squadron Leader was not amused. "Well what are you doing here, *Adam*?" He sneered, over-emphasizing my name. I remembered that whilst serving, if you struck a senior officer it could get you up to a year inside and then kicked out, but here, there was bugger all they could do to me. Tempted though I was, I let go the thought of belting the toffee-nosed bugger. I knew it would cause aggro for the people who had put themselves out for me, and were still doing so.

He made no effort to shake my hand, and didn't tell me his name so in my book, he was the rude and arrogant one. I looked at the name embroidered below his pilot's wings.

"Well, *Nigel*," I said, "I'm waiting for Patrick."

He looked across to where Patrick was standing talking to someone and clearly recognised him. The other flyer called him away and as they walked off I started whistling The Dambusters theme. Nigel turned and looked back. I couldn't resist saying to him, "tally ho, Ginger. Look after Nigger[10] for me."

---

[10] The name of the black Labrador owned by Wing Cdr Guy Gibson VC who led the infamous Dambusters raid.

The other pilot worked to keep him steered in the direction they were heading, probably to bag a Jerry in their Spitfires and then home in time for tea and medals. People like him were the reason I left the military in the first place.

I remembered the comment that these islands were retaken, and this war was won by a bunch of gutsy young men fighting, when it came to it, with fists, rifle butts, and bayonets. Probably whilst Nigel was still in nappies.

Back to Stanley

Arriving in Stanley, Patrick arranged to meet his other passengers back at the car in an hour or so after he had finished his business in town. With that we went our separate ways, I, in search of a postcard shop, the latest of Patrick's passengers in search of the nearest pub.

I picked a couple of cards to send to my family, and one to a very old friend, Maxine, whom I had not seen for about eighteen or nineteen years. She and I had lived in the same village on the Norfolk Broads but had gone to different schools. I had a bit of a thing for her but it was all very one sided, though we wrote to each other when I was on *Sheffield* in 81/82. One night, her mother walked into her room and unceremoniously announced: "the ship your friend is on has been sunk in the Falklands," and walked out again. Her mother had never liked me.

The day after I arrived home in '82, my mate Andy came round with some clothes for me. He was much bigger than me and the trousers he gave me were massive – I had to take about three steps before they even started to move. We went to the local village disco, where I knew there would be a good chance I would see Maxine. I told him to park away from the village hall and the floodlit illuminated car park.

He went inside to look for her. I was smoking at the time and got out of the car to light up a fag. There were two kids from my school there who saw me. They immediately disappeared back inside. I had a bad feeling about this.

That morning there had been a big write-up in the local paper about all the local lads from *Sheffield* who had returned home, including myself. Within seconds the village hall emptied and they all stood there staring at me. I stared back.

I saw Andy pushing his way through the crowd. Maxine was quite short and I couldn't see her. He shoved his way through to the front, then I realised she was behind him. Just before they got to me, Andy stopped and turned round, but Maxine kept walking towards me.

I opened my mouth to say hello but was stopped by Andy, who gave the assembled gawpers the benefit of his good nature and English language abilities. "What the fuck are you lot staring at? Fuck off!" Typical Andy, and needless to say, it worked.

Max was wearing a white rah-rah dress with big blue polka dots and had spiky hair, like Claire Grogan from Altered Images (this was the 1980's!) I asked her to come with us to the nightclub nearby. She hesitated then looked round. Two of her mates were watching from the door, as were a number of others. I had a feeling this was going to go on for a while, at least while the war was so fresh in everyone's minds.

"Maybe another night," she said, kissing me on the cheek. "It's good to see you, I'm glad you're home safe."

I wasn't to know then but that kiss would be as far as anything with Maxine would ever go.

My reverie was interrupted by the lady behind the counter of the postcard shop.

"Will there be anything else sir?"

I handed over the money and left, then hiked my way back up to Shackleton Drive where I sorted my kit into what I would be taking to Goose Green with me and what I could leave there. After eating, the only sensible course of action seemed to be, like Patrick's other passenger, to find the nearest watering hole.

I arrived at the once world-famous 'Globe Tavern' and found it had reverted to its original name after being re-christened the 'Globe and Laurel' by the Royal Marines, after their beret badge. It was a single story building with one long bar and a disco at the far end on a raised stage. Military memorabilia covered the rest of that wall, the paraphernalia including badges, caps, sailor's hat ribbons and even an old rifle (very well secured to the wall). I ordered a pint from the Chilean-looking barmaid who had been on my flight in from Punta Arenas with her husband, whom I presumed was a squaddie. I discovered to my dismay that the only draught beer they had was German lager. How could somewhere so English not have draught bitter? I scanned the fridges and shelves behind the bar praying that I would not be resigned to drinking some trendy modern lager like Red Stripe and spotted the familiar colouring of McEwan's. Yes! The very own Red Devils/Red Death – call it what you will. Perfect! So McEwan's it had to be. I savoured every drop and it was bliss, the Australians just cannot make good dark beer.

The beer was good but the pub lacked atmosphere so I went in search of a more homely place. As I crossed the road to The Victory, a gust of wind blew up from the harbour and found its way through every zip, pocket and gap of clothing I was wearing. It was freezing! I opened the pub door and before I had taken one step inside, everyone turned towards me to see who was coming in.

I took a seat on a bar stool and ordered another McEwan's. While I was waiting I asked the landlady why you could not get any draft beer here. We started with a scientific discussion of what beer is actually made from, i.e. barley, wheat hops, etc and it obviously wasn't grown on the islands, so therefore could not be brewed here. That all made sense. So the only other option was to import it by sea, again all very obvious. Given that most people here would want British beer, it would take three to four weeks to get here by sea. She told me that if kegged beer was in weather like the South Atlantic swells for any length of time, it would be ruined, hence they only imported cans. I couldn't see the difference personally, but there was no point in arguing.

After a few pints the bar started to fill up. I heard a woman's voice speaking with a broad West Yorkshire accent. I went in search of the owner. We exchanged a few words and she told me that after the war, she and her husband had decided they wanted to own a piece of their own land. Given the scarcity and cost of land in the UK a place like this might very well be the only place they could afford. They had relocated in 1983 and never looked back. I thought of a couple of nights out I'd had in Barnsley and Bradford and couldn't say I blamed her.

I knew that the following morning, I had to hire a car from Terry's daughter for the drive to Goose Green so I decided, quite responsibly, I'd had enough to drink. This was opposed to my usual trick of drinking until either the pub closed or I ran out of money.

As I crossed the car park, a voice came from behind me.

"Excuse me."

I stopped and turned around but didn't say anything. The man went on, "I didn't mean to eavesdrop but I heard you and the lady talking about the *Sheffield* in '82."

He waited for a response.

"And?"

He pulled a business card out of his jacket and held it towards me. I didn't take it but just stood and stared at him.

"Well," he said. "I'm from the BBC. We're down here making a documentary about the 20th anniversary of the war, and I was wondering if you'd be prepared to talk to us – on camera."

I hadn't seen him in the pub and wondered where he'd been eavesdropping from. I weighed him up, he seemed OK, but my distrust of journalists went back twenty years. The press had come to see me when I got home, they took a photo and I gave them my version of events. They didn't print what I said and I wasn't impressed. I'd seen other reports filed by journalists saying they had watched from the bridge of *Hermes* as *Sheffield* had slipped below the waves, still on fire with the ship's company desperately trying to abandon ship before she sank. A complete work of fiction; *Hermes* was about thirty miles away and all they saw was a plume of smoke.

"Sorry, this is a private visit," I said as I turned away and carried on walking. It was freezing and I pulled my woolly hat down over my ears, turned my collar up and shoved my hands deep into my pockets. I sensed someone next to me. It was the journalist. I can't recall exactly what he said, I wasn't really listening.

I interrupted him. "I'm sorry, I can't help you." I kept walking and turned left into Fitzroy Road.

"There could be a fee involved," he called after me.

I was pissed off now and felt like decking him. I'd had a good night and he'd just ruined it with his stupidity. I walked back to him. He could see I was annoyed and started backing away.

I came face to face with him and very calmly asked, "which part of 'no' don't you understand?"

He swallowed hard and stammered. "I… I just thought that…"

I interrupted him again. "That wasn't my question," I said. "My question was, which part of 'no' don't you understand?" Before he could gather himself to answer, I turned and walked off.

CHAPTER 19

Goose Green and Darwin

Terry drove me to the house belonging to Geoff Porter, the owner of the Jeep I was to hire. Geoff had a thick Irish accent, had previously been a squaddie, and met and married one of the local girls whilst posted down here. He gave me a safety briefing the like of which I've never had before. "Always park into the wind. Do *not* open the door without holding onto the handle, preferably with two hands in a wind like today's." I knew what he meant – I recalled the battle I'd had with the wind as I'd tried to climb Mt Estancia the week before.

Familiarising myself with the very basic vehicle, I backtracked west along the MPA road towards Darwin. Despite the fact that there is only one road, I kept stopping to check I was heading the right way because there weren't any landmarks. When the scenery all looks the same you start to lose faith in your ability to navigate. It was early morning; normally I would have checked my direction of travel by the sun, but on an overcast day like this, not a chance. I had been warned about driving on gravel in a small light Suzuki Jeep like this. It was quite high-sided, making it a wonderful wind catcher, and steering it in these conditions was about as easy as walking on ball bearings. It frightened me on a couple of occasions.

I found the turn off for Goose Green and Darwin and immediately came upon a sign pointing me in the direction of the Argentinian military cemetery. I took the turning and drove a few hundred yards down the track to the top of a small rise. There I found a white picket fence, beyond which were rows of neat white crosses, and a large white cross at the top of the cemetery near the brow of the hill.

Wondering along the rows of crosses, it seemed every one was draped with Rosary beads and pictures of handsome young Hispanic men in white tuxedos or uniforms, with names such as Luis, Diego, Rodriquez. The fighter pilots pictured were clad in black leather jackets covered with squadron badges and motifs. It was good to see that their airforce also has the standard regulation-issue moustache.

While many of the crosses bore names, a large number didn't, being marked only with, 'An Argentine soldier, known unto God.' Lots of the young conscripts had not worn dog tags or other means of identification. Some had been so mutilated in battle that such things were irrelevant anyway. Bizarrely, many of the unknown graves had been adopted by more than one family who had lost loved ones, but who have no known grave to mourn at.

I counted the crosses – 250. Argentina says it lost less than 650 men. The final figure of the sailors who went down on the cruiser ARA *General Belgrano* was about 360, which would leave around 300 killed in land battles and aircraft shot down. The Islanders say that even before the British air attacks began on 1st May, Argentinians were dying of exposure and starvation which would amount to even more bodies unaccounted for.

I was told by more than one person that to get rid of the Argentinian dead, their military commanders had them loaded into Hercules aircraft and helicopters and flew them out to sea, where the bodies were dropped out of the doors. I also heard suggestions that others were loaded into a container, put on a ship, then dumped at sea.

Of course that might all be hearsay, but I did meet an old woman at the war memorial in Buenos Aires who didn't know how her son had died or where his body was. Galtieri's government was renowned for making people disappear, so maybe it's not so unbelievable.

It was also common knowledge that some, though by no means all of the Argentinian officers were living comfortably in good accommodation with plenty of food and small bottles of whisky in their ration packs, while the conscripts were living in appalling conditions, frozen, and starving.

I walked all around and through the Argentinian cemetery, looking on these men not as an enemy we defeated, but as somebody's son, somebody's father, brother, husband. They were no different from me, us, except they spoke a different language. The volunteers and professional servicemen may have believed they were recovering Argentinian property taken from them on 2 January 1833, a story which had been drilled into them from school. I know there were also conscripts who had no idea what they were doing there, or even where they were. They were sacrificed on the altar of nationalistic incompetence by belligerent politicians.

I felt an intense loathing for Admiral Jorgé Anaya, who had been at the centre of the original Argentinian plan. Galtieri was his puppet, a naïve idiot but Anaya was a nasty piece of work. Right then, I longed to have ten minutes in a cell with him. What an unutterably evil man he was. I'd have cheerfully kicked him to death for the role he played in the destruction of so many lives.

The sum total of his life's achievements that we know of, was the death of 1,000 men, the destruction of the way of life of another 2,000 people, the desecration of a beautiful place, and countless families left with a lifetime's grief. I was so pissed off I turned and left the cemetery, saying a silent prayer for the men there who would never leave. I'm not in the least bit religious but I know most of the Argentinians were Roman Catholics so I made the sign of the cross as I walked out. It seemed the decent thing to do.

Climbing to the brow of the hill I looked out over the glasslike waters of Choiseul Sound towards the settlement of Goose Green. The houses, with their green and red roofs, were reflected in the waters, forming a perfect mirror image. How could such a place have borne witness to such violence, such bloodshed, aggression and killing? When I think of battlefields I picture the Somme, trenches, Passchendaele, mud, barbed wire, Ypres, huge water filled shell craters. The Normandy beaches, the 'bridge too far' at Arnhem. What was in front of me was not the kind of picture conjured up by the word 'battlefield'.

I drove round past the sign for Darwin, a sign which seemed to point towards nothing but by now I was used to signs for nothing. I took the turn off for Darwin to find the lodge, my accommodation for the night. I pulled up on the track at the foot of yet another hill. There was a large cross surmounting a stone cairn surrounded by a freshly painted white picket fence. This spot is the only place that overlooks both settlements, and the fields where the men to whom the memorial is dedicated actually fell in battle.

Lt Col 'H' Jones VC aged 42, Commanding Officer of the 2nd Battalion, The Parachute Regiment, commissioned into the Devon and Dorsets. Private Stephen Illingworth DCM aged 18, from a mining family in Doncaster.

What did these two men have in common? From opposite ends of the country and no doubt opposite social circles, they now lie, their names inscribed on a memorial, amongst many others remembered by the people they freed, in a land they liberated, the stones and cross erected by the people of Goose Green and Darwin for whom they had made the supreme sacrifice. Nothing separated these men now.

I laid poppies amongst the mass of other wreaths, some quite fresh, some faded from the harsh South Atlantic weather. All bore the same words – 'In loving memory of a beloved son. In our thoughts today and every day'.

Darwin Lodge was a couple of hundred metres down the track through the gulley which, on the 28 May 1982, had been the Regimental Aid Post (RAP) for 2 Para. All the casualties were brought into the RAP where the medics fought to keep them alive and warm. The gorse around them was on fire from the shelling and in the end the medics resorted to covering their wounds with dressings and then piling hot ashes from the burnt gorse over the men.

When I reached the lodge, the welcome was as warm as every other I'd received so far in the islands. Bonnie Greenland was a born and bred Islander, and Ken was an ex-military policeman (although that should not be held against him). After leaving the military police, he ran the island's civilian police force for a number of years before taking on the renovation and running of Darwin Lodge, and the attached self-contained and self-catering cottages. No sooner had I arrived than I was greeted by a cuppa on silver service.

I dumped my gear and took a walk around the water to Goose Green, carefully avoiding the barbed wire fence signposted 'Minefield'. The wind had died down. I stuck to the coastline and as I wandered round, I was trying to work out why the Argentinians would mine some of the areas they had, but not the obvious places. Blind Pew could see where an amphibious assault could come from, or more likely, attacking troops could advance under the cover of the cliffs and rocks.

Crossing a rickety old walkway across a stretch of water, I came across a penguin trapped by the wire on the walkway. It kept frantically running from side to side trying to get away from me. I eventually cornered it, and after numerous attempts managed to get a hold on it. It was an aggressive little bugger and its beak hurt when it pecked. I leaned over the fence and managed to release it into Choiseul Sound, where it pedaled away furiously like a clockwork bath toy.

At the end of the jetty, I studied the wreck of the *Vicar of Bray* which was the last of the gold rush ships taking prospectors to California in 1849.

After a ramble around the settlement I passed the community centre where 115 residents had been held for 28 days in 1982. The only remaining signs of a conflict here were the letters PoW daubed on the side of a shed. It beggars belief that so many people could be crammed into such a small building. It must have been horrendous.

I then went in search of Bodie Creek Bridge, the most southerly suspension bridge in the world. It connects the north part of East Falkland to the southern part, or Lafonia. I continued along the coastline and onto the stony beach, climbed a fence and jumped down onto what looked like a patch of sand. It was only when I sank knee deep into a putrid sludge of well-fermented sheep shit that I realised it wasn't. I dragged myself back up the fence and climbed along it towards more solid ground. Of course, the stinking gunk clung to my jeans, and seeped in through every lace hole of my boots!

The large peninsula of land hooked round at an angle of 180 degrees and went back north east, which meant I had to cut directly across country in a south westerly direction to link up with Bodie Creek. All I had between me and the bridge was any number of identical rolling hills grazed by hundreds of identical roaming sheep, not a landmark in sight. I wasn't sure whether I still had the navigational ability to get there and back before nightfall.

Checking the map against where the water lay and the angle of the sun I decided I could get myself to the bridge without too many dramas. Not even a sailor could get lost in the space of a couple of miles. After two or three hills though, I started to have my doubts. I kept checking the map, worried that I would be lost out here at night and wondering whether I should turn back.

I jumped a fence and happened upon a track which should have taken me to the elusive bridge. I continued along this for a few hundred yards, but as I crested a hill, I found it fenced off at the end, the equivalent of an agricultural cul-de-sac. It was no big deal to hop the fence but there were two sheep between me and the end of the track. They immediately started to panic, charging backwards and forwards across the track, head butting the chicken wire fence and its posts, anything to get out of my path. I stayed where I was so as not to worry them any further, but they carried on. I wondered if I could stop them before they did themselves any harm, but eventually I couldn't help myself; I started to laugh. They would race like lunatics from one side to the other, charging headlong into either the wire, or the wood of the posts, then would collapse dazed on the ground. Then they would struggle to their feet again, turn around and repeat the process, with predictable, identical, results. I was pissing myself laughing by this time, but I crossed to the far side of the track, to give the suicidal sheep an obvious escape route, and thankfully, they realised this was their best chance of escape before they became lamb chops. They took it and scarpered, and I couldn't help thinking that such stupid creatures deserved mint sauce.

I carried on; more hills, more heather, more hidden potholes and more ankle injuries. I was thirsty, and pissed off that I hadn't brought anything to drink, not even the hip flask. I kept on checking my map but it was pretty useless, the best a tourist shop in Brisbane could provide. It was that ancient it probably came with the first convict settlers. Dispirited now, I was on the verge of turning back when I crested a rise to see the girders of the bridge. It was only a short distance by military standards but I felt quite chuffed that I'd managed to walk a straight line towards it, without a compass or any landmarks.

I'd like to say that the walk was really worthwhile but the bridge was a bit of a let-down. It looked like the Humber Bridge or San Francisco's Golden Gate Bridge, but it was 1/100th of the size, far less interesting, and decidedly unstable. When the wind blew, it looked and felt as though it was about to fall apart and collapse into Bodie Creek.

It was closed, so I lobbed a rock onto the boards of the walkway, which went straight through, sending a shower of wood and splinters into the waters below. How could it have been allowed to fall into such a state of disrepair that it was not even safe to walk across? This bridge had cut miles off the journey round to Lafonia and Walker Creek and now all that had been lost. For a moment, I thought about crossing it, despite the notices pointing out that it was in danger of collapse. Then I remembered the rock, and I shelved that plan!

The sun was low in the sky and I knew it was time to head back. I guessed it was just over four miles (or six km), so I knew I needed to start making decent time.

I couldn't see any sign of life for miles and, again, I began to lose faith in my map reading ability. Using only an old tourist map, the angle of the sun and the water, I was attempting to find my way back to a small settlement in a large place. By the time I'd gone half way, the sun had gone down, it was almost dark and one ridge and hill looked very much the same as the next.

I eventually crested a rise and was relieved to see a house in the distance, so I headed towards it. It was pitch black when I arrived back at Goose Green. I met one of the residents who insisted that I come in for tea and cakes. They asked what I was doing here and we had the usual exchange of stories. What follows is theirs:

When the Argentinians first arrived there weren't any major changes. However, on 1st May when Harriers started bombing and the warships commenced shore bombardment, all that changed.

All 150 residents of the settlement were herded into the community centre. They were allowed out for exercise twice a day and on many occasions were lined up against the community centre, and made to face the wall. The Argentinians had troops manning tripod mounted .50 calibre machine guns. When the residents were lined up with their backs to the guns, the weapons were cocked and they thought they were all going to be shot.

As there were only two toilets, they were in constant use and got blocked the whole time. During the exercise period one of the islanders was unblocking the toilets. An Argentinian officer told him exercise was over and he was to go back inside. The man refused and said he would not go until he had finished. The officer drew his pistol and put it to the man's head, and told him if he did not go back inside, he would be shot. The man told him to fuck off. The officer cocked his pistol and told the man to put down his tools and get back inside. The man carried on working and told the officer to shoot, because he was not going back inside until he had finished unblocking the khazi.

The interred Goose Green residents heard of an incident over at Fox Bay where some of the islanders had been putting sugar and sand in the petrol tanks of the Argentinian military vehicles. One of the NCOs had been heard to say in English, that two of the islanders should be shot in front of the rest of them to teach them a lesson. His officer was not impressed and the sergeant was deported back to the Argentinian mainland.

The woman imparting the story to me paused for a while, and swallowed hard, I knew this was getting difficult for her. Her voice started to falter. "On a number of occasions, we were convinced that we were all going to be massacred," she said.

I asked if they really thought a nation would take away more than a hundred Britons, including the elderly and babies and then murder them with the eyes of the world on the conflict (which they were) and an enormous British Task Force of 30,000 personnel including the nation's most efficient fighting men on their doorstep. She very calmly and casually reminded me that they had allegedly murdered some 20,000 of their own people in the period of the 'dirty war' with no ramifications, so what difference would 100 enemy 'gringos' make? She certainly had a point.

The worst occasions, she said, were when the Argentinians told them that they were going to take their children and evacuate them to Argentina for 'safety'. I was told that it was believed in Argentina at the time, that the wealthy or well to do, or well connected families who could not have children, suddenly became 'parents' of newborns and infants without looking pregnant. The natural parents of the children concerned were told that the child would be offered a much better home and chance in life. The couple I spoke to are still convinced that if their children had been sent to Argentina they would have been sent to other families, and they themselves would then have been murdered.

The parents said they had made a pact; once they were convinced that their own deaths were inevitable and imminent and they could no longer protect their children, they would ensure that they died first at their own hands. They wanted to spare them either being abducted to Argentina and suffering an unknown fate, or seeing their own mother and father executed.

The children of the couple were the same age as my own little girl was as I listened to the story, so of course it made a great impact on me. The thought of how I would cope with having to make such decisions, planning to kill my own child to protect her from an unknown fate, was simply too much to bear. I started to cry. And when I looked up in an attempt at apology, the couple were crying too.

When we collected ourselves a little, they told me documentation had been seen stating that '*after 31st May 1982, occupants of Goose Green and Pebble Island will be removed*'. Had the 2nd Battalion, The Parachute Regiment not liberated Goose Green on 29th May, many people are convinced they would not have lived to see June.

I left the house in a state of shock, not knowing what to make of it all. I believed the couple totally, but I needed space away from what they had told me as it was so upsetting. I looked down at my hands which were trembling uncontrollably. My throat was dry despite all the tea and my stomach was in knots. My knees gave way and I pitched forward onto my hands and knees and was violently sick. I had never before believed that emotions could make you ill. I didn't doubt it now.

By the time I got back to Darwin lodge it was pitch black. Ken said he was starting to get concerned, knowing that I didn't know my way around. Once again dinner was a sumptuous feast, roast with everything. After relaxing a while, I had shed the previous nausea and was feeling OK again. The island's Governor, Donald Lamont was staying at the lodge, ready for a trip to Lafonia the following day. We exchanged a few words over dinner, and he asked if I thought it had been worth it all in 1982. He got the same answer as everyone else.

A bunch of RAF men were staying in the self-catering cottages and I went drinking with them. In the bar was an 'honesty book' – you simply helped yourself and wrote it down. Needless to say, I got absolutely legless.

I breakfasted with Governor Lamont on Saturday morning. He repeated the questions he'd asked the night before.

"Are you glad you came back? Do you think it was right in the first place?"

He had one of the posh Scottish accents that had been worked on to fit into diplomatic circles. Sometimes, inadvertently, he didn't do a bad Sean Connery. We exchanged pleasantries and talked about our agendas for the day and the rest of the week. They differed considerably!

"Did you sleep well?" asked Bonnie as she served the standard colossal Falklands breakfast.

"Excellent thanks," I replied.

There was a pause. "Do you sleep walk?"

"No. Why?"

"You did last night," she said. "Ken found you outside in the middle of the night. Ask him."

I sat back and scoured my memory. I couldn't remember a thing. I'd been drinking but it hadn't been over the top. As I headed upstairs to sort my kit out, Ken appeared from out the back.

"So take me through last night's escapades," I said. "I remember nothing."

He laughed and relayed his version of events.

"I heard the chimes rattle and sound out their tune as the front door opened. I wondered who it was at that time of night, so got out of bed. My first thought was that some of the RAF men from the self catering cottages across the way were coming to replenish their beer stock, but it was the middle of the night. The front door was wide open, as was the porch door. I checked my watch – it was 1:30am. I've been a copper all my life, so I'm used to investigating unusual situations, especially at night, so I wasn't worried as such. I just thought it was strange. I could make out a figure standing outside, but it appeared to have no clothes on, and I thought, surely, this couldn't be right. Half past one on a winter's night, you'd freeze in seconds.

I stood at the door and realised it was you, wearing nothing but white boxers, although they were hardly distinguishable against your lily white skin in the pitch dark. You were standing with your arms folded, looking away from the Lodge towards Goose Green.

'Are you alright?' I asked.

'It's OK, I'm British,' you said.

'Yes I know you're British, I'm British, we're all British now,' I said. 'Come back inside.'

'No I'm fine,' you said. 'Leave me alone. I'm a Brit.'

I know you should never try to wake sleep walkers nor force them against their will. There have been cases where they've become aggressive. So I ventured outside. It was absolutely bloody freezing, and I was wearing pyjamas, and there you were, you lunatic, clad in a pair of cotton underpants proclaiming your citizenship on the front lawn. So I moved around so I was no longer between you and the door of the Lodge and hoped that by walking towards you from that angle, I could persuade you to move back towards the door and get inside, before both of us caught pneumonia!"

I stared at him and said again that I had absolutely no memory of any of it. He carried on:

"I stepped towards you, telling you it was OK, and that we should go back inside as it was the middle of the night. You backed away at first, but then unfolded your arms and became agitated, although you clearly didn't know where you were or what you were doing. I couldn't decide whether you were awake or still dreaming. So I took another step towards you and said something like, 'it's OK, just calm down. You're going to freeze if you stay out here. Let's go back inside'. Then you blinked, and the look on your face said you knew something wasn't right, but you still weren't with it, so I ushered you into the porch and through the hall. Then, I thought you'd woken up, so I pointed you in the direction of your room, and off you went."

I shook my head at him, hardly able to believe it. He said he noticed I was wearing my glasses. Not many people sleep in their glasses so I must have put them on when I got up to come out, but if I was sleep walking, why would I do that? And if I wasn't sleep walking what the hell was I doing walking round in my boxer shorts at 1:30am?

CHAPTER 20

Battlefield Tour of Goose Green

Goose Green, a name that was at one time synonymous with violence and aggression, is actually a beautiful and peaceful place.

Our first stop was the grave of Lieutenant Nick Taylor RN. It was in a fenced plot at the edge of the airfield. He was a Sea Harrier Pilot from 800 Squadron aboard HMS *Hermes*; he was killed the same day *Sheffield* was attacked. He had been involved in a low level bombing raid with an RAF pilot, Flight Lieutenant Ed Ball, and another Naval pilot, Lieutenant Commander Gordon Batt. They had attacked in daylight at low level, flying into a barrage of 35mm anti aircraft fire. Lt Taylor's Sea Harrier disintegrated before he had time to eject. His body was found by the local Argentinian commander and buried with full military honours. The inscription his parents had put on his headstone was to the effect – *He died bravely, fighting for a country he believed in, and a cause he believed just.* Large bits of the wreckage of his aircraft had been gathered up and placed around the cross at the head of the immaculately maintained plot. It seemed fitting. I left a single poppy.

Ken took me to the start line where 2 Para had advanced forward. He gave a good account of the advance of each of the four companies' individual battles and when and where they were held up, pinned down and so forth. Given that the battle, which began at 2:30am and was intended to be over 'before breakfast' continued into the following day, and much of the fighting took place on open fields in broad daylight, it's a wonder the casualty figure wasn't far higher. Ken and I walked around Darwin Hill to where Col H Jones fell. There was no doubt about it; the Paras had achieved an incredible victory.

Ken told me of a wounded Para Captain who had lain all night on the battlefield until he was found hours later. He had major trauma wounds to the stomach, and no one could understand how he was still alive. It was later found that his blood had retreated to his major organs, and because of the cold, his body temperature had lowered significantly, keeping him alive. Thanks to that discovery, it has become accepted medical practice to lower the body temperatures of major trauma victims.

On the way back to Stanley, the wind became gale force again, so much so that it was almost tipping the Jeep over. I was going to go via Bluff Cove to the scene of the Sir Galahad bombing, but I was worried about damage to the Jeep, so I returned it to Terry's daughter and walked back to Shackleton Drive. I spent the rest of the day wandering around Stanley, doing nothing in particular.

It was Saturday night and I thought 'when in Rome' and headed off into the town for a couple of pints. The Victory seemed a good a place to start. It had the décor of any English country pub and it livened up as the evening wore on. I had selected a quiet corner where I could observe the bar and both sides of the pub to do my first bit of people watching, to see if it was like anywhere else with a British flavour. It was. The young servicemen could be spotted a mile away, as could the local girls they viewed as 'fair game'.

After a couple of hours and a couple of cans of McEwan's, a group of girls came in dressed in St Trinian's outfits, complete with straw boaters, freckles and pig tails. I hadn't seen that for years and of all the places to find it, here. It brought a smile to my face. They were going round with charity tins, rattling them under the customer's noses and not taking 'no' for an answer. One girl pushed her way through to me. She thrust the tin at me and I saw it had SAMA82 painted on the side.

She burst into a well-rehearsed spiel. "Would you like to make a donation for SAMA82, it stands for…"

I interrupted. "I know what SAMA is. Of course I'll make a donation."

I pulled out a red Falkland five pound note and pushed it into the tin. Five quid I thought, that's nothing compared to what some people gave. I drained my glass and headed for the bar. The McEwan's was going down well.

The woman with the broad Yorkshire accent I'd talked to on the Thursday night was with the St Trinian's girls. We exchanged greetings and she introduced me to some of the others. The young girl who had accepted my fiver heard the conversation and butted in.

"Were you here in '82?"

I opened my mouth to reply but before the words came out, one of her friends answered.

"Yes, he was on the *Sheffield*."

The look on the young girl's face was a mixture of sorrow and pity, yet she wasn't even old enough to know anything about it. "I'm sorry," she said. "I didn't know. You can have your fiver back."

I laughed. "Actually, they need every cent… I mean, penny."

She bought me a drink and when the St Trinian's girls crossed the road to The Globe, asked me to come too. Free beer is good at any time but when it comes from a bunch of women in fishnet stockings and suspenders, and you are the only bloke in the crowd, it adds somewhat to the flavour!

The one thing that was constant (apart from the free beer) was people saying how sorry they were for what had happened to us in 1982 and it was starting to get me down. I decided I'd put a diplomatic stop to it. Sure enough, it came again, and I turned to face the girl concerned. She would have been old enough to remember the war and occupation, and there was an older lady with her, probably around my mum's age.

"Much as I appreciate the hospitality," I said quietly, "I don't need anyone's sympathy, thank you."

She didn't speak, but the older lady who had heard me did. She stepped forward and rested her hand on my arm and said with total sincerity, "Son, it is not our sympathy you have – but our gratitude for what you did for us."

As she spoke, I saw unshed tears in her eyes, and without warning, I found myself filling up, the tears spilling down my own cheeks. A grown man, I stood with a beer in each hand, crying my heart out along with the elderly lady, and nobody said a word.

All in all it was a good night out, as nights without draught beer go, but it wasn't over yet. As all the pubs kicked out at 11:30pm a group of youngsters I'd been drinking with asked me along to a party. As there were no nightclubs, it seemed the only sensible thing to do. I piled into the back of a long wheel base Land Rover with what seemed like scores of other people, and crates of beer.

One youth pointed at me and asked in a strong West Country accent, "Who the fuck is he?"

One of the girls answered him. "This is Adam. He was here in '82."

I couldn't hear his response because the Land Rover engine roared into life but it looked like he'd said 'so fucking what?' I hoped it wasn't going to be another case of civvies versus military people, which happens in all military garrison towns, whether it be Portsmouth, Aldershot or wherever. Surely if that was the case they wouldn't have invited me in the first place.

The Land Rover made its erratic way through the streets of Stanley. A lot of the corners are right angles but I'm sure we took them at about forty five degrees. It was now pouring with rain. We stopped and everyone piled out. I had no idea where I was, it had been impossible to talk in the back of the Land Rover because everyone was shouting at everyone else, and being thrown about as the vehicle careened round the corners. I followed the party goers and crates of beer into a house, where I wandered through various rooms until I found the beer in the kitchen. Everyone was younger than me but they were all very welcoming apart from the youth who had originally asked who I was. He was still being obnoxious and made a derogatory remark about the events of 1982. I walked out and sat in the living room with half a dozen people. I asked one of the girls how old he was, she told me he was eighteen, so he wasn't even born until two years after the war that had liberated his parents.

I decided then that he had used up all his chances. The night wore on and the beer flowed, and every now and again, Mr Obnoxious appeared at the entrance to the living room and then turned and went back into the kitchen. I got up to get the beers in and walked through into the kitchen where he was with a bunch of other teenagers. I introduced myself by name, leaving out my reasons for being in Stanley; I grabbed a couple of beers and made to rejoin the serious drinkers. One of them asked what I was doing here and before I had time to respond, one of the others chipped in.

"He was blown up on *Sheffield* in '82."

"Serves the cunt right for being here in the first place."

I don't know if Obnoxious intended to go on, but he never got the opportunity. I switched the beers to my left hand and as I turned around I smacked him in the mouth. I carried on walking as he hit the kitchen floor. I was sitting down in the living room when all the lads appeared at the arched entrance into the lounge. Obnoxious was bleeding, complaining that I'd started on him, and that they were going to come in and 'do me'. The room went suddenly quiet and people moved away from me. 'Shit, this has got out of hand', I thought. I knew if I got into a scrap and someone's house got wrecked that Terry would be really pissed off and it could damage relations between the locals and SAMA82, and the veterans who would be here later in the year.

156

Despite the mouthy threats, there was no action which was reassuring, because if they actually meant to do it, they'd have charged in by now. I stood up and told them this was between me and Obnoxious, and that I had no quarrel with any of them. He was obviously a mouthpiece and did the 'we're all mates and we stick together routine'. Time to leave I decided, but how to get out and get my boots was the problem.

"Look fellas," I said. "Give me my boots and I'll go, OK?"

One of them walked towards the front door and re-appeared at the archway with my boots, which he threw into the kitchen, which meant I was going to have to pass them all to get to them. I didn't fancy fighting in bare feet if it came to it. I remembered then though that I'd seen an arch at the other end of the kitchen so I walked round the dining room and into the far end of the kitchen where my boots lay. I snatched them up and pulled them on whilst they all stood watching me. If I was going to rush someone, I'd have done it whilst they were getting their shoes on.

Obnoxious walked in and the others followed, they were now completely blocking the exit to the front door. Obnoxious took a couple of steps towards me with his mates close behind. I backed up against the kitchen bench and felt around behind me for something to use if the need arose. I picked up the first thing I put my hand on, which was the kettle, which was thankfully cold.

Time to bluff my way out. I pulled the kettle round in front of me and said, "You lot way outnumber me so I know I'll get a good kicking in the end, but the first one to come near me, the very first one… I will kill you. Not just hurt you, I will kill you. So who wants to be the hero? Who wants to be the martyr? What about you?" I said, staring at Obnoxious.

I was shitting myself, but clearly so was he, because at that point he stood aside and the others followed suit. How could such a tosser be the kingpin of this group? I could hardly walk out with the kettle but I had to run the gauntlet through them and as I did, I was waiting for the first blow from behind, which would be the signal for a bloody good hiding for me. I reached the front door, lifted the latch and was never so relieved to walk out into driving rain and freezing wind in my life.

I heaved a sigh of relief, and found myself wondering whether if they had called my bluff, would I have had to stand up in court as the charge was read out, 'that he did wilfully kettle him to death'.

I stopped to get my bearings and realised I was as far from Terry's house as it was possible to get. Still, the walk would clear my head. I'd walked for a couple of minutes when a police Range Rover stopped me. There was a female copper who resembled my friend's daughter. She lowered the window.

"Where've you been?" she asked.

"To a party," I answered in all truthfulness.

"Was there any trouble?"

"No," I lied.

"Are you OK?"

"Of course I am," I said. "Why wouldn't I be, there wasn't any trouble – honest."

"That's not what I heard," she said. "On your way home, NOW!"

Way home, my arse! Where the bloody hell did she think I was going at that time of night in that weather.

"Give us a lift please?" I said.

She glared at me. "Piss off!" Then the Rover sped off into the rain.

"Bloody coppers," I yelled after her.

CHAPTER 21

Battlefields and Memorials
Pebble Island

On Sunday morning the weather was clear and fine. I walked through the 1982 Memorial Garden, where there is a tree planted in remembrance of the 255 men and the three local Falklanders lost. With the islands almost devoid of trees, this was a place that could really capture the imagination as well as stir the emotions. The trees would of course continue to grow as other memories faded, and the garden would help those memories stay alive.

The road stretched all the way down to the airport and round to Cape Pembroke. When I got to the 'road sign', so called because of the hundreds of signs pointing towards people's homes and other far flung corners of the world, I had to laugh. The first two were from Hull. One had a sticker from Hull AFC – 'The Tigers' the other a sticker from Northern Divers, a company started and run for many years by some of my dad's best mates. It's a small world.

At the Cape there were some beautiful beaches, with silvery pristine sand. Unfortunately though, they were all unusable because they are mine fields. No one in the Argentinian military had had the sense to map where they had laid the mines, they were scattered indiscriminately. It struck me that had they managed to keep the islands, the beaches would have been unusable for them too, unless of course they made some of the conscripts walk on them.

I took ages walking around the unfenced beaches and headlands through virgin ground untouched and untrodden by man. The names of the places made me smile – Seal Rocks, Surf Bay; I could have been back in Australia. This Surf Bay hosted a mid-winter swim for the clinically insane and those who are tougher than old boots. The participants brave the freezing waters for a dip on mid-winter's day as the spectators stare in bemusement.

There is an enormous amount of history in Stanley associated with the days of sail, and the early days of steam ships. Many vessels would pull into the harbour after a battering whilst rounding Cape Horn, and some would never leave. Stanley is one of the greatest graveyards of 19th century shipping in the world. The *Charles Cooper* was the last sailing packet to leave America and has lain in the islands since 1866. The *Lady Elizabeth,* an old 228 foot, three masted iron vessel rests at the end of Stanley harbour. She has been there for almost 100 years. She was built in 1879 and some of the materials for the Christ Church Cathedral were shipped to the islands on her. I had heard tales of the SAS and SBS hiding in there during the occupation; I could only assume that that was rubbish.

I settled down into a recess behind the sand dunes and took some photos looking right up the harbour towards Mount Longdon and Two Sisters. I sat for hours just watching and thinking, not about anything in particular. There was nothing bothering me, or puzzling me, no awkward questions playing on my mind. I felt relaxed and strangely at peace, contented in my surroundings. It was dark by the time I left for the walk back to Terry's.

I arrived at Stanley airport the following morning hoping there would be no problem with the wind speed across the tarmac for take-off this morning. I looked at the nine-seater Britton Islander; it was rocking alarmingly in the wind.

The aircraft was full and we were crammed in like sardines. If one of these aircraft ever went down, there would be no chance of getting out. Whether it was land or sea, we were that tightly packed, it would be curtains if it wasn't a wheels landing. We had only just started taxiing along the runway when the nose wheel came up and the plane actually started leaving the ground. I couldn't understand how anything so slow could actually fly.

We climbed over Stanley. It was easy to make out where the 'newer' buildings were, newer being post 1982. Stanley had been a very small place. I looked over towards Tumbledown Mountain, Wireless Ridge, Moody Brook and Mount Longdon. The final fighting had not been far from Stanley, and that couldn't have been much fun for the civilian residents. We flew between Mt Estancia and Mt Kent and continued North West towards Pebble Island. The weather was dull and overcast and it had started to rain, making the place look miserable and bleak. Also, the wind was stronger up here and the plane was being bounced around. It struck me that this was the best laxative known to man, far better than sitting in the Shankill Road with a gun in your hand.

We crossed over the sound at the narrowest point of the northern entrance and started our descent into Pebble. The pilot pulled a sharp left hand turn; the rocks on the mountains looked so close I could almost touch them. I was watching the wing tip, trying to judge how far it really was from the mountain. No doubt it was further than it looked, but I was terrified, although I tried not to show it in front of the islanders on the plane with me. From out of the gloom, Pebble Island airstrip came up very quickly and we kangarooed quietly down the grass strip.

As I climbed out, my bag was produced, and the aircraft was already taxiing back to start of the strip for the run up into the wind. Ray introduced himself, and I did the same, adding, "How many people on the island Ray?"

"Just you and me," he said, grinning. I looked as far as I could towards each end of the island. It must been at least twenty five miles long and in some places five miles wide. It was, and still is, run as a sheep farm.

We piled into the Land Rover and headed for the settlement. A couple of the houses looked well kept, but I could see that some were falling into disrepair. There were long, dark, dirty marks like rust stained the once white washed walls. Rather than getting out of the Land Rover each time we met a fence, Ray had built a stile for it to go over, which was hairy, but efficient, and it also meant there was no danger of the livestock escaping. Another example of the Islanders' ingenuity.

After settling in at Ray's place, I went for a walk around the settlement. It was deserted. There was a small stone cairn with a brass plaque mounted at the airstrip where the SAS had pulled off their audacious raid on 15th May. Choppers from *Hermes* had taken them in, supported by shore bombardment from HMS *Glamorgan*. It had been carried out by the men from G Squadron, with whom I was onboard *Resource*. I wondered if Roger had been there.

I climbed the hill to where the memorial to HMS *Coventry* is positioned. It looks out towards the position where she went down with nineteen men aboard her. She had been hit by three bombs dropped by A4 Skyhawks. I climbed to the top of the hill, where there were some spectacular views, the mountainous western half contrasting with the grassy plains of the east and marshy wildfowl breeding areas. On the far end of Pebble, a Lear Jet had crashed after it was hit by a Sea Dart missile fired from HMS *Exeter*. The 'plane was on a photo reconnaissance mission at 40,000 feet and the pilot presumably imagined he was outside the missile's maximum performance envelope. The jet wouldn't have been fitted with missile lock-on warning device, and the first the crew of five would have known about the attack would have been the impact. The lucky ones would have died instantly when the missile blew the tail off.

By that stage of the war, the British had infiltrated the Argentinian frequencies. The operations room crews of some of the British warships listened to the screams of the Lear Jet crew as it spiraled out of control to the ground. The aircraft is not fitted with ejector seats or any other means of escape. Free-falling at the optimum speed of 120mph, it would have taken approximately six minutes for it to fall and hit the ground, to what the crew would have known was certain death. Fast jet aircrew know they will not survive high speed collision with terra firma. Not a pleasant way to spend your last six minutes. When the wreckage was found following the surrender, the bones of the crew had been picked clean by vultures, seagulls, and caracaras.

Out of the wind, I found a sheltered spot and sat down for a moment of quiet reflection, thinking about the past few years, where I'd been and what I'd done. Jobs that had come and gone, holidays, girlfriends. Which of any of these had had any lasting impact on my life, and why and how? I didn't come up with any answers, but it did make me wonder how much of my inability to settle to anything for long was attributable to the events that brought me back here.

I thought of my daughter Lucy, now seven years old. She had been born with a thick mop of jet black hair. Over the years and with the Australian sun it had faded to a beautiful silky fair colour. She had the creamiest skin and big blue eyes, a perfect little English rose. I closed my eyes and I could smell her hair, and hear her squeals of delight when we played in the surf, her innocence when I tucked her into bed and read her a bedtime story, and how she would say, "I love you Daddy". She would give me her special hug, which she called a 'huggle'.

Right then, as always when I allowed myself to think of her, I missed her so much. I needed one of her special huggles. She had her heart set on being a vet, or an artist, or a ballerina, all typical of a seven year old girl with a life of fairies and enchanted castles. How long would it be before she was exposed to the harsher realities of the world?

Having gathered my thoughts, I started off towards the northern coastline of the island for a long walk back. The ground was pitted by what I took to be penguin burrows, clumps of grass, and hidden holes, which of course made for difficult walking, so I tired quickly. Looking for somewhere to rest for a moment, I saw ahead of me the wreckage of an aircraft with huge parts of the fuselage and cockpit intact. Despite the fact that someone might well have been killed when it crashed, just then, for me, it was ideal. I was knackered, so this was no time for sentimentality. I curled up inside and soon drifted off to sleep. When I came to, it was dusk, which told me I must have been asleep for a couple of hours. I climbed out of the wreckage and made my way as quickly as I could back to Ray's place. It was fairly straightforward but I didn't like the idea of getting lost here on Pebble as there was no shelter at all.

The following day, I walked right around a large part of the coastline. The cliff-top scenery was breathtaking, and I sat absorbing it, enjoying it, for ages. It was somewhere along here that the remains of an Argentinian pilot was washed up in his dinghy the following year. He had ejected safely out of his aircraft but no search and rescue mission was ever launched for him and he was listed as 'missing, presumed killed'. The sea is no respecter of nationality, rank, creed or religion. It treats everyone the same, a bit like cancer, and lottery wins.

Getting back to my feet, I noticed some intriguing clumps of seaweed. I took one step towards them, and suddenly, I was up to my knees in some sort of stinking quicksand. Panic set in, because it wasn't only stinking, it was also freezing, but the more I panicked to get out, the deeper I went. Eventually, common sense told me to stop panicking, and I realised that when I stopped wrestling, trying to free myself, I stopped sinking. Taking a deep breath, I leaned back, and moved first one foot, then the other, backwards, an inch at a time.

After almost an hour, I made it to solid ground, exhausted. I lay down to recover my strength and get my breath back. The quicksand must have been made up of rotting seaweed and decayed fish remains, I almost gagged. My jeans were sticking to my legs and they were freezing. After a short rest, I started trudging back to Ray's. It was heavy going and I was tired and ached all over.

When I arrived back at the settlement Ray looked at the state of me and said, "had fun then?" I nodded and asked what was for tea.

"Pick one," he said.

I looked at him puzzled.

He pointed towards the sheep. "Pick one," he repeated.

The penny dropped. "*You want me to sentence one to death?*"

He laughed. "Well, they're all going to be slaughtered anyway."

I looked around, and finally settled for the one that was grinning at me. Ray stood astride the sheep and placed a hand on the back of its head and one on it jaw. One quick twist and snap and the sheep dropped to the floor. A swift and painless execution. When he was done, he threw the garden spade at me. "We need some vegetables too."

Despite my not wanting to go, I knew the following day would be important; I was going to Sealion Island and the *Sheffield* memorial. I needed a good night's sleep and to be refreshed and ready for whatever tomorrow brought.

Soon it would be time for me to leave.

CHAPTER 22

Sealion Island

We left Pebble and flew to Carcass Island. It looked great in a desolate sort of way. Maybe this was the land that time forgot. If I ever came back, this would be on the agenda. Then I found out we were taking the scenic route to my destination via Port Howard, Stanley, Port Stephens then Sealion itself.

We took off from Stephens and the feeling I had felt as the aircraft from Punta Arenas came into land at Mount Pleasant returned, as did the goose pimples. I started to have second thoughts. I felt like I was finally confronting a school bully who had pushed me around and made my life a misery. My bully was about to get his comeuppance.

We began our descent into Sealion. This is the place where I had expected to fully confront the past, to finalise it and leave it behind when I left. I wasn't sure I had identified or clearly defined what 'it' was. I knew the feeling but was unable to articulate it. Whatever form it took, however it came to me, (and I was sure it would,) I knew it would not be in my rucksack when I re-boarded that plane. It was mental baggage that I was leaving here for good.

The ground crews were excellent, the aircraft had hardly stopped when the doors were open and the gear was swiftly unloaded. A smallish man was throwing huge bags around. I grabbed my own because I knew it would be the biggest and heaviest. He snatched it from me and treated it the same as the rest. It stuck me that he must have been extremely fit. He looked South American, possibly Chilean. As he walked off I saw he had a long pony tail, it matched the moustache and slicked back hair.

In the shelter of the Sealion Lodge, he introduced himself as Juan. He was here with his family, his wife Martina, daughter Jessica, son-in-law Roberto and grandson Robertino. I was to find out what wonderful people they all were.

Sealion is the most remote of all the inhabited islands. It is five miles long, one and a half miles wide, and with a resident population of just four. The nearest land is Bull Point, some eight miles distant but the nearest inhabitants are at Bleaker Island, miles away. Sealion is isolated, has a rugged coastline, and no harbour, so only the hardiest souls make their homes here, but at least The Lodge was modern, and comfortable. Jenny Luxton, a native Islander introduced herself and made me feel welcome. She showed me round and pointed out the courtesy bar.

I read through the guest book. A man called Allan Knowles Jnr had signed it very recently. He must have been the son of the late LMEM(M) Allan Knowles who was lost in *Sheffield*. I remembered him well. The late Allan Knowles had bright blonde hair, a reddish tinge to his skin, was always smiling, and was a thoroughly decent bloke. Allan Jnr would have been about six when his father was killed. I would have liked to have met him. The thought of my own Lucy being told at six that I'd been lost and she would never ever see me again was too awful. I went back to my room and cried – alone. I didn't feel bad about it because I had allowed myself to come here and do this. Afterwards, I knew I had to get out of the lodge. Cosy and inviting as it was, it would have been too easy to stay all afternoon drinking tea and reading. I needed the fresh air; I wasn't sure what else I needed.

I walked down to the nearest beach, which was littered with solid seaweed, thicker than anything I'd ever seen before. On one part of the beach, huge elephant seals lounged, flicking sand with casual flicks of a flipper, while just a couple of yards away lay the carcass of a dead seal on which birds were feasting. It was a naturalist's dream, like a scene from the beginning of time, surely the only remaining frontier country on earth. I had never seen so many albatross. They fought the skuas and striated caracaras over the slashes torn in the seals skin. I went much closer than was safe or healthy and got some excellent close-up photographs of them all. They weren't interested in me; their only concern was ripping the guts out of the seal.

The aggressive caracaras eventually vanquished the last of the albatross, which started its clumsy, running take-off like an overloaded jumbo jet. No sooner had this oversized seagull completed its ungainly take off, than it entered its own realms to become the most graceful and majestic of winged creatures. The caracaras then launched a full scale air raid on me. I had to smash one of them with a heavy camera before the rest of them retreated, leaving me petrified! The caracaras look like a smaller version of a golden eagle with brilliant bright yellow beaks and talons. Here, they were definitely kings of the skies.

The heaving South Atlantic was in impressive form. Enormous rollers powered along before breaking, sending spray for miles. I took out my map and took a rough bearing. Somewhere approximately forty miles south-east of here, at the bottom of the sea in approximately six thousand feet of water, lay the ship that had once been my home. HMS *Sheffield*, D80, Type 42 Destroyer, first of her class. She held the trophy for High Seas Sea Dart missile firings and for Naval Gunfire Support with the 4.5 inch gun. Now she was a designated war grave, the final resting place of 19 of her ship's company. I looked around and once again felt that lack of understanding, of impotence. I took my frustration out with my boot, on a massive clump of seaweed, which repaid me by splitting, and covering me in gooey crap. So I swore at it.

I found a sheltered spot from the wind and decided to recap on some thoughts. If I was going to get it all out in the open, there was no time or place like this. I allowed my thoughts to drift to the past, to the events of 4th May and the subsequent weeks on RFA *Resource* and the m.v. *British Esk* until our return home.

How and why had it all happened in the first place? I'd never truly got to the bottom of that one. I knew it was politics, or more correctly, politicians. The ones who purport to be holier than thou, who then get caught with their fingers in the till or some other unholy mess. The next time a politician advocates going to war to fix an international problem, I really think they should be invited into the war zone themselves to 'fix bayonets'. Even more effective would be to invite them to send their own sons and daughters to do their dirty work for them. Does it ever occur to anyone to ask how many children of politicians are currently serving in front line military units actively engaged in combat?

I remembered the celebrations, the victory parades and wondered about the 'accidental' nature of things, how and who decided who would live and who would die? Life is a jigsaw puzzle and the final piece falls into place when your number is called. You can control practical things like the job you do, the house you live in, but how do you control your fate?

If the ship had turned to starboard to narrow the angle of the target for the missile as it approached, it would still have hit us but further for'ard. If that had happened it would have impacted even closer to where I was or maybe even in the same compartment. Then, the only evidence that I had existed would be in the hearts and memories of my family and friends. Maybe I'd also be a name carved on a memorial somewhere, with a photo on a wall. Maybe I'd be a tree in a garden of peace, or perhaps a park bench. There were a whole range of things that could have happened on *Sheffield* which would have spelt my demise, but they didn't happen. I was spared – it just wasn't my time.

After getting over the first impact and shock of the war, the memorial service and then the few months of violent and alcoholic suicidal lunacy back in the summer of '82, I had not thought about what happened. There were a couple of incidents that brought it all back. I had just joined HMS *Nottingham*, newest sister ship to *Sheffield*. Coincidentally, I joined her on exactly the same day, 9th November, but one year later. I was given the same watch, the same part-of-ship and the same mess. I asked the Chief Ops, Dave Nunn to change some of it, which he did. He understood; he'd been on HMS *Coventry* and had a triangular burn scar down the side of his face around his eye socket. When a bomb detonated below *Coventry*'s operations room, the fireball came up through the computer room hatch and raced across the operations room. The rest of his face was saved by his anti-flash hood. Dave was one of the best Chiefs I ever worked for, indeed one of the best managers. A lot of civilian managers could have learnt things from him.

It wasn't the events of war that I had to live with, they couldn't be changed. It was the way I dealt with them and reacted to them.

A bitter wind blew up, and I pulled my woolly teacosy hat down over my ears as far as it would go and turned the collar of my jacket up. My best friend Kim had bought the hat for my birthday the year before when I'd had my head shaved for charity. I never realised then that it would come in this handy. My feet were freezing. I pushed my hands deeper in to my jacket pockets but no matter how I tried, there was always somewhere that my clothes rode up or down, letting the wind through.

Hundreds of penguins were running around, some diving into the water and some scampering up the beach. It struck me they were either very brave or absolutely mental to do that in this weather. I thought of all those maniacs in the seaside towns doing the swim between two piers on New Year's Day. The incoming waves would have been magnificent for surfing if you could have stayed alive for more than five minutes. If the cold didn't get you, an orca or sea elephant probably would have done. The place seemed so impossibly remote and inhospitable, and I remembered when I had told some people where I was going, their response had been, "what on earth for, there's nothing there, is there?"

I went back to the lodge and brewed some tea in the biggest mug I could find, which must have held about a quart. Jessica came out and asked what I wanted to eat that night. We had a choice? There was a menu, what a bonus! The only other guest was a Japanese tourist, who naturally had the biggest camera lens anyone could carry. One day man will land on other planets in the solar system. As the astronauts climb out of their spaceship, odds on there'll be a Japanese tourist already there with a phallic camera.

It was still early and I had a lot to cram in, in a couple of days. I decided to go and look out for the sea elephants and the *Sheffield* memorial at Rockhopper Point. Taking a more southerly route I walked through the short tussock grass to the edge of the beach and the low cliffs. Spread out in front of me, only a few feet away on the solidly covered seaweed beach were dozens of sea elephants. Some were fifteen feet in length and the same in girth and tonnage.

Some burped a deep and hollow warning to some of the younger and more ambitious red blooded males that they were keen to keep their harems intact and would pursue a conflict to the death if necessary to protect it. Dozens more of the huge blubbery creatures lay hidden in the almost impenetrable tussock grass, burping to each other. Coming between these colossal creatures and the sea, or their pups, can be fatal; despite their lumbering appearance they can cover short distances extremely quickly. I sat back on the edge of the cliffs gazing at the whiskery creatures – they put me in mind of some of the clientele of the nightclubs in Plymouth and Portsmouth I used to visit decades ago.

I set off for the memorial at Rockhopper Point. Carefully threading my way through the massive tussock grass, some of which was ten feet tall, I could hear a variety of burps, and snorts, and snores. The thought struck me that if I'd heard farts, and the sound of someone wanking, I could have been back onboard a warship! The grass was almost impenetrable. If the rest of the islands had been covered in this, we'd still have been trying to find the Argies. It was between six and ten feet tall, and was knitted together to form a freezing wall. Some of this ground would never have been trodden by man before, it was completely virgin. I kept backtracking, to find a route through. Some of the area had been flattened down into perfect walkways, like Hampton Court Maze. I suddenly found out why when I almost stepped on a sea elephant, which woke up and roared at me, I almost shit myself and tried to scarper but the grass was too thick and high. The thing didn't move though. It just flopped back down again and went back to its snoring.

I wound my way inland past a big pond with the most wonderful array of birdlife; king cormorants, egrets, herons. I managed to work my way from there back down onto the beach. There was a lot of wood, covered in seaweed, and the rocks and stones were greasy and slippery. I moved away from the edge of the sea and back towards the cliffs. I heard a noise similar to a sea elephant but not as loud. Looking towards the sea there was a beautiful gooey-eyed sea elephant pup. It was obviously calling for its mother. I crouched down to level my camera at it, but had to turn my back to the wind to steady myself. As I pivoted, from the corner of my eye, I saw something moving fast. Somehow I managed to spring backwards as tons of enraged and protective sea mammal launched itself through the spot where I'd just been debuting for National Geographic. The pup's mother had clearly been resting at the top of the sand dune, and used the pathway down as a runway to the sea, where I had come between her and her baby. Lesson learned. When you're told no closer than fifteen feet, then fifteen feet it is.

I found a spot to climb back up the sand dunes to the top of the cliffs and decided that safety was the best policy. I wasn't familiar enough with the environment to be taking stupid chances like that. I walked around the headland to where the memorial was marked according to my map, but it was nowhere in sight. I looked around for ages, lining up the fences and coastline and still could not work out why it wasn't there. I was sure I was at Rockhopper Point. Really annoyed with myself,

I went back down to the beach and walked around the headland until I could get no further and dejectedly climbed the cliff to head back to the lodge. When I got there, I looked at a photo of a caracara perched atop the cross that surmounts *Sheffield's* memorial. I was determined to find it the following day.

The day dawned in usual Sealion Island fashion – it was blowing a gale. Juan asked if I could help him with a few tasks around the lodge and then he would take me to the memorial. We drove along the south coast of the island, and I asked Juan to stop a couple of hundred yards from the memorial. It was perishingly cold. Appropriately enough, some rockhopper penguins were huddled against the small stone wall surrounding the cairn and silver cross that serves as the memorial. I stood in front of the cross and looked out to the south east, to the direction where the ship lay. The rollers of sea water were phenomenal, long and lazy, yet surging onward with such power. As they crashed into the cliff walls, the wave tops were whipped up into a veritable frenzy of spray which stung my face, and I tasted the salt on my lips. The wind didn't howl here, it roared. I looked around; Juan had stayed in the Landover. Whether because he knew I'd want to do this alone, or because the weather was an indicator that we were only 600 miles from the Antarctic Circle, I didn't know.

I took off my hat out of respect and wished I had a mop of thick hair. The rain lashed against my head and face, stinging my ears. I crouched down in front of the memorial and opened the case containing some wreaths and read some of the cards attached to them. I recognised all the names, and I pictured a lot of the faces. The names may have been different to the others around the islands but the messages were the same, as were the sentiments. My hands were already freezing and I could hardly feel my fingers. I sucked them to try and get some feeling back into them and the salt tasted foul. I took the poppies out of my bag, twisted them together and placed them with the others. I closed the lid and stepped back to survey the scene one more time. Droplets of seawater leaked in through the casing and dripped onto the flowers like tears. As the drops fell onto the cards attached to the wreaths, water and ink merged into one, like sailors and their ship merging and becoming at one with the sea.

I bowed my head and recited the words to the sailors' hymn, "For those in peril on the sea", then I turned and walked away. I had thought I would probably become emotional at this point, but I was pretty much cried out and felt strangely calm. After the scenes at San Carlos Water and in the pub, I was simply accepting it. That was good – it was what I had come here to do.

I walked back to the Landover, where Juan asked if I was OK. I nodded and we drove off. We had some work to do at the slipway where the supplies are hauled up a steep ramp from the supply boat. There was a sea elephant in the way, but it had no intention of moving and it stank. We walked around and went down a natural staircase in the cliffs. At the bottom in the rock floor were rock pools in perfect circles, as if they'd been machined. As we drove back to the lodge, we paused to watch a caracara assassinating a goose. The goose was much bigger but it was no match for such an aggressive raptor.

171

I sat with Jenny when I got back and she asked what I thought of the place. I told her the truth – it was beautiful, one of the most beautiful, if not the, most beautiful places I had ever been. As we talked, a chopper arrived with some RAF personnel for a couple of days R & R. We had a few beers and whiled the evening away talking about the usual stuff. I surprised myself in that I didn't feel a lot more on Sealion. I was just glad I had held it together, as that was the place I had gone to with most trepidation.

Later, I packed my kit ready for the flight to Port Howard the following day then crashed out. It must have been all the fresh air and exercise because I was asleep before I knew it.

The following morning, I reiterated to Jenny what a wonderful place the Islands, especially Sealion, were and how much I had enjoyed being there.

"I wish more people like you would come," she said.

CHAPTER 23

Port Howard to Tumbledown Mountain

The pilot Paul gave me the seat beside him and we chatted about the usual stuff. He had lived down at Port Stephens during the war, and gave an interesting perspective on the conflict. I mentioned the sharp bank to port between Mt Estancia and Mt Vernet on the flight from Pebble to Stanley.

"Oh yes, sorry about that," he said. "I wasn't really paying attention and left it a bit late."

"But it was thick fog!" I reminded him, stunned.

He grinned at me and didn't seem even remotely concerned. "You get used to it," he said, with a shrug.

We touched down at Bleaker Island, and never was an island more appropriately named. A five minute hop saw us calling in at Goose Green; it looked even smaller from the air.

We cleared Packes Ridge by far less than we should have done and swooped down onto the grass airstrip at Port Howard, coming to a stop in about ten feet. We were met by the staff from the Lodge, led by Henry, a Scottish Farmer. Port Howard is a sheep farming settlement from which the 200,000 acre farm is operated.

After checking in and being shown to our rooms, we reassembled downstairs to go on the first excursion of the day. I piled into the Land Rover with Henry and a Reservist Army Captain called Thelma, and we headed off back east towards Packes Ridge that we had come so close to becoming a part of, on the approach to West Falkland. Henry and Thelma stopped to fish, and I headed off up to the top of the Ridge. Prior to starting the climb, a Land Rover stopped en route from the farm in front of me. I had a quick chat with the woman driver who insisted I should drop in for tea and cakes on the way down. (What else would one expect?)

I took a zigzag route up the hill but it was still hard going. The view from the top though was magnificent, well worth the effort. I could see the length of Falkland Sound, right down past Swan Island. There were gun emplacements left made up on the rocks, where the Argentinians had built them. I came upon the place where Captain Hamilton of the SAS had been killed and Sergeant Fonseca had been captured. I took a direct route down the hill to the farm, and when I got there, I knocked at the door but there was no answer. The woman in the Land Rover had invited me to 'help myself' if she wasn't back, something you would never dream of doing anywhere else. I made some tea. I'm not sure whether it was because I actually wanted it, or because the thought of flashing up a brew for yourself in someone else's house is so foreign, it just has to be done. I washed my cup and went on my way, still with no sign of anyone around.

Since Henry had dropped me off, the tide had gone out a long way and exposed all the mudflats. It was a long walk round so I opted for the short cut and regretted it. However, once my feet were soaked I saw no point in trying to climb back up the high banks, so I just pushed on. I crossed the first of the two river forks and then pulled my map out. I switched direction to head more westerly as I wanted to pass by the cemetery en route to the lodge. I wandered briefly around the graveyard until I found Captain Hamilton's grave. I tied a poppy to a small wooden cross and left.

The next day Henry, Thelma and I set off early for the trip down to Fox Bay. Fox Bay was one of the places I'd had computerised reference points on when we crossed into the Total Exclusion Zone almost twenty years earlier. We soon saw the first lot of aircraft wreckage, and there was plenty of it. The attacking Argentinian pilots would make their runs either up the sound then swinging away across West Falkland, or straight across East Falkland already on a course for home, having delivered their deadly cargoes. Those that were hit over East Falkland, or over the sound came down on West Falkland. A number were chased by Harriers and were also brought down here. We stopped by one wreck and beneath the now-fading paint and scored camouflage, we could see the six pointed Star of David. Obviously one of the Mirages or Daggers procured from the Israelis.

A couple of hours later, Henry pulled off the road beside a large lake full of Black-necked Swans. I'd seen a few on Pebble, but there were masses of them here, one of only two places I'd ever seen them. Thelma and I walked around the water and she asked about the events of 1982, and how it felt coming back. It all seemed surreal. Somehow, I couldn't relate the reasons for this visit to the original events. I started by telling her how events had begun to 'replay' about five years previously and had got progressively worse. I jumped forward to the time in New Zealand when I discussed the subject with my sister. Then I came back to the present and talked about my reflections as I was sat atop the hill on Pebble Island just a couple of days before.

There was no logic to the order of what had happened. I started talking about one thing and then found that I was going on about something else. The subjects were all linked but I wasn't giving Thelma the bridge between them. No wonder she looked confused. Maybe she thought it was too late for me and I'd lost it. Either that or I was born a retard. And I have to admit, I was as confused as she was. We stopped talking and stared out over the lake. It was full of wildfowl, so we found ourselves talking about that instead. We got back to the Land Rover where Henry had set up a picnic.

After eating, we drove on towards Fox Bay, stopping to view some rock formations. I picked up a few fossilized shells which had probably been around since the islands were part of the Gondwana super-continent a few million years before, prior to Africa and South America separating. We went past the settlement and down to the bay, where a pod of black and white dolphins were frolicking in the surf. We gingerly climbed down the rocks towards a penguin rookery with Henry pointing out various forms of sea bird life. I saw one of the reviled Snowy Sheathbills that the airstrip at Port San Carlos was named after. They looked a bit like white doves with a sea bird's head, certainly not like they lived on shit! But they were having dinner, and it really did stink. I almost gagged. We drew back and watched the King Cormorants, Rock Shags, Gentoos and various other birds, all doing their individual bird things.

On the way back to Port Howard we called in to see Gavin and Deirdre whom I had met in the store on my first day here. They lived in the cook house like Jenny and Tony in Port San Carlos, though this place looked even bigger. We were sitting in the kitchen chatting when their daughter, Rachel, came in. She was all tousle haired with bright red rosy cheeks, smiling and laughing. It would have made the most wonderful photograph captured naturally. All who had hosted me in camp seemed like older versions of Rachel – rumpled clothes, rosy cheeks, perpetually happy. They seemed genuinely interested and warm in their welcomes.

We were invited to overnight at Port Howard. Apparently, there was a bit of a 'do' on at the community hall. Sadly though, we were not able to accept this offer as Henry and Thelma had to get back to the lodge. On the drive back I spotted a crested caracara nesting on a huge mound of earth. I got out of the car to take a photo and closed on the bird a step at a time, always checking the range between the Land Rover, myself and the nesting site. Before I got halfway, I raised the camera which was the signal for the bird to take to the skies. Remembering well my encounter with the birds on Sealion, I turned and raced back to the safety of the Land Rover.

When we arrived back at the lodge, a group of RAFs had arrived, and I couldn't escape them. We had dinner together and swapped a few stories, got pissed, then retired to bed. Before I left for Stanley the following day, we were given a tour round the lodge and the museum. The museum houses artifacts from the conflict, amongst them an old field gun and an Argentinian ejector seat – used.

The lodge had the most fascinating telephone system, which the whole islands had used. The handle was wound in a certain code for who you were calling. Everyone had their own code but anyone could pick up the handset in their own home and listen in. No secrets here then!

Tumbledown Mountain

We touched down at Stanley where a bloke introduced himself as one of Terry's mates. He drove me back to Shackleton Drive so I could sort my kit out for the next couple of days. I had decided I was going to bring my flights forward to get to the UK earlier, because I was missing Lucy terribly. I had originally intended to go down to Ushuaia and do some trekking in Tierra Del Fuego but that seemed unimportant now. I knew that once I'd completed what I had to do in Buenos Aires, I would want 'out'. I visited the Lan Chile office behind the cathedral in Stanley and made the necessary arrangements; instead of going back to Punta Arenas and south, I would go to Rio Gallegos and connect straight north to Buenos Aires and London.

I went to see Dave Eynon, the ex-North Sea diver who ran South Atlantic Marine Services. I wanted to see if there was any chance of getting a dive in while I was there. That would be one for the log book. Unfortunately his divers were sick, he was preparing for the entry of the sail ship *Endeavour*, and he would have had to borrow some gear from the Navy too, so all in all it was a non-starter. As I left I spotted a big notice in Dave's shop window – *When the people of Argentina recognise our rights to self governance, then they will be welcome.* You can't say fairer than that.

I walked all the way west along Ross Road and then back from the far western end of Stanley Harbour. The town, along with its 1914 war memorial was mirrored perfectly in the dark waters of the harbour, which looked like glass.

When I got into town, I checked my hotmails. One of the girls at work had sent me an e-mail: *I hope your trip is having the desired effect.* I thought it was a nice touch and I quite fancied her anyway. I printed it off and shoved it in my jacket pocket.

That night I went for dinner with a mate of a mate, Les Briggs. His grandmother had been one of the three Falkland Islanders killed during the war.

We had a couple of beers and he asked me straight out, "Do you know who killed my granny with the shelling? I know it was either HMS *Cardiff*, *Exeter* or *Glamorgan*."

"In all honesty Les," I said, "it could have been *Arrow*, *Alacrity*, *Yarmouth*, *Plymouth*, or anyone else for that matter. I'm sure they're sorry for it and it could only have been an accident."

I didn't ever want to use the nonchalant 'well it's just one of those things' phrases to someone who had lost a relative, civilian or military. He said the reason for his asking was that if some poor sod had been torturing themselves over it, he wanted them to know that they were forgiven, and that he didn't hold them responsible. I thought it was a thoroughly decent thing to do, and said so, to want to let someone know they'd been exonerated.

I went for a pint on the way home. The pub was quiet but I struck up a conversation with a Glaswegian bloke at the bar whose accent was sometimes almost impossible to understand. He asked me what I was doing there. I decided he was probably another 1982 veteran so told him about my visit and my impending trip to Argentina. It turned out he had been here in '82 with the 2nd Battalion, The Scots Guards. They'd assaulted Tumbledown Mountain and he said it had been vicious hand to hand fighting at the end. I told him I was going there the following morning and asked him if he'd come with me to take me through what happened. He thought for a while.

"No," he said eventually. "I won't come with you – but let me give you an idea of what it was like." He hesitated, ordered another couple of drinks for us and cleared his throat.

"There are three false crests to the mountain. We got up one, then stalled for a while at two. Then next thing we were running along with machine guns, towards the summit."

He swallowed hard and took a swig of his pint, and I noticed his hand was trembling. Then he descended into broad Glaswegian.

"I wiz runnin' alonga torp o' the moontin, wi' ma bess mate fae school when a roond hits him reet in a middla his fuckin' face. Blew the back o' his heed off. An' I thought, 'reet, youz bastards are goney fuckin' get it noo.' So I guz doon an' fixes ma bayonet. An we went in and did 'em, wi' fists and rifle butts an' bayonets. If you meet any o' the 5th Marine Battalion, tell them fae me, that they were good, bloody good but on tha' night, no' good enough. On that night, no one would hae bin good enough tae stop us. That night, we were unstoppable."

Listening to him, watching him delivering this sent a shiver down my spine – I believed him.

It was only after we'd swapped stories that we swapped names. He was actually Jimmy from Glasgow – I couldn't believe it. I told him I'd be having an early night given my intention to climb Tumbledown the following morning.

"You'll need it," he said. "You'll need it."

Terry had arranged for Tony Smith to take me on tours of all the mountains encircling the overland approach to Stanley. He reckoned he was probably the most knowledgeable on the history of the 1982 sites. We drove to Tumbledown Mountain, scene of a bloody hand-to-hand battle between the Scots Guards and the Argentinian Marines. Approaching from the northern end of the mountain, the first relic we came across was an old Argentinian field kitchen. It was rusty, but the insignia of an anchor was still clearly visible on its side, though what looked like a palm tree was somewhat faded. We were below the summit of the mountain and Tony said we should approach from the west to get an idea of what the Guards had had to do that night.

Skirting around the southern edge of the mountain was fairly tough going and we arrived at the start point around mid-morning. Tony explained that the Guards had designated their attacking sections after the rugby union positions – left flank, right flank and full back, the Guards – what else? The north face of Tumbledown which looks towards Mount Longdon, was almost a sheer drop. There was a steep and open valley between them.

We started up the west face of the mountain, with Tony pointing out where various sections of troops had attacked, been pinned down by machine gun fire, counter attacked, and so on. Initially it didn't look like it was going to be that big a job, getting to the highest elevation of Tumbledown, although I knew it was quite an elongated structure. As we approached the second crest, we could see many of the old Argentinian gun emplacements were still in situ. This was a point at which the Guards advance had almost halted, not because they lacked the courage or military know-how to overcome the defenders, but because they were short of ammunition. Such had been the rapid advance up the mountain and the fire they were laying down, they had used up almost their entire personal stock, plus all that their platoon sergeants could bring up from the rear.

It was here that soldiering took on its truly brutal nature, the kind which hadn't changed in a hundred years. The young jocks, the boys from the shipyards of Glasgow, the docks of Leith in Edinburgh, and the working class families of Aberdeen, fixed bayonets and charged, as had so many of their countrymen centuries before them, to the skirl of the bagpipes. They charged up the mountain, clearing out enemy machine gun posts in a well-worn pattern – grenade, explosion, bayonet, stopping only when the second crest was secured and fresh stocks of ammunition for the final assault had arrived. I found myself thinking about Jimmy, the bloke I'd met the previous night, wondering how old he'd been at the time. Eighteen? Twenty, maybe? The Guards had lost eight men in the attack plus one Royal Engineer attached to them. I wondered which one was Jimmy's best mate from school. The attack had taken place on the 13th June, the day before the surrender; it was one of the final battles of the war, with the goal of Stanley actually in sight.

I looked north towards Mount Longdon, another foreboding structure; we'd be scaling that after we'd finished here. It was unusually warm for the time of year, making it difficult to envisage the full horror of what had happened here. The sun was shining, there was little wind and the views across the islands and out to sea were beautiful. Falkland's peace and tranquility was in abundance. We arrived at the summit, marked by a skillfully crafted wooden cross and glass box of wreaths bearing the names of the fallen. The view before us wouldn't have been available to the Guards, who had taken the mountain at night. All they would have seen was the tracer and fireworks from the final attack of the war, that of 2 Para on Wireless Ridge to their front left.

As dawn broke in front of them, the sun would have risen over Berkeley Sound, Stanley, and the harbour, revealing the white flags. Those who had survived Tumbledown had survived the war. They had come through the bitter South Atlantic winter, the hours in a landing craft, the likelihood of being shelled by a Royal Navy destroyer who detected those landing craft unidentified, and in the wrong place at the wrong time. For them, their war had finished at the summit of Tumbledown Mountain. I doubt any would have been aware of the untouched and unspoiled nature of the place they had just saved.

Standing there, I knew with absolute certainty that this trip was the right thing for me to do, despite the months of trepidation and self-examination I'd put myself through. The wind suddenly blew up cold and I shoved my hands into my jacket pockets, my fingers closing over a crumpled slip of paper. I pulled it out and unfolded it. It was the e-mail the girl from work had sent me the previous day – *I hope your trip is having the desired effect*. The weird synchronicity unnerved me. That I should read those words at that moment. I edged a large rock aside and scraped a hollow in the earth, then folded the paper and put it in there. Then I covered it over with earth and set the rock back on top of it. It's probably still there.

Tears started then, but this time of a different nature; tears of relief and contentment. I had already shed one lead overcoat, though I didn't kid myself that there wouldn't be another, bigger, overcoat to shed when I reached Buenos Aires.

CHAPTER 24

Mount Longdon and Onward

I had specific reasons for wanting to visit Mount Longdon. A mate of mine from Brisbane Steve 'Oz' Staughan had been in 3 Para at the time and fought his way up Mt Longdon with a GPMG. His wife Caroline, had lost her first husband there during the battle to take the mountain. Steve had never talked about that time, but I knew Caroline had visited on her own pilgrimage ten years before.

Tony and I drove to the foot of the mountain and then skirted around to the west where the Parachute battalion had approached from the direction of Estancia House. I looked up at the foreboding structure before me. It looked huge, probably longer than it was tall, and the sun glinted off a cross at the summit, which I knew had been placed there in memory of those valiant young men who had laid down their lives. As I gazed upwards, I felt a shiver down my spine.

The start was easy going, and we quickly reached the foot of the first steep incline where the Regimental Aid Post had been. A number of poppies and crosses were stuck in the ground here, marking out this place where a shell had landed, killing several of the Paras. How many were wounded, being tended, and how many were tending them, I didn't know.

We were climbing up the face, varying between west and north, most of which had been assaulted by the three companies of the battalion. In the final approaches to the summit, the granite rose in vertical slabs, making gullies a few yards wide. How easy it would have been for the enemy to have waited until their attackers were trapped in the gullies, and then to have rained down the fires of hell on them. There would have been no way forward, and no way out. Tony pointed out where Sergeant Ian McKay VC had fallen, and took me through the action. Sergeant McKay was platoon sergeant of 4 Platoon, B Company, which was ordered to clear the northern side of the long east/west ridge feature, held by the enemy in depth, with mutually-supporting positions and they were putting up fierce resistance. As 4 Platoon's advance continued, the heavy fire increased from a number of well-sited enemy machine gun positions on the ridge, and the Paras received casualties. The Platoon Commander ordered the platoon to move from its exposed position and seek shelter among the rocks of the ridge itself and link up with part of 5 Platoon. The position of the platoons was becoming increasingly hazardous as the enemy fire was becoming heavier and increasing in accuracy. The Platoon Commander took Sergeant McKay, a corporal and some others, and whilst covered by supporting machine gun fire, they moved forward to carry out a recce of the enemy positions. The Platoon Commander was hit by a bullet in the leg, and Sergeant McKay assumed command.

Sergeant McKay decided instant action was needed if the advance was not to falter and even more casualties sustained. He decided to convert this reconnaissance into an attack, in order to eliminate the enemy positions. Whilst in no doubt of the strength of the enemy, without hesitation he issued orders, and taking three men with him, broke cover and charged the enemy position. The Paras assault was met by a hail of fire. One private was killed, the corporal and the other private were seriously wounded. Disregarding these losses Sergeant McKay, with total disregard for his own safety, charged onto the enemy position alone. On reaching it he threw in grenades, killing the enemy and relieving the pinned-down 4 and 5 Platoons, who could then continue the attack onto the remainder of the mountain. Sergeant McKay, however, was killed at the moment of victory, his body falling on the bunker. Heroic indeed.

The last part of the battle for the mountain had been vicious hand-to-hand fighting, using grenades and bayonets, just like at Tumbledown.

When we reached the summit, Tony got the flask out and we sat down with a brew, which by all accounts is exactly what 3 Para did, though whether that's true or not, I'm not sure.

My thoughts went back to the summer of '82, when the late Steve Mulcahy and I had gone to the Union Jack club just outside Waterloo station for a weekend or two. The rooms were always very basic – a bed, a locker – not too dissimilar from a military barracks really. The welcome was always warm, the scoff was always good and the company was always the same – people who could relate to you, and you to them.

The bar was furnished pretty much as you would expect a serviceman's club to be – crests, flags, paintings of battles in years gone by, maybe with some of the protagonists who had once frequented this same bar. The crimson and gold carpet was worn down by years of hard drinking and party games, and its pattern was interspersed with random cigarette burns. Solid plastic ashtrays adorned the tables. They did less damage to the people and fittings they collided with on a fairly regular basis than a glass one did.

We'd gone drinking on the Saturday afternoon with some Paras and Marines who had been down south and undergone the usual good natured rivalry and drinking competitions. We'd had a fairly heavy session on the Friday evening when we arrived, and Saturday afternoon was just a bit of a top-up. During one of the story swapping sessions, I'd heard an account by one of the British troops, who said he had snapped his bayonet in half when attacking an Argentinian defender, such was the ferocity of the attack. He had bludgeoned the enemy to death with the jagged remnants of the steel blade, although apparently he took an age to die, and screamed out 'Madre'[11] until his dying breath.

After that story, came another, equally horrific. A young soldier threw a grenade into a bunker, then followed up with his bayonet. Of the three occupants, two were already dead, though he bayoneted them anyway, just to make sure. The third man regained consciousness after the blast, and realising what was happening, tried to duck out of reach of the blade. However, he wasn't quick enough, and the bayonet went straight into his eye socket.

I'm told that bayoneting someone to death is very up close and personal. You're aware, of course, of their every move, their thrashing and writhing, their screams in your face, their flailing hands. And also, inevitably, their blood and spit, which you end up covered in. It is unlike shooting people from a distance, which is clinical by comparison, much more impersonal.

When those tales were being told, there was no sense of bragging. They were told in a quiet and matter of fact manner, and I couldn't help wondering to what extent those men were bothered by their actions, or whether they simply accepted them as 'part of the job'.

Back on the mountain, I came back to present day and reality, looked at the plaque at the summit; it bore the parachute crest and motto *Untrinque Paratus*[12]. The names and ages of the twenty three men who died

---

[11] Mother
[12] Ready for Anything

183

were inscribed on the plaque, and as I stood and read, I pondered on these 'men'. In one instance, Private Jason Burt aged just 17, the same age as I had been. Then I remembered the young rosy-cheeked Para' who had been at Douglas when I was there. His age was irrelevant, his (in)experience irrelevant to him. When it came down to it, he would fix bayonet and fight with the heart of a lion, just like those who were 27, or 37.

I looked back down at all the gullies Tony and I had climbed up, the same ones the Paras had. How on earth had they managed to fight their way up there without losing half the battalion? I know 23 men killed is 23 too many, especially if you, or a loved one are one of them, but as military achievements go, it was incredible. They weren't known as the Maroon Mafia for nothing.

At each memorial, there is a yellow duster and a tin of Brasso metal polish. I spent some time polishing the plaque, as I did with most of them, and as I did so, I was humming the hymn, *Abide with Me*.

As the sun rose on the morning of 13th June, with both the battle and the war over, it revealed a mountain littered with bodies. I can only imagine the scene had it been snowing; the snow would have run red. Tony pointed out a spot where two of the Paras had been checking the Argentinian dead. One of the enemy who had been wounded was laying still; he'd been told horrific stories about what the British would do to him if he was captured. The Paras actually thought he *was* dead until he suddenly grabbed hold of one of them by the leg. Thinking he was attacking them, the Para shot him in the head. Years later, having also survived that wound, he told the story to a British Paratrooper he met.

Tony and I walked down onto Wireless Ridge, which was taken by 2 Para. This was the scene of the last battle before the Argentinians capitulated, and was taken at the same time the Jocks were attacking Tumbledown to their right. Although most of the rock is the same dull, granite grey, there are bright pink pock marks all over it, much of which represents small arms and shrapnel damage. The rock shrapnel itself caused as many injuries as the flying shrapnel from ordinance did. Tony then took me to a small pool where he had recently found what looked like a grenade; he'd marked it with a flag. When we found the pool, the grenade had gone, which was a worry, unless the EOD from Stanley had been up to remove it, although Tony hadn't told anyone about it.

We looked across to Moody Brook barracks, the original home of the Royal Marine garrison. It looked so close, and just across the water was

Stanley itself. No wonder the British commanders didn't want the fight to spill over into the town. We backtracked to the Land Rover and Tony pointed out the spot where the British troops had been ordered to stop, now named 'Holdfast Road'. The commanders believed that if the troops pushed on into the town and the fighting continued, the civilian casualties could be unacceptable and the collateral damage to the town quite possibly massive.

We drove along Ross Road from west to east heading towards the airport. Tony pointed out where various Argentine defensive positions and anti-aircraft batteries had been. We drove across some rough terrain and stopped next to a large water-filled hole, which was one of the bomb craters made by a 1,000lb bomb dropped by the RAF Vulcan I had tracked on radar almost twenty years before. The idea had been to drop the bombs in a diagonal row, straddling the entire length of the runway, to stop the Argentinians using one side of it. This was the first that many on the islands, (of either side), knew of how close the British Task Force was and when it intended to begin operations to retake the islands. That operation was followed by low-level Harrier bombing raids, and then shore bombardment by the ships of the Task Force. This action also marked the first realisation for many that this was actually going to turn into a shooting war, that both sides were prepared to fight for the islands, and that a lot of people were likely to be killed.

Beyond us, in the water, a number of old trawlers, half sunk at their moorings, creaked and groaned in protest at the straining ropes still holding their gunwhales above the water. Each tiny ripple brought a grunting request that they be allowed to slip quietly beneath the surface and rest peacefully on the bottom of the harbour.

Afterwards, Tony dropped me back at Shackleton Drive, where Eli handed me a cup of tea, and Terry handed me a beer. I'd never combined the two before; I don't think I'd do it again.

"So," Terry asked. "What do you think?"

I knew the question would come. I just wasn't sure how I was going to answer it. There was no doubt about it, the achievement of the British troops had been a feat of military magnificence, a lesson in pure discipline, professionalism and above all – courage. Those mountains should have been impenetrable after they'd had two months to prepare.

I looked at Terry. "Do you want to tell me about it?"

He drew on his scotch. "No," he said. "No, I don't thanks."

Just like Steve, he'd never spoken about what had happened on the mountain. In common with all the other assaults on all the other mountains, there had been bitter hand to hand fighting all the way. I totally understood why he didn't want to talk about it.

I had wanted to take Terry and Eli to the pub for a meal and a few drinks as a 'thank you' for their hospitality and for arranging the rest of the trip. Terry always refused, and Eli quietly asked me not to repeat the request. I asked whether the new diner, 'Shorty's' might be an option, and it seemed that was acceptable. We all went up there that night, and I paid for the most salubrious meal on the menu, all the time wishing I could have done more. It was a pittance in comparison to what they had done for me.

Terry is a great and courageous man, and they were a wonderful couple.

Mount Harriett, Goat Ridge, Two Sisters

We started at the foot of Mt Harriett near the start line of the assault by 42 Commando. Looking up, the mountain appeared to have the best natural defences on earth. As we neared the top, many of the sangars built by the Argentinians still held their last occupant's possessions; white canvas plimsolls, bits of blankets, food cans, left over ration packs, most of it untouched since it was last used, twenty years ago.

I sat inside one of the sangars and looked down the mountain. I recalled a conversation with a Royal Marine back in late 1982, when I'd asked him about attacking and defending the mountain.

"If we'd been defending those mountains," he said, "we still would be. A monkey with a catapult could have defended those mountains."

I believed him.

Tony pointed out how close 42 Commando had got before they were spotted. They were just metres away. Whether this was due to the Marines' fieldcraft skills, the Argentinians lack of, or the fact that the defenders were expecting an attack from the northern face, rather than the southern face from which it came, I never found out. Given that the British were known to be in force and attacking the mountains around Harriett, you'd think it would be a good idea to keep an all-round look out.

Having got past the first row of defences, we went on to the summit. It was difficult enough in daylight and calm weather trying to find footholds that didn't give way under loose shale and rock. We navigated a long way round the assault course, to the peak of Harriett. There, a wooden cross set in a stone cairn had been erected. As with all the other memorials, I laid a poppy and remembered the sacrifice it marked. All around the summit were the remains of Argentinian machine gun emplacements. Although some of the defending troops in all the battles on all the mountains had held out well and fought bravely, they should still have been able to beat off the British attacks. Military strategy quite clearly states that to capture a stronghold, the attackers need to outnumber the defenders by a ratio of at least 3:1. That was simply not the case.

As we started down the north face of the mountain I looked over towards Goat Ridge. Although not that high, it was a real spiny vertebrae, a dinosaur back. It looked to be a few hundred yards away, and not all that big, so I anticipated reaching it in a few minutes. However, no sooner had we come off the mountain and onto the boggy ground, than I knew that would not be the case. The soggy peat was heavy going and the grass was long and thick. We stopped a couple of times for a breather and the ridge seemed no closer. As we pushed on, the size of the ridge seemed to increase exponentially, and we drew nearer, it rose up suddenly to monolithic proportions. Halfway along was a large gap which we headed for. Even that was a hike to get through. I couldn't believe the land could be so deceptive. I looked around at how the rock formations had been created. What incredible geological structures these things were. Over millions of years, the layers of the earth's crust had rotated through ninety degrees so the horizontal layers of rock, which is like a cross between granite and flint, is now in vertical rows up and along the mountains. Again, like Mount Longdon, the rock formed perfect valleys in which you could entrap hundreds of men, but only if you used it to your best advantage. We stopped for a brew and something to eat, knowing that the other side of Goat Ridge to Two Sisters was going to be exactly the same tough going. I was already knackered and we'd yet to climb the southern spur of the twin peaks in front of us. I knew that was going to take some fairly serious energy reserves.

The start of the slope up Two Sisters caught me by surprise. I'd had my head down, plodding along, one foot in front of the other, trying not to twist an ankle, the same action I'd been undertaking for the past two weeks. Within minutes, I was puffing and panting because the angle was so steep, and demanded maximum leg exertion. Tony asked if I wanted to stop but I didn't even have the breath to reply. He was making a good pace and I was struggling to keep up. At least the ground had firmed up now, and the bloody grass didn't grow on the mountain.

Having used up virtually all my energy and effort on Harriett, Goat Ridge and the trek between the two, I was now calling on non-existent reserves to get me to the summit. I cast a thought back to the days of 1987 in Devonport Field Gun Crew when every day, we were called to expend effort that had long since run out. We always found it. Then of course, I'd been young and fit, and had trained regularly for the preceding three years. This was different. I was already in pain, probably laughable by most military people's standards but I wouldn't let the side down. Tony was being very encouraging, "one more step," and "keep going, we're nearly there". I knew he was lying.

As we reached the first plateau, I pulled up for a breather and gulped some water down; I was sweating profusely. I looked towards the summit and found I couldn't see it. All I could see was the way up.

"Ready?" Tony asked. I just nodded, unable to speak.

I tried to forget the painful task at hand and focus on my rhythm, remembering how the mad Club Swinger from '87 had coached us on our breathing techniques. I started to pace my breathing with my climbing and focus my thinking on all the good times we'd had in HMS *Drake* during the Field Gun season. If I'd had any spare breath I would have laughed. 'Clubs' was Welsh and if Wales lost at rugby at the weekend, Monday morning PT was guaranteed to be absolute torture. Although that was never funny, because it meant spells of sprinting up and down the 'Seven Sisters', the hills outside Devonport Naval Barracks, the fact that he could get himself so worked up about things amused us enormously. Tony stopped. "You ok?" I pulled up too. The wind was powerful up here, but even above the din it was making, I could hear my own efforts at breathing. It sounded more like wheezing. I was aiming to draw in through the nose, to fill my lungs, and then to gently exhale through the mouth to lower my heart rate.

I stood looking down, and was surprised. We'd come further than I imagined, but I knew we still had a fair way to go.

"We'll have to slow down and step carefully here, it's a bit tricky," Tony said.

He took off as sure footed as a mountain goat but this time with a little less alacrity, and he used handholds from time to time. As we neared the top, the wind picked up further and the hand and foot holds became less stable. The angle of ascent was steeper but the pace was more novice friendly, which was actually a pity because I'd just got my second wind. I'd started enjoying the 'fizz,' as we used to say when I trained in Hull with a former Royal Marine, Ian 'Popeye' Holtby, who had been on Mt Harriett.

He and I met doing civilian fitness instructor's courses and hit it off immediately. I'd suspected he was an ex-Marine because he was wearing 'Ron Hill' tracksuit bottoms. No one else in the world wore them except the Bootnecks. He must have been the fittest man I've ever known, absolutely obsessive. One night he'd been out for a run in Hull and got hit by a car. He rolled across the bonnet and landed in the gutter, and when he got up, the driver was only interested in inspecting his car to see if there was any damage. He was so pissed off, he walked away because he knew that if he'd confronted the driver, he would probably have killed him. He decided to leave his rucksack full of short scaffolding poles at a mate's house, then he ran home. The following morning, when he came round, his thigh was black and blue.

Tony pulled me from my reverie. "Take it easy from now on," he warned. I looked down and realised immediately that that was a stupid thing to do. I've never been a great one for heights and it looked steeper and higher than it actually was. I cursed myself. The wind was phenomenal now, and I couldn't hear a word Tony said. I could see he was shouting something. I picked my way up to where he was standing, although there wasn't room for two people. He cupped his hands around my ear and shouted, "it's only a bit further, and there's only one way. You lead."

He was letting me get to the top first.

The summit was now in sight, and I had to let my sense of self preservation override my enthusiasm. Just below the peak, I could see a ledge big enough for two people, and it was in the lee of the wind. We stopped and I took my camera bag and backpack off, and handed Tony the camera. Then I started up towards the summit where the stone cairn is mounted. What a feeling when I reached the top, and what a fantastic view. I could see the whole of East Falkland, a spectacular view of bugger all in reality, but it felt like magic. My legs were on fire, my lungs on fire but I'd hung in there, and here was the payoff. I looked back down the mountain, across to Goat Ridge and Mt Harriett. The usually dull colours of the Falkland landscape had become much sharper, and I had never felt so alive in my life. I felt euphoric, really proud of myself. I looked out to sea from the direction where *Sheffield* lay, then to the Narrows of Stanley harbour. I thought of the motto of SAMA82, 'From the sea – Freedom'. And it's true. The freedom came 8,000 miles, in frigates and destroyers, aircraft carriers and ferries, tankers, tugboats and cruise liners.

Tony and I sat on the ledge and shot the breeze for a while. I think I probably bored him shitless because I couldn't stop going on about how good it felt to be up there. Then he gave me the good news.

"That was the easy part. Now we have to get down in one piece."

I knew that if I'd been injured on the way up and hadn't made it, I'd have been very pissed off, but of course, I'd achieved all I'd set out to achieve. I'd climbed all the mountains, I'd left a poppy at all the appropriate sites, I was almost 'over the line'. It felt fantastic.

Going down was nothing like as difficult as Tony would have had me believe, and I realised, he just couldn't resist pulling my pisser. As we hit the grass I remembered what a pain it was to go through. We slogged onto Goat Ridge, stopping for a quick brew, before heading off for the Land Rover. I was totally done for. Tony dropped me back to Terry and Eli's on Shackleton Drive, and for the second night on the trot, I couldn't stop talking about what a fantastic day I'd had. Terry smiled as he sipped his scotch. I tried to articulate my thoughts to him, although I'm not sure how well I managed it. Very soon, a tidal wave of tiredness came over me. I managed to get a shower, though my efforts to sponge away some of the aches and pains of the day were a total failure. I was dog tired, and I don't remember falling into bed.

CHAPTER 25

Last Days

I had climbed all the mountains that lie outside Stanley and the effort had totally knackered me every time. I was about twenty or so years older than those who did it in '82. I climbed in broad daylight with only my backpack of tea, sandwiches and camera. Also, I'd had a good night's sleep in a warm bed, and three decent meals a day for the last three weeks. Furthermore, the weather was reasonable for the most part. Because the terrain was so rough, I had to be very careful where I put my feet, otherwise I risked falling, or twisting my ankle. So of course, when I was out drinking with the Paras, the Marines, or the Guardsmen who did all the nasty stuff, in dreadful conditions, I asked them how on earth they'd done it.

If I could hardly manage it now, even taking into account the age factor, how had they, who had been crammed in a scabby North Sea ferry for three weeks and 8,000 miles, had waded ashore in waist-deep, ice cold water, and stayed wet because they were sleeping in dug out holes in rain and snow soaked ground? Further, they ate only cold rations, marched fifty miles, carried a 100lb Bergen[13], together with weapons and ammunition and everything else they needed to fight with. Then, they tackled these incredible geological features, the best natural fortifications in military history. At night, they would have been crossing minefields in appalling weather conditions. They would have been heavily outnumbered and under heavy fire from people intent upon using their nipples for target practice.

"So how the hell did you do it?" I asked.

The response was unanimous. "I don't know. We just did it. Because we're British. No-one else could have done it!"

I found myself agreeing with that last bit, though I kept it to myself. I shook my head and gave thanks for small mercies, like the fact that I

---

[13] Military Rucksack

selected the Navy when I joined up, all hot showers and warm bunks whilst the cannon fodder roughed it out here.

I wandered around Stanley taking in the fresh air and enjoying the time to relax, and to start putting my thoughts into perspective. I was pleased that when I rang the bank, the telephone was answered with, "Good morning. Can I help you?" rather than an automated machine telling me to "Press 1". Real customer service does exist in remote locations.

My first call was to see Lisa Riddell, the editor of Penguin News, the island's weekly newspaper. I asked her if she would put a note in the paper to thank all the islanders for their hospitality and understanding. She said she would be glad to, but asked if I would grant her an interview before I left on the Saturday. I knew the only day I'd have to do it would be the following day. I didn't have any firm plans, but was still a bit wary and skeptical of journalists as a whole. I remembered the prick outside the Victory two weeks earlier. But Lisa was different, she was a born and bred islander who had lived through the conflict herself as a twelve year old girl. We agreed that I would meet her at 10.00am the following day.

I stopped by the Bomb Disposal Squad office and bought an old sign taken off a minefield fence. It had a skull and crossbones, and proclaimed 'Danger Mines', so I thought it would make a good souvenir for the bar in my house when I eventually got one built.

I hadn't had a beer for a couple of days so slipped into The Globe for a pint. There were a bunch of lads in there, obviously servicemen. The haircuts and mixed accents were a dead giveaway. I sat at the bar remembering what it had been like as a 'twenty something' matelot – a bloody good laugh as I recalled. One of them nodded a greeting. "Alright mate?" I nodded back. One of the older blokes, who still wouldn't have been twenty five asked me, "Were you here in '82?"

"Yes, what made you say that?"

A couple of the others looked over. "You're obviously not in the mob now, you look about the right age, there are some others here from '82, and what else would you be doing here?"

I laughed. "Well deduced, Dr Watson. You're wasted in the RAF. Can I get any of you a beer?"

They insisted on buying me one, and I felt it was good to see that some military things don't change – like respect. They asked which service I'd been in, and which ship. When I told them, one of the youngsters exclaimed, "Wow, really? How cool! Good shit." He wasn't being offensive, just naïve.

The older bloke chastised him. "Don't be a dickhead. Things like that are not 'good shit' or 'cool' at all."

The kid stared at the floor and shuffled his feet, then he apologised. I told him it was OK and that I knew he hadn't meant it in a disrespectful way. He told me he was only 18, and when I told him I'd been the same age as he was at the time, he went very quiet. I let him think for a while; I knew exactly what he was going to say.

"I can't imagine having to do that sort of thing right now," he said.

He was a nice kid but too sheltered to be serving in the armed forces. I told him that he'd better start considering it, because there was unrest all over the world, and would continue to be. We went through the old 'Queen's shilling' routine, joining up because you get to travel, a regular wage, and a uniform which gets the girls every time, was no justification for his career choice. Sooner or later, the time would come when he was going to earn his money the hard and shitty way! His face drained, and even a couple of the older ones swallowed hard and necked their pints.

I had a couple more beers and shot some pool with the lads. They told me the youngster had come from a wealthy family and had fallen for every trick played on new juniors. His dad had sent him to the RAF to try and make him wise up a bit. We had a laugh about it, but I asked how any of them would feel going into action with him on their squadron. Their silence was answer enough.

They invited me down to The Narrows Bar at the end of Fitzroy Road. I had nothing better to do so we headed off. In the pub we were engaged in conversation by a group of locals. One of the older men lived out towards Volunteer Point and invited me up there for a few days. I was leaving on Saturday so I had to say no, which was a shame because I would have loved to have gone, and maybe seen the king penguins. I'd seen everything else I wanted to.

Soon afterwards, I decided I'd had enough to drink and was planning to go back to the diner for some food. Outside, I cut through to the road where I thought the diner was, but I was clearly mistaken. I was also a bit pissed and the more corners I turned, the more lost I became. I stopped and got my bearings and back-tracked to a point of reference I knew. Once I'd established the direction I needed to go in, I saw the actual short cut. However, the ditch I tried to jump was much bigger than I'd imagined, and I landed up to my thighs in cold and filthy water! What a way to sober up. And I knew, nowhere in Stanley was likely to let me in looking like I did. I clambered out, cursing my stupidity, and then, to make matters worse, it started to rain – hard.

I spotted some new houses close by and chose the porch of the first one to shelter in. I thought I'd just hang in there for a few minutes until the rain eased off, but suddenly, the front door opened and a woman appeared.

"Can I help you?" she said, not even mildly perturbed.

I felt more than a little sheepish. "I'm just sheltering from the rain," I said.

Her husband appeared, and the two of them invited me in. Needless to say I wasn't used to such treatment in the cities I'd lived in, but this kind of hospitality seemed normal for the islands. I stepped in, just beyond the door and pointed out I couldn't go any further because of the state I was in. The woman disappeared, then came back carrying a massive pair of woolly tracksuit bottoms.

"Slip these on and I'll throw your jeans into the dryer," she said.

I couldn't believe it. Total strangers not only inviting me into their home, but also insisting I strip off, and offering me dry clothes.

Her husband peered at me from the living room. "Well what are you waiting for? You'll catch your death of cold like that."

I grinned at him, then dropped my jeans and socks and pulled on the tracky bottoms, then I went through and sat down. A mug of tea was thrust into my hand. It was far too sweet, but sitting there, wrapping my hands around the steaming mug soon had the blood forcing its way back into my bony white fingers.

Half an hour later, feeling much better, I pulled my semi dry jeans back on and thanked them as I left.

To this day, I wish I hadn't been so pissed. I can't even remember their names.

My last full day in Stanley, in the islands, came, and for the first time in three weeks, I was depressed. Terry asked if everything was OK.

I told him straight. "I don't want to go Terry. I love it here, I want to stay."

He was very sympathetic, but he knew enough to know that wasn't what I wanted.

"You'll be back with your little Lucy soon," he said.

I thought about her, and wondered if she was missing me. My brother-in-law had flown to Australia to pick her up; she was already in England with my parents, not expecting me for another two weeks.

She was a major positive, but much as I tried to think of her, and all the other positives – seeing my family, going to the *Sheffield* twenty year reunion, I couldn't shake off the gloom. I walked to the far western end of Stanley and had a look around the museum, which I found fascinating as it gave an excellent insight as to what life had been like for the islanders under the occupation. There was a small room off to the side, housing exhibits that for some might well have been simply too painful for viewing. There were photographs, last letters, berets and a multitude of military paraphernalia all to remind you that ultimately war means death and permanent loss. A loved one you will never see, hear, touch or embrace again. Everything in there was a part of someone and every one of them had left people behind. As I thought of them I wondered if the grief ever subsided, and if it did, what it was replaced by? I could only think of a hollowness, a void that could never be filled. Displayed as they were, those who couldn't bear to see these reminders could bypass them. I walked out into the cool fresh air, it was only then I realised I was drenched in perspiration from the visit to the museum.

As I looked around, I was very aware that this would be the last time I would walk this road, the last time I would tread in the footsteps of the liberating troops who had taken this route in their march into the capital.

Because I knew there had been some offshore exploration drilling done around the islands, and also because I'd kept up an interest in oil and gas from my days in exploration drilling on oil rigs, I went and chatted with the Director of the Department of Mineral Exploration. Bonnie from Darwin Lodge had taken a brilliant photograph of a semi-submersible drilling rig which was framed and mounted in the Lodge. I hoped I might get the chance to work there one day.

After that, I went next door to The Secretariat. I'd made an appointment with the Human Resources Director of the Government and Council. I was interested to find out about how their HR Department functioned and the day to day issues they faced, and how it compared with what I knew. While I was in there, I noticed a brass and wood plaque on the wall. It was then I realised I was standing in the room where the 1982 surrender was actually signed. The re-taking of the islands back in 1982 had signified that Great Britain was still not to be messed with. We might only be a small nation, and an island nation, but once we'd ruled the world. In this very room was a reminder to the watching and waiting world of why that was so. How many people had actually ever been in a room where a world shaping event had taken place? Not many I thought. It seemed to me the significance was colossal, the two Generals had sat across from each other at this very table. I said "this is where the surrender was signed wasn't it?"

"Yes," she replied.

"Here, in this room?"

"Yes."

I was speechless and tried to imagine the atmosphere in the room as the victors and the vanquished confronted each other. We sat there in silence, I've no idea how long for.

While we were talking, the Director asked me the same questions many others had done – was it worth it? What it felt like coming back. How I felt about it all. We discussed the sacrifices that had been made, and the benefits that had come out of it. As she talked, the two of us became very emotional, and it wasn't long before she began to cry. Before I left, she told me how glad she was that we had all come back, and I could sense it was heartfelt gratitude from a genuinely warm person.

Outside I stood for a moment and studied the 1982 memorial which is set in a semi-circle. It features plates with the names of all the fallen and pictures of various battles. In the centre is an obelisk bearing the names of every ship, unit, regiment and squadron that participated in the conflict.

Turning away, I crossed the road to the office of Penguin News to meet Lisa, the editor I'd promised an interview with. I was having second thoughts about it now, but I didn't feel I could let her down. All I actually wanted from her was a printed 'thank you' to the islanders who had hosted me. They had shown overwhelming kindness, hospitality and warmth during my stay, making it a visit I would never forget.

In the office, she asked if I minded if she recorded the interview as opposed to writing it, and she produced a Dictaphone. She asked me to give her my version of the attack on *Sheffield*, which I did, but every now and again she'd ask a question, or request more detail. At one point I had to ask her to stop the tape as the whole thing became very emotional. Here is the transcript of what she wrote in the Islands newspaper:

'I CAN say with absolute sincerity that employment by this organisation offers a consistently stimulating existence and for that I am grateful.

At the same time one must accept that while an interesting life is very much a fulfilling one, it is often achieved with just the right degree of discomfort.

The latter was a sensation never very far away when I interviewed HMS Sheffield veteran Adam Lawton, not simply because of his unusual and uneasy personality, but because as an Islander I was forced to deal with emotions triggered by his very powerful account of that harrowing incident.

The comment that gave me most food for thought though, was one uttered after the interview ended.

I asked him whether he believed the trauma had affected his personality. He said, 'I went to war at 17: my personality wasn't really fully formed so it's incredibly difficult to tell to what degree I have been affected, or whether I was just going to be this way anyway.'

Lisa asked if I thought it had been worth it. I was fairly sure she would, and even though she was an Islander herself, I still couldn't bring myself to say something I knew she would print. I wouldn't hold anything against her for printing anything – that was her job, but the way to avoid journalists printing things you'd rather they didn't, is to keep your mouth shut. I exercised that option. I tried to say in a roundabout way that some things in life, and the world too, are worth fighting for, but when it comes to it, someone is also going to die for them.

I wondered if any of the men who didn't return had felt that way. How appalling to think of them dying for something in which they didn't believe in the first place.

The sail ship *Endeavour* was making her way into the harbour after rounding Cape Horn. I wandered down to watch, as had lots of other people. Once the ship was secured alongside, there wasn't much else to do so I decided I'd go for a bit of a dinner time session and wandered off to The Victory. I ordered a McEwan's and a curry.

"I'll get that," a local piped up.

I dropped the money for the curry on the bar. "Thanks," I said. "The beer's fine."

He grinned at me. "That's all I meant."

We had the usual chat, others joined in, and as usual, I found myself being treated to endless pints.

"You know those wankers thought they would be greeted as liberators like the allies in Paris," one bloke said. "All flowers and kissing girls. Told them exactly what we thought of them. They came begging at the doors, they shat in our gardens and they stole our chickens. Probably the cats too."

I looked at him. "This isn't going to be solved easily is it?"

A few puzzled looks came my way, but without waiting for answer, I said, "This problem over sovereignty, it's not going to be easily fixed for the Argies, is it?"

That didn't seem to go down too well. The response was in chorus. "It is fixed, it's not a problem, not for us anyway. We're Brits and that's that. If they have a problem with that then fuck 'em, we don't care."

They were right. The atmosphere in Stanley is friendly, rural, typically English countryside really; no traffic lights, no parking meters or traffic wardens, not even a cinema. People greet each other on the streets. The Falkland Islands are a beautiful, peaceful place and although they have computers and play stations, the atmosphere makes you feel you have stepped back in time forty or fifty years. A few pints later I ambled off home for a siesta.

It was Friday night, so where else to go but the pub. One of the girls I'd met came in and bought me a drink. Knowing I was leaving tomorrow, she asked what I thought. I told her that was a massive call which couldn't be decided over a couple of pints.

"But," I said, "there are some things I definitely feel."

I talked about the fact that the kind of lifestyle she and her fellow islanders lead didn't appear to have changed in decades. They know what community spirit really is, they have very little in material terms, but are content with what they have, they have a passion for their home and a tireless determination to keep it the way it is. There is no crime, and old fashioned values such as friendship and neighbourliness are still the norm. They have retained values much of our own society lost sight of years ago. They are very special people who deserve the right of British sovereignty, and their freedom, though whether freedom is the right word I'm not sure. Could freedom be the price we pay for war? The place was beautiful and still relatively unspoiled, (bar the minefields) and I hope it stays that way. What better memorial could there be to my comrades and the other men who had lain down their lives?

"So what do you think of the Argies?" she said.

I shrugged and told her I didn't know any, I'd never been there and couldn't comment until I had.

"So what did you think about them coming to the islands?"

Politics was never my strong point so I turned it on its head, asked her what she thought of them. She didn't hold back.

"Filthy Argie fuckers! Not one of them should ever be allowed to set foot here ever again," she spat.

"But you can't go round hating every single one of them forever," I said. "What about the conscripts and their families? What if they want to visit the graves of the people they lost?"

I was stunned at the ferocity of her response. "Tough shit," she said, "they started it. Let them in, they can have a British Military escort to their cemetery and straight out again to Argentina. No filthy fucking Argie cunt should ever be allowed in my country again! You didn't see what they did to my mum and dad. You are one of the people who has earned a right to your opinion. You're entitled to express it, as is everyone who came here in '82. But we are equally entitled to ours. If you don't live here, or you didn't fight for the place, then it's nothing to do with you."

This was serious hatred and it struck me, she was so young for this, far too young to be talking or feeling that way. I decided to steer the subject to talk of wildlife instead, and as I ordered more drinks, she smiled, and clearly knew what I was up to.

"OK, OK," she said, her hands up in mock surrender. "New subject. But when I have children I will take them to tend the 1982 graves and memorials and I will tell them why, and my grandchildren too. And I will make sure my grandchildren know to teach their grandchildren too, and so will every one of the friends of mine you've met here, and everyone in this pub. That's how long it is going to take before the Argies can even start thinking about getting near this place. It's not going to happen as long as my grandchildren are alive."

We adjourned to The Globe and found Jimmy, the Scots Guardsman, in there. He was drinking with the lady whose house he had been billeted in after the surrender. They were like a long lost mum and son. Jimmy and I went outside into the cold where it was quiet."

"So, what did you think?" Jimmy asked.

"Christ Jimmy," I said, "how did you do it? How did you take that mountain with such massive defences, when you were outnumbered and outgunned?"

He necked his pint. "Adam," he said, "you were British military, albeit Navy, the majority of whom are fucking poofters and queers, so you'll know how we did it. We just fuckin' did it, and if it came down to it, I could do it again, so could you, so could we all. Let's get pissed."

We went back inside. The place was heaving, all the *Endeavour* crew were in. We were talking to a couple of girls who were finishing their stint aboard at the next port, wherever that was. They couldn't understand a word Jimmy said, and by now, neither could I. Their accents were familiar, they were both Australians. I asked them where they were from.

"The Gold Coast, it's near Brisbane," one of them replied. "So is this a regular night out for you guys then?"

The last thing I remember is saying, "Dunno, I live near you."

Departing

My last day was the Queen's Birthday parade on Ross Road. Everyone was there in full ceremonial uniform and medals. I made my way down town with Terry and Eli. Terry was in his red beret and Parachute Regiment tie, having had the honour of being made an honourary member of the Parachute Regiment by the CO of 3 Para in 1982, Lt Col (now General Sir) Hew Pike.

No sooner had we got down to the harbour than Terry linked up with Para veterans of 1982, Thommo Thompson, a then 18 year old private from 2 Para, and Harry Harrison, now the RSM of the Resident Infantry Company. We exchanged pleasantries and Harry informed me he had been a "gobshite eighteen year old private" in 3 Para at the time. Thommo remembered Oz Straughan as the 'Tasmanian Toothbrush Taker' – something about Steve nicking his toothbrush on exercise somewhere. He had also joined up with Mark Dodsworth, Caroline Straughan's first husband who was killed on Longdon.

Parading for the ceremony was a detachment of each of the resident British Forces, as well as the Falkland Islands Defence Force, looking, acting, and being just as professional as their full-time counterparts. The Governor arrived, resplendent in his ostrich feather hat. There was lots of saluting, presenting of arms, firing of cannons, hoisting of flags and the obligatory military fly-past. Then it was over. I wanted to stay, but I knew I had to go.

I thought I'd have a final pint in the Globe and the Victory. I'd got to know some people well in there and had struck up quite a friendship, almost an acceptance. I went round and said my goodbyes to those I knew.

"I have to ask, was it worth it for you?" one of the ladies asked.

"It is your way of life and your freedom," I said.

"It was worth it from our point of view," she said, "but what about you,

200

the men, the boys who had to come here? You must have an opinion."

I could only tell her the same as I had told the others. "I cannot answer that, you must go and ask 255 British families without sons, fathers, husbands, brothers. They are the ones who made the sacrifices for you. Ask the widows and mothers. Only they can ever tell you if it was worth it."

There was still a question in her eyes.

"Yes," I said. "I'm glad I came."

"We're glad you came, both times," she said, giving me a bearhug. When I let her go, she was in tears.

It started to snow as I walked back to Terry's. I threw my gear into the van reluctantly; I really didn't want to leave the islands, despite how much I wanted to see my family.

We drove in silence to Mount Pleasant Airport. The mountains of William, Challenger, Harriett, still looking like buried dinosaurs, just as they had three weeks ago and would for a few more million years.

At the airport, I checked in, and in what seemed like the shortest wait ever in a departure lounge, I boarded the Lan Chile flight to take me to Argentina, once enemy territory. The storm clouds gathered and the sky turned black. What a surprise.

I thought of the wildlife, the scenery, the views, the untouched and unexplored beauty. I remembered Ailsa Heathman telling me that one of the locals had said to a well known journalist who had been negative in a report about the islands before, "Why don't you just fuck off and write something positive about us for once?"

This little slice of Britain was one of the last wild frontiers on earth; a place where nature was still in charge. It had asked things of me that I didn't know I was capable of anymore. It had answered many questions that had eluded me for two decades, for the entirety of my adult life. It had touched my heart and soul. It had triggered previously unknown emotions in me, and had dusted cobwebs off feelings that were long dormant or I didn't know I had – relief at my final arrival; sadness and anguish at the war and the waste of life, peacefulness and contentment, fulfillment at managing to climb the mountains, and anger at the teenage tosser who'd picked a fight with me. The only thing that had given me a bigger kaleidoscope of feelings was the actual war and immediate aftermath itself. Since then I'd spent twenty years wandering around a mental wilderness without a map. Much more of the mental jigsaw puzzle was now complete. I was leaving the Falklands feeling awake and alive.

As the aircraft thundered down the runway, the rain started to fall; I arrived in the rain and left in the rain. As we climbed towards the clouds, I started to hum the tune to the hymn 'I vow to thee my country'. I now knew the answer to the question I'd been battling with just an hour or so earlier. All those who did not return in 1982 did not die in vain. I was almost complete.

I was so glad I had made this journey.

CHAPTER 26

Confronting the Demons – The Argentine Story

We circled over Rio Gallegos an hour or so later. It looked like a dump. During the war, A-4 Skyhawks and other aircraft had flown from here. I wondered if there'd be anything interesting to do during the two-hour wait for the flight to Buenos Aires. I'd been on the flight with Terry's prospective daughter-in-law, who was Argentinian; she'd said the place was as bad as it looked. There were no customs or immigration, no one checked passports or visas, and I was quite surprised to see my bag had even made it off the plane.

I wandered around the deserted buildings, eventually finding someone who was supposed to be working at the airline ticket desk so I could pay for and collect my re-issued ticket via Brazil. That done, I went in search of a beer. Near the entrance to the terminal was a security office in which a fat little security guard sat watching re-runs of Diego Maradona's golden goals.

"Maradona is God. God, si?"

I was hard pushed not to tell him he was actually a little, fat, drug taking, cheating bastard and Argentina's top wanker, but that wouldn't have achieved the required taxi into town for a couple of beers. He summoned one from somewhere for me and I could still hear his shrieks of delight as the taxi careered across the pot-holed surface, weaving between obstacles placed to test someone on an advanced defensive driving course. I negotiated a fee of $10 for a drop-off at the appointed bar and a pick-up in half an hour's time. $5 now and the rest on completion seemed fair enough.

Inside, the pool hall was immaculate with polished floors and gleaming mirrors. No one took any notice of me as I took my place at the bar, ordered a jug in Spanish and retired to the corner to watch the evening's sharks sharpening their cues. The half hour passed too quickly; I was just settling in. No matter, I stood waiting at the corner. And waiting. But no taxi; the bastard had ripped me off. Well that was hardly going to break the

203

bank, but there didn't seem to be many other cars about and I had a 'plane to catch. Eventually a taxi trundled into sight and I said just one thing, "aeroporto". The driver, who had clearly recently graduated from driving a donkey and cart, ambled across four lanes of traffic oblivious to the hoots and yells from the other cab drivers, then headed back in the other direction.

At the aiport, the ground crew and cabin staff stood at the bottom of the boarding steps. They didn't look happy. It was Saturday night; they probably had homes and families to go to. Goodbye Rio Gallegos, I thought to myself, hopefully a place I shall never have the misfortune to visit again. The 'plane took off, then bumped its way through the cloud. I was asleep before we came out.

We started the descent into Buenos Aires in darkness, though the city could be seen from miles away. It was lit up by an orange glow for what seemed like forever. It looked bigger than London. Half of Argentina's population of thirty six million people live in Buenos Aires and its suburbs.

I went through passport control and the immigration officer stopped me and started questioning me in Spanish. If I hadn't been so pissed I would probably have understood him, I wasn't too bad at the lingo. He wanted to know how I had arrived on an internal flight with no entry stamp into the country. I tried to tell him that at Rio Gallegos, there had been no-one on duty at any of the customs desks. He summoned other immigration officers. It was midnight, I was hungry, thirsty and tired and in no mood for pissing around with these flashy-uniformed, power crazy idiots.

"Que British Malvinas si?"

I thought, Oh Christ. Here we go. They'd found the entry and exit stamps to the islands in my British passport. I should have given them my Australian one.

There were frantic exchanges between various different uniformed personnel, all seeming to be about me. I reached out my hand, indicating I wanted my passport back, but it was jerked away from me. A police officer, very like the rest of them, but older, quite a bit older, appeared. He had a chest full of medal ribbons, and as he approached, he muttered something to the others that I couldn't quite make out. They all fell silent and my passport was handed over to him. He flicked through it until he found the Falklands stamp, then he came over to where I was standing, and stood up close.

"How many times have you been to Las Malvinas senor?"

I glanced at the men gathered around him and I knew they all knew.

"Twice," I replied, feeling more than a little intimidated.

"You are lucky," he said. "I have never had the chance to return. I too would like to go back one day."

"I hope you get the chance," I said. "It's a wonderful place."

He stared at me with dark eyes. "Wonderful enough to fight for?"

"Wonderful enough to die for," I said, meeting his gaze.

He paused for what felt like a very long moment, then stuck out a hand. "Welcome to Argentina," he said, handing over my passport and dismissing me.

Relieved, I shoved the luggage trolley towards the exit and into the midnight humidity in search of the airport's taxi rank.

When I found it, I was accosted by a couple of cab drivers competing for the fare. They started arguing, dragging my bags off the trolley towards their cabs. I was battling to stop them and keep all my gear in one place when the veteran Malvinas copper appeared. The cabbies, it seemed, were unlicensed and touting for business, and though he couldn't stop them, it was clear they were wary of him. He advised me to go only with the licensed cabs, so I scrummaged my way into one and showed the driver the address Terry's prospective daughter-in-law had written for me.

The driver nodded briefly, then took off like he was coming out of the pits after a Formula 1 tyre change with a few laps to make up. I was soon to realise that this is the way you drive in Buenos Aires! We arrived at the Juncal Palace Hotel, which didn't look much like a palace to me. At the reception desk a man tossed a registration card and pen at me and pointed to the tariff sign.

"Quatro," I said. He took my credit card and swiped it, and I asked him if there were any snacks available. He shook his head. I asked if there was anywhere open to get anything to eat. He shook his head. I asked him if he had a map I could look at. He shook his head. I asked if there was anywhere I could make a coffee. Again, he shook his head. I felt like asking him whether he wanted to live to see morning, to see if I got the same response. Right then, I would gladly have obliged him.

I chucked my rucksack in the shed of a room I'd just rented and went in search of sustenance. I had to settle for Argentina's finest golden arches. McDonalds is a place I avoid like the plague (mostly for fear of contracting it there). Two burgers and a couple of cups of tea later saw me back in my shed at the Palace. When I awoke, I felt surprisingly refreshed. Following a shower in a bathroom I doubt would pass a public health inspection, I went downstairs to explore the once-enemy country. I asked for a map at reception, but there weren't any. Or if there were, the bloke behind the desk was not interested in finding them. He was too engrossed in yesterday's football results. Breakfast was dire! I've never been a fan of continental breakfast and they hadn't heard of a fry up. The bread was like rock and nearly broke my teeth, and the coffee was the strongest I'd ever tasted. It was like drinking tar, and was served in thimble size cups, which was probably a blessing. In the guest's lounge I checked the racks for tourist information but there was none, so I set off in search of the nearest tourist information bureau. All in all, not a good start to the day!

Wandering around, I found myself in the slums of the city. It appeared everyone had a dog, and Sunday was the day for walkies. Negotiating the footpaths was tricky as there was dog shit everywhere. There were also beggars in the streets with old and ragged clothing. One particular young man I noticed was wearing boots held together with lurid green masking tape. The area was practically derelict, many of the buildings were boarded up and defaced with political graffiti. I could have a pretty accurate guess as to what it said with half the nation starving, little money around, queues to buy bread, and the banks all closed. It was grimy, dirty and rundown, yet when I came across a couple of old buildings with ornate decorations, they were covered in Argentinian flags, as were others in the area. Clearly, despite everything, this was a very proud nation.

A couple of streets further on, I reached the plush residences where, in complete contrast to the area I'd just left, there were BMWs and Mercs parked outside the houses, and carefully tended trees and gardens. Eventually I came to a marketplace, a series of stalls set around an expanse of manicured grass. Nearby, I discovered a cemetery, the sort with tombs above ground. I've always found them rather macabre so I didn't stay. Instead, I went back to the grassy area and sat and watched the world go by.

From the oppressive military bullies who had ruled this country for so long, it seemed a world away. I had watched the Argentinian media prior to departing for the trip. They had turned over a number of different presidents in the space of a few days. People had lost their life's savings, and there wasn't enough food to go round, even for those with money. There were mass civil protests, rioting in the streets, and the entire country was teetering on the verge of civil war. How could they possibly run the Falkland Islands?

Here though, it was all very cosmopolitan and could have been any European capital though I still couldn't find any tourist information or maps anywhere. By now I was desperate for a pee, but I couldn't find a public toilet. Eventually I spotted two female police officers and the thought came, 'when in doubt, ask a copper.' As I approached I was encouraged to see these two particular coppers were rather aesthetically pleasing.

"Buenos dias," I greeted them.

"Buenos dias senor, how can we help you?" they replied in their perfect Spanish.

"No entiendo Castellano," I continued, indicating that I didn't understand Spanish, and required some assistance. I couldn't imagine how bad my accent must be and this was long before I got to even asking for the toilet. I was hoping and praying it wouldn't require hand signals. If they misinterpreted, they'd throw the key away.

The taller of the two was wearing stripes so I assumed she must have been a sergeant. "Are you English?" she said.

Normally I would have come out with a firm and proud "yes", but on this occasion I hesitated. I thought of taking the easy way out and telling her I was Australian, which strictly speaking is now true, but I couldn't do it.

"Yes, I'm British," I said, waiting for the first signs of contempt. They didn't come.

"Welcome to Argentina," she said with a smile. "I hope you like our country and enjoy yourself here."

She looked a bit like Gloria Estefan, only prettier. These were the Latin-American beauties I had heard about. She extended her hand, I took it. She shook hands firmly for a woman, especially for someone who was much smaller than me. "How can we help you?" she continued.

"Cuando los serbios, por favor," *Where is the toilet please?* I said.

They rattled back in Spanish as I felt my bladder get fuller and fuller.

Right now, it felt like the size of a zeppelin, and my eyes were starting to water.

"Cuando los serbios, por favor," I said, more desperately this time. They tried various interpretations, until finally, I scrabbled for my phrase book and shoved it under their noses.

"Ah! Los serbios. No problemo," Gloria Estefan said with a grin. She explained that you could walk into any café and use the toilets without being a customer.

She directed me to a café nearby; it looked rather posh from the outside. I opened the door and strode in and everyone in the place looked up. They were quite obviously all dressed up for their Sunday Lunch outing, which is a big thing. I was in a well-weathered jacket and trekking jeans and boots. The maître d' took one step towards me and I saved him the trouble of embarrassing us both. I'd about-turned and marched out before he took another pace. The two policewomen were outside.

"That was quick," Gloria Estefan said.

I smiled, embarrassed and still busting. There was a whole row of cafés and restaurants, all dining al fresco, but two doors up there was a Guinness sign! That's more like it, I thought.

Guinness is an international language or at least an international word. I went straight to the bar and ordered a pint, and while it was settling, I dashed upstairs to find the gents.

Coming down again, and feeling so much better, I found my Guinness had settled nicely. I drew a smiley face in the top to see just how good it was. The two eyes stood out like aroused nipples. This was good Guinness, I was going to enjoy this. And I did. I turned and walked out of the bar and spotted, just across the pavement, a beer garden fenced by trellis with climbing and creeping plants. The tables nearest the pavement were occupied, but up at the back there were a few empty ones and I made my way to one of them, one which gave me sun on my body and shade for my eyes, plus, a view of the talent walking past – perfect! It was a beautiful warm spring afternoon, couples strolled hand in hand, families chatted and children played. This was the kind of scenario where lyrics were dreamed up. *And in the streets the children screamed, the lovers cried and poets dreamed...* I mused.

The nearest company I had was two young men in football shirts from one of the local sides. They were a couple of tables away engrossed in a discussion of match tactics using salt cellars and wine glasses for players and goals. The flowers around me were just coming into bloom, the birds were singing their best spring courting songs, when *Crash!*

The two teenagers were picking up the remains of their glasses and a bottle of red wine that one of them had sent to the floor as he knocked the table. A waiter appeared and started shouting at them. The teenagers were drunk and blaming the uneven surface, a wonky table leg and anything else they could think of. The waiter shouted even louder, then a dour looking woman appeared. The three turned on her, each giving their version of the events. The woman raised her hands to signal calm, then she turned to the waiter and asked him what happened. Before he could open his mouth, one of the youths leapt to his feet, gesticulating, pointing first at the table, then at the floor.

The woman spoke to him sharply as though he was a child, then his friend stood up and catching his arm, tried to persuade him to sit down. He was having none of it though, and shoved him away, making him catch a nearby table. The crockery leapt into the air, and the youth sprang towards the woman but was stopped in his tracks by the waiter. Next thing, Gloria Estafan appeared with her mate, both of them wielding truncheons, and arrested the wrong lad. The culprit was still doing his best to get at the bar owner but Gloria swung her baton and caught him right behind the knees. While he yelped and let go of the waiter, she hooked the baton round his neck, whipped out her handcuffs, threw him to the floor and with one knee in the small of his back, she cuffed him by the wrists.

She looked up and let out a grunt, then seeing me, she did a double take, an 'I've seen that face somewhere before' kind of look. I raised my glass then offered a mock round of applause and she laughed out loud. Then back to business, she stood up and dragged her quarry to his feet just as two male officers arrived looking the part in black leather bomber jackets with flashes and patches. They were even wearing mirrored sunglasses and had the obligatory big black moustaches.

They grabbed the youths, making the stroppy one cry out in pain. The two policewomen spoke to the waiter and the woman in charge and as they turned to leave, I raised a hand to Gloria and she came over. Not knowing how good her English was I refrained from making jokes about her arrest technique, or Cagney and Lacey.

"I am sorry if this has spoiled your afternoon," she said. "Not everyone here in Argentina behaves this way. We are a civilised people."

"I am impressed," I said, "and no, it didn't spoil my afternoon but actually livened things up. Cheers!" I raised my glass again and she smiled her beautiful smile.

"Cheers," she replied, looking confused. As the two women walked away, she looked back over her shoulder once, and was gone.

I was sitting replaying the afternoon's free entertainment when I realised someone was talking to me. I looked up to see the woman who ran the bar.

She was holding a pint of Guinness, which I was sure I hadn't ordered. She had a thin face, with high cheekbones and a perfectly formed nose and her hair was pulled back into a bunch. She was made up perfectly, too perfectly. She looked like one of the guitar playing doll-like women in the Robert Palmer video *Addicted to Love*. She wouldn't have been out of place on the catwalk or cover of a magazine, but not my type. I prefer 'the girl next door'.

"Complimentary," she said, setting the glass down. "I am sorry for the behaviour of those two."

I'd had a bit of a show, been in no danger, got to watch two good looking girls wrestling (albeit fully clothed) and here was the woman who had been confronted with the aggro buying me a pint. Gloria was right, this was a civilised country.

"Are you OK?" I asked her.

"OK? It would take more than a boy like that to worry me," she said as she drew herself up. She was tall and quite imposing.

"Do you get a lot of trouble here?" I asked.

"No, not here, never," she said. "But I have had lots of practice." She smiled at me and there was a glint in her eye. "Enjoy your Guinness."

She turned and walked back into the pub as the staff materialised to clean up the debris around me. The audience, namely the families and couples having their Sunday lunch had already returned to their meals as if nothing had happened. I thought of her remark, "I've had lots of practice." She certainly didn't look like a bouncer. Maybe she'd been a copper? But no, she would have said something to the other two. Whatever, I made a mental note never to get on the wrong side of an Argentinian woman.

Two Guinnesses later I ambled off towards the markets feeling quite contented. I stopped at one of the stalls that was absolutely bedecked with Argentinian flags, pennants, badges, maps, t-shirts and a myriad of articles adorned with their flag and national colours. One flag in particular caught my eye. Emblazoned across its white and sky blue stripes was the outline of the Falkland Islands, with the words *Las Malvinas est la Argentinas,* which roughly translates as 'the Falkland Islands are Argentinian.' I picked it up and studied it.

"One hundred pesos por favor senor. "

I looked up at the wizened old woman who owned the stall. She must have been 95 if she was a day. Her skin had the look and texture of a walnut shell. I smiled to myself, 'a plastic surgeon's dream'. You could spend hours teaching plastic surgery students and actually use her for practice and she probably wouldn't even notice. Her clothes were shabby and old, there wasn't a thing she was wearing that didn't have a hole in it.

She snapped at me in Spanish. "Do you agree?"

I assumed she was asking me to buy the flag. What I did not know at this point, was that the woman was asking whether I agreed that the Islands belonged to Argentina. I shook my head and replied, "No thank you," and attempted to hand the flag back to her. She was enraged and started ranting in Spanish.

I couldn't work out why she was so offended. She folded her arms in defiance indicating she would not take back the flag and I wondered if there was some Latin American custom that if you handled the goods they were considered sold. I reiterated. "Mucho gracias, no I don't want it."

By now she was incandescent, jabbering away at me. I decided I'd had enough of the cantankerous old cow and was in no mood to have a purchase forced upon me, but that didn't impress her. She was worse than any used car salesman I'd ever met! I was getting seriously pissed off now.

"No!" I yelled back at her. "Non. Nien, niet. What's Spanish for 'no I don't want to buy it'?"

She snatched the flag off me and started waving it around and yabbering on about God knows what, and sticking her finger in my face. I didn't really care but I noticed people had stopped and were listening to her and glaring at me. This was not good. I couldn't think what I had done that was so bad, or what she might have implied I had done to make these people look so potentially hostile.

The hairs on the back of my neck were standing up and I sensed an imminent 'kick-off'. A short fat man who was sweating profusely sidled up to me and said out of the side of his mouth, "Senor, you must leave. She thinks you are disputing that the islands belong to them."

I was staggered! "Well they bloody well don't!" I said. "Tell the old cow that!"

The man was all reason. "Senor," he said. "There are hundreds of Argentinians around you who feel very strongly about this. You would be wise to leave it."

Here I was, arguing over one of the nation's most emotional issues in a place crowded with 'the enemy'. I looked around at the faces of the people, old, young, men, women. They all glared back at me. I was still in my old dirty jeans and hiking boots, I had my sunglasses on and with my head freshly shaved that morning and two days' facial growth, I hoped that when I pulled myself up to my full six foot, I would look sufficiently intimidating to deter anyone from starting on me. If I didn't, if anyone there wanted to take the discussion further, I was up shit creek. I've always preferred to bluff my way out of trouble rather than actually fighting my way out. I'd been filled in too many times in my teens by starting situations I couldn't handle. The fat Chilean was yanking at my arm, so I followed him. Then he started breaking into a trot.

"Amigo," I said, resisting. "I will walk away, but I will not run, so take it easy." We put some distance between us and the crowd, then stopped at the bottom of the hill, beneath the shade of a large tree.

The man let go of my arm and offered his hand. "I am Fernando José Gonzalez," he said.

I just couldn't help myself. I burst out laughing! His face was a picture, a weird mix of confusion, annoyance, hurt and embarrassment at this foreigner whose skin he had just saved. Luckily the confusion part meant he was not entirely sure it was his name that was being mocked. I remembered the warmth and hospitality of the Chilean family on Sealion Island and how much Juan had said the Chileans and Argentinians disliked each other.

"Thank you for saving me from a public lynching," I said to him, grasping the proffered hand. He pointed out his family, who were sitting on a huge tartan rug, enjoying a picnic in the park. They had clearly seen what had happened, and with the next breath, I was asked to join them. Fernando, I thought, must have been in his late fifties, his wife Martha the same age, though the wrinkles on her lower neck and hands did not match those on her face. There wasn't a trace of 'crow's feet' in the corner of her eyes, which struck me as odd until I realised that she has probably had a face lift. Fernando introduced his son, Diego, a Latin-American soccer player look-alike. He was with his wife Veronica who was cradling their daughter Anita. Veronica was tiny, much younger than Diego, and she didn't actually look big enough to have had a child. I sat down and accepted their offer of tea, though there was no milk, and it tasted bloody awful! Then the biscuits came round and they were a slight improvement, even more so once they'd been dunked.

Veronica burst out laughing. I asked her what was so funny but she spoke no English. Diego translated. "She says she has never seen anyone dip biscuits into this tea before. So, you are English?" he said.

I hesitated, not because I was wary of admitting that I was a Brit in Argentina after his dad had just rescued me, but because I wanted to know how it could be so obvious. Maybe we're the only nation that enjoy 'dunkers', I thought. Surely as a typical fair skinned, blue-eyed Caucasian I could have been of any northern European descent or even a yank or an Aussie but both he and the copper had immediately assumed I was British.

"Yeah I'm a Brit," I said eventually, "but I live in Australia now. What made you think I was British?"

There was no hesitation from him. "Your interest in the old Malvinas woman. I know you call them the Falkland Islands but I find Malvinas easier to pronounce. It's all I've ever heard them referred to as, no offence meant."

I nodded at him. "None taken Diego. What's her story, the old woman? She seems pretty caught up with it all?"

Diego paused for a moment, then looked directly at me. "She lost her son, and also maybe another relative there. She is not the person to start discussing who owns the islands with. You will never change her opinion that you, the British, are the invaders and aggressors."

I found myself feeling sorry for her. She had grown up being brainwashed. I bet if I took her to the islands and showed her all the kids waving Union flags, and the houses with their picture of the Queen, and the flags painted on the brightly-coloured roofs, and the banners declaring that the Argentinians would be welcome only when they recognised the Islanders' right to self determination, she would probably still say, "They are ours".

I remembered the comment made by the young girl on my last night in the Victory in Stanley – 'Never, as long as I'm alive.' No doubt she will teach her children, as the Islanders have taught all the children since 1982, and those children now tend the memorials and graves of men who gave their lives for the freedom of their mothers and fathers.

I was dragged from my thoughts by Diego's voice. He had clearly been addressing me for a couple of minutes judging from the frustration on this face.

"Excuse me, excuse me, were you there, in the Malvinas in '82?"

"Yep," I said, returning to the tea and biscuits in order to shortcut the conversation. My thoughts were with the old woman. She hadn't singled me out, she was on everyone's case, thrusting her flags at anyone foolhardy enough to pass closely by her. It seemed she got a lot more attention and nods of agreements than she did sales. I couldn't help thinking, what if things had been different and I hadn't been so lucky in '82. Would my family be like this?

I decided it was time to go. I stood up and shook hands with Fernando and Diego and nodded to Martha and Veronica. As I walked away Fernando strode after me.

"Senor," he called out, "Argentina is more peaceful now, but there is still a lot of internal unrest due to the political situation. *Please* be careful what you say, if you understand."

"Cheers mate," I said, patting him on the arm. I walked away briskly, feeling really good for some reason.

I wandered around for a while and came upon a square lined with cafés. I heard it before I saw it and when I got there, there were lots of couples, dancing the tango. The women were all gorgeous. I think every female I saw in South America was gorgeous, they must drown the ugly ones at birth. I made a mental note to learn to tango when I returned to Australia. Once again, the pavements were covered in dog shit and it struck me that that was probably what they were dancing around. Maybe that's why you learn the Buenos Aires shuffle in the first place.

Eventually, I arrived back at my hotel room, which didn't look very inviting. Still, it had a bed, however crappy, and I was tired.

The old flag woman was fluctuating between hysterical sobbing and wild bouts of screaming but unlike this afternoon she was in perfect English. She was yelling abuse at me for murdering her only son and calling me all the names under the sun, then falling to the floor and beating the ground in frustration. For an old woman she got up quickly, her fists raised, the undersides bloodied where she had beaten the ground in torment. As she came towards me I backed off and put out my hands to stop her, but her strength was unbelievable and I could not push this apparently frail old woman away. Her fist landed hard in the centre of my chest.

I woke up with a start, my throat and airway closed up as if I was being strangled. I began to cough and staggered to the bathroom gulping down brackish water which tasted as if it shouldn't be drunk straight from the tap. I returned to the bedroom and realised I was sweating profusely and the mattress was drenched, so wet that it looked like I'd pissed the bed. The room was in total darkness and when I flicked on the light, I found it was 8:30pm, and I was starving.

Too tired to shower, I toweled myself off, pulled on my old clothes and went in search of something more appetizing than the previous night's efforts in McArgentina. After a number of right turns and left turns, which I memorised so I could perform exactly the reverse on the way back, I came across a modern looking eatery. I approached the counter and asked for a menu. The waiter gestured for me to sit down. I said I'd like something to drink straight away. He simply nodded. I tried in vain to get the attention of any one of the waiters who seemed to be playing 'ignore the foreigner'. The reason soon became apparent – someone scored and the restaurant erupted with cheering. There were a number of televisions around the place and I realised the local team was playing.

The fans ranged in age from around three to ninety three. I stood up and waved to the waiters behind the bar and the people behind me shouted at me, I presume to sit down. I pointed at the bar indicating to them that when the waiters came over I would sit down. A woman started shouting at the waiters in Spanish, and with her, and the noise of the televisions, it was total chaos.

Eventually, a bored waiter appeared and attempted to take my order without taking his eyes off the screen. I did my best to make life simple for everyone by ordering steak, chips and a couple of Cokes. When he apparently failed to understand, I varied the wording, then the pronunciation, then both. The woman next to me quickly became irritated by my continuing attempts, whilst the waiter continued to stare at the screen and made no effort to understand.

"Senor, senor," she snapped at him.

"Si si," he responded, notebook and pencil poised. She rattled off another sentence, pointing at me.

"What is it you would like?" she asked in perfect English. There was a slight American twang but she could have held her own at Royal Ascot or Henley, without question.

"Just the steak, cooked medium please, with chips and two glasses of Coke, big ones por favor senora."

She clapped her hands and laughed, repeating my order to the sour faced waiter, who was clearly disappointed that he would now have to miss a fraction of the game whilst taking my order into the kitchen. I asked her where I was going wrong with the phrases I had been using and she assured me that my first attempts were quite near the mark. The waiter knew I was not fluent and also knew that I wouldn't know how accurate I was being.

So the more I changed the wording the worse it got, and the longer he could stand there ignoring me and watching the game. I didn't care. All I really wanted to do was complete what I had come here to do and get to England to see my daughter, whom I was missing desperately by this time.

The waiter re-appeared with a Coke and put it down without so much as a word or even looking at me. He was starting to piss me off. He had only brought me one Coke when I knew the woman had asked for two and he had acknowledged two.

"Senor," I said, "dos Coca-Cola por favor. Dos." I held up two fingers to underline the point. He glared at me. I smiled and held up two fingers again, pointing to the Coke bottle. The slight movement of his lips told me he was cursing me in Spanish. I didn't give a shit whether he didn't like Brits, Aussies or any other English-speaking people. As the second Coke arrived I looked up. It was delivered by a much older grey haired waiter, who smiled. He must have sensed that his young protégé and one of his customers had not hit it off. He also brought out the steak and chips, which I have to say was one of the most perfect meals I've ever had. I concentrated on enjoying it, trying to ignore the shouts, gasps, sighs and groans all around me. It sounded like a massive orgy. As I ate, I couldn't help smiling to myself, enjoying my own joke.

Settling the bill was much easier than I'd anticipated. It was so cheap I threw the old waiter a note for a few thousand pesos, which more than covered it. He handed me back a handful of 'shrapnel', which I pocketed as the final whistle went. The entire restaurant was jumping up and down like it was their FA Cup Final. Maybe it was! I went out into the street, and though it was getting late, there were still plenty of people about. I was keen to not take any wrong turns on the way back to the hotel. I had visions of ending up in some dark and dodgy alley from which I might never re-emerge.

I retraced my steps. By now it was cold, and I shoved my hands deep into my jacket pockets, wishing I'd brought my 'Benny' hat to stop my head from freezing. A car approached from behind blaring its horn. I looked around and gawped. It was a tiny Fiat weaving all over the road virtually hidden by massive flags. It was weaving because the driver couldn't see out! Kids were hanging out of the windows waving flags. I recognised the team's colours from the supporters in the restaurant. Two more were standing up in the car, poking out of the sun roof. They were ecstatic; there was a chorus of car horns and frenzied whistle blowing, and it struck me, they were all going to be deaf before the night was out, or at least suffering from bad tinnitus.

A few minutes of quick pace found me back at the decidedly un-palatial Juncal Palace. The front and downstairs décor was very ornate; pity it didn't reflect the rest of the place, but all I had asked for was a bed and somewhere to dump my gear. There were two residents sitting in the downstairs lounge reading newspapers. The room was thick with *Camel* cigarette smoke. I knew because I hate the stink of it. It took me back to 1987, shortly after I'd joined Devonport Field Gun Crew in Plymouth, when one of the older field gunners, Bagsy Baker (who actually ran for Portsmouth but was billeted in Devonport for a few days whilst waiting for a ship) took me to a 'poor student's nightclub'. He said the students were so poor, they would smoke anything in roll-ups including 'camel shit, tea leaves and bus tickets'. As I climbed the big ornate staircase, I thought about that night out in Plymouth. It had ended up as a 'damned good run ashore' for all the reasons that sailors deemed it so. I wondered what had happened to Bagsy. I'd thought of him when I was at San Carlos. In '82 he'd been an AB gunner on the *Ardent* when she was bombed and sunk and we had swapped a couple of stories in '87 but we soon realised that neither of us wanted to talk about it. I made a mental note that I would try to track him down when I got back to Australia.

The night was hot, and humid. I opened the windows and pushed out the shutters in a search for some air. The window opened onto grey walls that extended upwards about another three storeys. I looked down into a small square, no more than ten feet along each wall, the sole purpose of which appeared to be to collect rubbish. It was impossible to see the ground beneath the piles of old newspapers, milk cartons and fast food wrappers. I thought of the rats, the flies, and the stench of rotting milk when the summer came. I lay down on the bed and realised I never did find a Tourist Information office or get a map. Right then, I could have killed for a pint of Guinness.

CHAPTER 27

An Appointment with History

The next day I got up earlier. The streets were bustling with people and cars and blaring horns. I didn't bother with the Palace breakfast, despite it being included in the bill. Any more of that coffee would stain my teeth black, that's if there were any left after gnawing the bread. I found a corner café selling toast and half decent tea and while the breakfast was ok, it seemed everyone else smoked, and they chose those bloody awful things like Gauloises. Maybe they got free packs after passing their driving test. I then gave myself a kick back to reality regarding the driving, the food, the smoking rules – this is someone else's country and you are a guest here. If you don't like it – leave, which is exactly what I intended to do in about forty eight hours.

I went to pay the bill clutching a few paper pesos. Two women were sitting behind the counter, one reading the Spanish equivalent of the Women's Weekly, the other knitting. They both looked up at me, looked at each other, then carried on what they were doing, clearly hoping and expecting the other one to get up and sort out the European customer. Nobody moved so I turned around and started towards the door. The reader jumped to her feet and started yelling. I turned and walked back to the counter and put the pesos down in front of her. She was still ranting on about God only knows what, and got more and more carried away. I couldn't help myself, I started to laugh, and she got worse, ranting and raving like a mad woman. I turned and walked out, it still makes me smile to think of it now. There seemed to be no half measures, everything was either calm, or it was a colossal problem to rant and rave about. It was beyond me. Why would anyone waste so much energy over such a small thing?

I rang the journalist Nick Tozer and got his answering machine. The message was all in Spanish but then what else would you expect in

Argentina? I knew it was the right number as I recognised his name and accent. I didn't have my mobile phone with me so he couldn't call me back, so it was obvious I would have to kill time until I could get hold of him. I continued walking, making a note of which way I turned so I could find my way back until I found a map. I called Nick again from another phone box and this time he answered. He gave me his address and told me to come over when I was ready, so I hailed a cab. It might have been the same bloke who picked me up from the airport. Same sort of car, same colour, same rosary beads hanging off the mirror, could even have been the same photo on the cab drivers license for all I knew. He certainly had the same moustache and the usual Spanish three names which I couldn't be bothered to try to pronounce. He drove the cab like a ballistic missile, just like the rest of the drivers there. I couldn't work out how motorcyclists and scooter riders stayed alive so long, and why would they be mad enough to ride without a crash helmet. Maybe they all shared the same collective death wish. I had a couple of feeble attempts at pronouncing the journalist's address, which drew nothing but confusion and frustration from the driver. I'm sure that wasn't helped by the queue of vehicles behind him, all of which it seemed were blaring their horns.

I showed him the address I'd written down when Nick had spelt it out to me letter by letter. There was lots of "si, si senor" and nodding and smiling as we carved our way through the traffic towards trendy and 'down-town' Buenos Aires. We turned left onto the main drag, which was about ten lanes wide, or rather ten *vehicles* wide, all weaving as though they were trying to shake off heat-seeking missiles. We approached a major intersection where there was a backlog of traffic, and the driver joined in with what I took to be shouts and curses at no-one and nothing in particular. He'd been babbling on incoherently since I first got in the cab and even my one attempt at "no entiendo Castellano" hadn't shut him up. I was starting to get a headache and also pissed off, which for me, is not a good combination.

"Oi! Oi, driver!" I yelled at him finally. "For Christ's sake, pack that shit in. There's obviously something wrong up there and you sitting there blasting away on that and shouting at everyone, isn't going to change anything, so just fucking chill out – comprehendo?"

He turned round and looked at me. First he was surprised, then offence took over and he started mouthing off. I'd had enough. I reached for the door handle and he quieted a little and said, "No, no. OK." We sat there in silence, with him twitching nervously and itching to get the horn going again, then slowly, the traffic started to move and he started up his weaving actions again, which I had now accepted as the norm.

I knew I could never spend any length of time in a place like this, or God forbid, think about living and working here. I had come here for a quiet time to sort out some private business and keep a low profile. I did not want to think what it was going to be like if English football fans ever came here.

We came upon the scene responsible for the current chaos. There were fire engines, ambulances and police cars everywhere. A car was embedded in a shop window with paramedics attending to someone still trapped in the front. Just behind the car, a new Jeep or four wheel drive was on its side, with lots of emergency service personnel buzzing around it, and firemen still pouring foam onto the petrol which had spilt onto the road from the ruptured tank. One fireman stood by, holding the 'jaws of life' in his hands as some of his colleagues tried to free a trapped passenger. On the ground next to him was a stretcher with a sheet covering someone who obviously hadn't been carrying their rosary beads today. I felt my opinion of South American drivers had been fully vindicated.

The cab stopped on a busy street corner and the driver asked for his money. I didn't understand how much he wanted and I tried asking him exactly where the address was but either he didn't know or didn't give a shit. He won. I dumped a load of pesos in his hand and was glad to be back on foot again.

I opened the piece of screwed up paper with Nick's address on and looked around at street names for any sign of similarity – none, bugger! I tried asking a couple of people in the street but as in London, they brushed past me in too much of a hurry to assist.

I turned the corner and was relieved to see the street name I needed. The building numbers were difficult to locate but I took a punt and rang apartment No 8, then recognised Nick's voice through the intercom. Bingo! A result at last. He came down to meet me as the security in most buildings, was pretty tight. He wasn't what I had expected, but then again I hadn't known what to expect. We did the introductions and the thought came to me that here was the man who would be introducing me to the Argentinian pilots. We climbed the stairs to his apartment, which seemed to be in marked contrast to the exterior, older, un-modernised.

When I looked around, I saw there were books everywhere; most about the war. I chose one written by a British officer which I'd also seen on bookshelves at Terry's house in Stanley. There was a photo of the author on the back cover; I asked Nick if he knew the man, and he made a scathing remark. I remembered looking at the book in Terry's study and he had said the photo on the back was a true reflection of the type of man the author was. It was a picture of him in his red evening dress tunic with medals, looking every part the British, Sandhurst, terribly spiffing chap.

"He's a right Rupert wanker," Terry had told me. "He used my photos and drawings and diagrams, without my permission, intimating they were his and when I gave him some facts he still refused to acknowledge them, preferring his own opinions in his book."

Obviously the man wasn't good at making friends. Nick offered me a coffee which I gladly accepted, the first decent hot drink since I'd breakfasted at Terry's on Saturday morning.

He asked what I wanted to do and I didn't really have a plan. I knew I needed a map and information for finding my way around the city but that was about it. The company I was then working for had an office in Buenos Aires. I told him I wanted to send an email to the Director to see if I could meet with her and her staff. He typed it in Spanish for me, giving his mobile phone number as the contact. The coffee was good, I had another whilst flicking through the masses of literature he had on the war. Of particular interest was a thick document compiled by the Argentine military intelligence. It was all about the British military capability, the types of ships, their weapon fits, their specifications even down to names and pennant numbers. There was also a lot of information on the Royal Marine Commandos and the Army which I didn't pay too much attention to.

A highlighted part in the document was on the Sea Harrier and its capabilities. I don't know how accurate it was because although I served on an aircraft carrier for three years which bore a squadron of these and I tracked them on radar, it was a long time since I'd studied their airborne capabilities. The information collected in the document was dated from late 1981 to early 1982, which meant the bastards had been planning it for at least six months. Part of our fate had been sealed before I even left Naval Training School to join *Sheffield*. Bollocks to it, I thought. Chamberlain knew what Hitler was going to do and never stopped him and there is evidence that points towards the British knowing that the Japanese were going to attack Pearl Harbor but they let them get on with it because they knew it would definitely bring the Americans into the war. Then suddenly I found myself in a real rage.

Fucking politicians! Give me the shits so they do, I thought, then wondered if I'd actually said it. They're happy enough to cause endless trouble, or sit back and let trouble be caused, then they expect youngsters to go and sort their crap out for them while they revel in the glory of the victory. No wonder they want to be politicians. If it fails, you blame the military, the people on the ground. Not the facts, such as that Type 42 Destroyers like *Sheffield* and *Coventry* had been designed decades before to fight high altitude, long range, Russian bombers and not combat the sea skimming missile, so the need for a point defence capability had been ruled unnecessary and too expensive. Too expensive! Try telling that to twenty families, that is twenty sons and how many widows? How many fatherless children?

Clearly my inner rage was showing, as Nick asked, "What's wrong?"

"Nowt," I said.

"Just history eh?"

I shrugged. "Yeah Nick, just history."

I calmed down then and drained the coffee. Of course I knew the world had always been like that. It's human nature to try to 'big-note' yourself when it goes right and point the finger at someone else when it goes wrong.

The mail arrived, and as he opened it, Nick let out a cry of astonishment. One package contained a video of a documentary about the attack on *Sheffield* that he had done a lot of research for. We stared at each other, wide-eyed. Strange coincidence indeed.

"Do you want to watch it now?" he asked.

"Bloody right I do," I said. "Get it on."

He only had a TV in the bedroom, so we both settled down on the bed, which seemed a bit strange at first.

As the video started rolling, I stopped and stared. There on the screen was my best mate from our radar training days, twenty one years previously in HMS *Dryad*, Mark Booth, who had joined the carrier HMS *Invincible*. He hadn't changed except that he was completely bald. I laughed, amazed at how he looked, running my hand over my own shiny pink cranium.

Mark went into the details of the events I already knew. He and George had argued black and blue that aircraft had appeared on their radar. The senior officer had pulled rank – shit had happened. After we all got home, I'd gone onboard the *Invincible* at the invitation of Steve and Buster whom I'd joined up with and been in radar training with in HMS *Dryad*. We had a few beers onboard and then went ashore. It was the first time we'd seen each other since we left the radar training base. We were in a quiet pub in Portsmouth, an unusual feat in itself.

"So?" Steve asked me.

I wasn't exactly clear about what the question was, and said so.

He spoke again. "So, do you blame us for what happened to you, for ignoring the contacts and the rackets? For not vectoring the Harriers onto the Etendards? For not giving weapons free, calling zippo one – fuck me Joe, for any of it?"

I hesitated, not because I needed to consider whether I held these two men, the rest of my class, the *Invincible*, her AAWO or anyone else responsible, just to give myself time to compose my response.

"No fellas," I said, after a moment. "I don't blame you or anyone else. I know how and why it happened. It's happened, it's just something I'll have to live with."

Buster chipped in. "No Joe, it's something *we* will live with, all of us, that's why you have oppos, shipmate."

Steve nodded – they were both good men, the salt of the earth. We got mindlessly drunk. Steve was later killed in a car crash driving home for his son's 6th birthday in November 1991, I was absolutely gutted. That was the last time I had cried prior to this trip.

Nick jolted me back to reality with questions about what Mark was saying on the video. He was convinced the Ministry of Defence had orchestrated a cover-up. What if they had? It was probably done in what they viewed as the nation's 'best interests' at the time. Maybe they'd been right, the nation wanted heroes not villains.

Nick asked if I wanted some lunch and given that decent scoff had been a bit sparse on the ground save for last night's steak, I jumped at the chance. It was only about midday, a bit early for me to get stuck into a hearty lunch, never mind heavy red wine. He knew just the place. The restaurant had a massive stuffed bull in the window. Obviously it was steak again. After much introducing to the waiter whom he knew well, and 'forgetting' to mention my reasons for being here, we were served with wine. It was only in small glasses which I'm not very good at making last a long time.

I told Nick I wanted something really 'local' to eat, not something I could get in the UK or anywhere else. More conferring with the waiter who assured me in a language totally unintelligible that it was going to be absolutely divine. That's what his mannerisms and actions suggested anyway, he reminded me a bit of Manuel of Fawlty Towers, I wondered if he was going to say 'que?' The waiter was right; the entire meal was fantastic, as was the wine, even if it was too early for me. Afterwards, we went for a walk round town to get some fresh air and walk off the 3lbs of steak and mashed potatoes I had just put on.

Because I wanted to leave the country on Wednesday rather than waiting until Saturday, my first task was to change the final leg of my ticket, and get it routed via Sao Paulo. Everywhere Nick and I went, every building, every office, we had to show ID. There were security guards all over the place, probably the only ones getting paid.

We walked into the gardens fronting onto the Presidential Palace, the *Casa Rosada*. Once upon a time, and on many occasions, the captivating and enigmatic Eva Peron had held the Argentine people in the palm of her hand on the balcony of this very palace. Evita, wife of Juan Peron, developed a cult following in the 1940's and 50's for her work on behalf of the poor, labour unions and women's rights. She delivered her passionate speeches from the balcony to the crowds gathered in Plaza de Maya, the square where I was standing. Over two million people came to her funeral in 1952 when she died of cancer, aged only 33. She had been tremendously popular but was hated by the upper classes. Her vault in the ostentatious Recoleta cemetery, which is normally reserved for the super rich aristocracy, still attracts floral tributes to this day. Don't cry for me Argentina indeed. It was a very photogenic city, and there were flags flying everywhere. There should be more of that in England.

We carried on to an Argentinian war memorial where there was a large sculpture of a soldier with a hole right through his middle. It was dramatic and macabre. Right next to it was a real old tank.

Nick took me to an old church or cathedral. Out of respect, we did the crossing ourselves thing on the way in, then he showed me a framed flag. It was an old white ensign (Royal Navy flag) that the Royal Marines had flown during one of yet another of Britain's colonial forays. Whilst we were there, the Director from the Buenos Aires office of the company I worked for rang him on his mobile. He arranged for me to visit them tomorrow lunchtime.

We then went to the 1982 Las Malvinas war memorial, a beautiful piece of curved stone in a dark reddish mottled colour. On the top at the left burned an eternal flame, common to many war memorials. Two Argentine servicemen stood guard like sentinels over their fallen forefathers.

On the walls facing us were raised plaques of over 650 men, men just like us, boys just like me. Sons, brothers, fathers, husbands, uncles, nephews, friends. Whatever they once were, they were now photographs on walls and tables, and memories and names carved in hearts. I took out two of the poppies I still had left. I twisted their wire stalks together and wedged them behind the centre plaque, then I stood with my head bowed for a moment. They may have been on a different side and worn a different uniform but these men were all someone's son, and they were all dead.

I sensed Nick behind me. "What you just did means far more than all the politicians going on their goodwill handshaking, publicised visits," he said. "Thank you for letting me share it with you."

I looked at him ruefully. "I suppose the difference is that I *mean* it. It's for genuine reasons, not for public point scoring. I have nothing to gain by coming here and paying my respects to some very brave men." I paused for a moment, then added, "Fancy a pint?"

Nick was too accustomed to the South American way of life; the 'pint' had him stumped.

"A beer," I confirmed.

A smile spread across his face as if he had just been offered it free. He led the way. We found an Irish pub where Guinness was on the menu, and bloody good stuff it was, and cheap as well. Nick did all the ordering and struck up a conversation with the barmaid. She fired a question at me. I was tired of telling everyone that my Spanish was crap and asked Nick to do it for me.

Just like the majority of the world's population she spoke English, which was one in the eye for me. I gave myself a major mental reminder that my foreign language skills would improve on my return, instead of me adopting that typical attitude of the English speaking world, that everyone speaks English so I don't need to learn another language.

We got on well, she asked where I was from and why I was in Buenos Aires. I took the easy way out and said I was an Australian backpacker, which, technically speaking was true. A few Guineses, Kilkenny's and Caffrey's later we were best mates. She was full of intentions of visiting me when traveling to Australia the following year. Her main interest was how far from my house would she have to go to see kangaroos and koalas. I told her in all honesty, only about twenty kilometers. She was thrilled. I didn't mention the bit about the zoo.

She mentioned that there was a big party that weekend and asked whether I would like to go with her. I knew I'd be in England by Thursday, but I thought about exploiting this opportunity prematurely. I told her I'd think about it and let her know tomorrow. That would buy me time to see how the evening progressed.

I was hungry again by then and the pub didn't serve food. After demolishing a couple of packets of crisps and peanuts I was still hungry so it was time to find another establishment. I bade her farewell and promised to return the following evening. It was a promise I had every intention of keeping. We happened upon a pub called the Kilkenny. The food was excellent and plentiful and the beer was cheap. It was simply made for me, I was feeling great.

As we sat there, Nick said, "Can I ask you a question?"

I'd been prepared for lots of difficult questions from all sorts of people and angles on this trip, so this couldn't be any worse than I was expecting.

"Let's hear it," I said.

"What is the purpose of this trip? Why do you want to meet the pilots Mayora and Bedacarratz?"

It was a good one. I didn't have an answer to give him because in all honestly, I didn't know myself. I took a long hard pull on my pint.

"Nick," I said, "war and its effects are like a cancer reaching out into all the separate cells and organs until it overtakes the body. Then it can become the basis for revenge, an eye for an eye."

He stared at me. "So is this about retribution?"

I shook my head. "No but it turns the body's perspectives on right and wrong, good and evil upside down."

"So are you the good and the right, and Colombo, Bedacarratz and Mayora the wrong and the evil?" he continued.

"We probably both thought that about each other at the time," I said. "I suppose I'm trying to get it back into perspective, back to normal."

He paused, took a drink and some thinking time. "What is normal – I mean normal for you? Do you mean the normal for you the way it was before the war?"

Again, I didn't have an easy answer, and admitted as much. "I don't know. I think I'll know it when I sense it, if you know what I mean."

He wasn't letting me off the hook. "How do you think others will think about you meeting these men? They sank your ship, they killed your shipmates, they were the enemy."

I thought about that for a moment before I answered him because again, I wasn't sure I knew the answer. "We all have to do the things that are best for us and live our lives the way we choose," I said. "So no, I don't feel any guilt about meeting the pilots. It's important. Forgiveness should conquer hatred. I don't think I should feel guilty – I just hope the healing process has turned full circle."

"You're quite a philosopher for a…" he began.

"For a what? For an uneducated moron, is that what you meant?" The look on his face told me I'd replied far too quickly.

"No," he said. "But philosophy like that usually comes from… well from…"

Once again I interrupted, "from Generals and Admirals and politicians, from university professors, not from ex-Junior Seamen?"

He stared into his pint for a while, then looked up at me. "Yes, I suppose you're right. It is a bit surprising. You don't *look* much like a philosopher."

I had to concede he had a point, and I knew there was no ill-will in his questioning. "I suppose Nick," I said, "in layman's terms, I want to find a peace with myself. I can never make peace with the world and with others if I can't make it with myself first. Those I've come to meet, were once the enemy. I wanted an opportunity to reminisce and reflect on all the things that had happened; how and why they happened; what the consequences were, and to see if I could gain an understanding of what drives men to do the things they do. I wanted to find out first hand about the suffering that was inflicted upon the islanders, the sacrifice, by both those who had lived, and those who had died. To see whether that sacrifice was worth it. I wanted to see the Islands as they really are and as they should be seen and experienced."

There was a pause, then Nick asked me how I wanted to handle the meeting with the pilots the following day. He said that if I wanted to go 'outside' with them and go at them 'hammer and tongs' he'd understand, or that if I wanted to get the story on the front page of *The Times* or *The Buenos Herald* (of which he had been editor), as a journalist he could facilitate that. That pissed me off. I felt I had made my reasons clear for doing what I was doing, and it wasn't about press coverage.

"Look Nick," I said, "the purpose of this meeting is to help me come to terms with the events of twenty years ago and to put it behind me. I do not want it sensationalising or anything else like that."

He accepted that and said, "well if you want some pictures with them, I can do that if you want." It was the inevitable journalist in him coming out.

"No Nick, no," I said, underlining the point. "There are to be no tape recorders, no notebooks and I'm not even taking my camera."

Despite my determination, he still said he would take his camera, just in case, and I made a mental note to make sure he had no obvious journalistic paraphernalia with him tomorrow. After a few more pints, he was feeling the effects and made his excuses to leave.

CHAPTER 28

Meeting the Locals

There were six women at a table by the window. They beckoned me over but I was in no mood to talk so I just waved and turned back to survey the rest of the bar. "Hey," a woman's voice came. "We saw your friend leave, do you want to join us?"

The girl had been polite, and introduced herself as Anna; I introduced myself by my nickname only. She looked very sophisticated and spoke good English, it would have been rude not to answer her. I went over to the table with her and sat down. There were two small dark girls who spoke no English. Anna had a friend with her whose English was also perfect. She introduced her as Juanita, they were marketing executives and had been to university in America. The remaining two looked somewhat dubious. One was clad, it would be fair to say, 'somewhat scantily', the other was wearing black knee length boots with massive soles. Her skirt was so short it was more like a wide belt and she had a top on that looked like it had been sprayed on, or she had been poured into it. She had the most enormous cleavage, the majority of which was on show. You didn't need a degree in social behaviour to work out what those two did for a living.

I couldn't understand why two educated, sophisticated executive professionals were hanging out with them. No sooner had I sat down than the cleavage started demanding I buy her and the other five a drink. I politely told her to forget it and buy her own. She banged her elbow on the table and pointed at me, all the others agreed. I was confused, I looked to Anna.

"She is saying you are a Jew, tight with your money."

I laughed but more from surprise than from the insult. It was years since I'd heard the expression 'Jew' in the context of all Jews being mean with their money. From a personal point of view, it was absolute bollocks, I was always first to get the round in, I just didn't see the point in lashing up a bunch of women I didn't know, especially when I couldn't even talk to some of them.

The expected conversation ensued of what I was doing in Argentina, I told them I was a travel writer and had only just arrived so could not really give them an opinion of the place. They were in their element, talking about all the places I should go and what I should do and see. It was interesting and I enjoyed talking to them. They were switched on and asked about Australian business and the economy. It made a change to talk about something different.

The cleavage was getting more pissed off because she had done the rounds of the pub and no-one would buy her a drink. Juanita asked if I knew of the current economic state of Argentina. I told her that I knew it was on the verge of collapse but had not discussed it in detail with anyone. She said that she and a number of her colleagues had not been paid, or partly paid for ages. It wasn't too bad for them, being single, but the families with children to feed were in dire straits. She asked if I wanted to know more. It was late, I was pissed and politics and finance had never been my strong points. She asked me to dance instead. I wasn't sure I was going to be able to string more than a couple of steps together, I was struggling to string more than a couple of words together at that point.

We cavorted around the dance floor for a while, with me generally knocking into people and making a nuisance of myself. She took hold of me to steady me, and caught me totally unawares as she stuck the lip lock on me, passionately.

She pulled away.

"Sorry," she said, looking a little embarrassed.

"Don't be," I said, as I returned the favour. It was turning out to be a good night out. She was better looking and more shapely than Anna. I had discounted the two smaller girls from any potential because they spoke no English and the other two for obviously being hookers. The cleavage returned more pissed off than ever because I had bought a drink for Juanita and myself. She was becoming a real pain in the arse. Juanita was drinking Daquiri, the same as the rest of them. It cost virtually nothing, so I gave Anna a few US dollars and told her to get a round in for her and the other four, anything to shut the cleavage up and stop her ruining a potentially promising night for me.

I half finished my pint and didn't want any more. I was tired, I wasn't interested in anything other than sleep. I told Juanita I was leaving, kissed her, and got up and left. I had just about made it to the taxi rank, when she called out after me. I turned and waited for her to catch up.

"Can I come with you, to your hotel?"

I was flattered, it wasn't every day that things like this happened to me. Sure I was knackered but I thought, what the hell?

"OK," I said.

She walked to the other side of the taxi and as she opened the door said, "it's $50, OK?"

I knew the hotel wasn't far and the cab fare was actually about five or ten dollars so I corrected her accordingly.

"No, no. Me and you in your hotel room is $50."

It was like there was a big brick wall in my head and suddenly all the bricks started falling out.

"Pay? You expect me to pay for it?"

The look on her face was a mixture of surprise, shame, guilt. "Well what did you think?" she asked.

"I thought I'd fuckin' well scored!" I retorted. I was furious, mostly at myself for being so naïve, but also with her for thinking I was the kind of man that would go round shagging hookers. The blokes I'd always gone ashore with in the Navy were all of the same attitude – 'if you're not smooth enough to trap, then you don't deserve it'.

She'd been silent for a while. I walked round the other side of the taxi. "Well?"

She looked up and I thought she was going to cry. "I'm not a hooker, neither is Anna."

I was confused. She drew herself up and I knew she was getting defensive.

"It's OK for you," she said. "You have a job, I saw all the American dollars in your wallet, but do not think I like you just because you have money. I've enjoyed your company, you are interesting and fun and maybe you think badly of me for wanting to spend the night with you."

If I had thought that, then the words kettle, pot and black would have been more then fairly applied.

"I don't think badly of you for that, not at all. But I thought we liked each other, even if it could only be for a couple of days. Now you're asking me for money and you're the one who has asked to come and stay in my hotel. I have never paid for it and I never will, ever! So it's your call."

She took a couple of steps away and said 'I am not coming back with you, not because you won't pay but because I think the affection that we have just formed in the last few hours, has just been destroyed by you thinking I'm a prostitute. We are desperate for money. You have probably gone home with a woman you have known for only a few hours before, haven't you?"

I nodded an acknowledgement, it was pointless lying.

"But the girls you've done it with before, have done it for the same reason as me, they like you. But unlike me, they probably don't wonder where their next meal is coming from."

I did feel sorry for her, but this wasn't my problem. "Well if that's the case, you should have suggested we go out for lunch or dinner tomorrow. I would have paid." Let's face it, for US$50, you could have fed a family for a week.

I opened the taxi door.

"You bastard," she spat. "You don't care about me."

"One hundred per cent correct," I told her. "I don't care about you any more than you care about me. Good luck with finding your next meal."

I considered making a very sarcastic and crude remark, which was already making me smile. I didn't, she had it hard enough without me making it worse. She stood in the road watching as her missed meal drove away and round the corner.

I wondered how many times I had actually 'paid for it'. Taking girls to the movies, out to dinner, nightclubbing, drinks, taxis everywhere, weekends away and so forth. How much had that cost me over the years? Perhaps it would have been easier to give girls like her the money and get it out of the way without all the time and effort necessary to invest in someone you like. But investing in someone I really like is something I enjoy doing and I do not consider it a waste. I think it's a very worthwhile investment with the right person. I decided to stick with the strategy.

The day dawned and I hung out of the window and craned my neck round to see what sort of light was coming down the small shitty vertical passage. The answer was good – it was sunlight. I went downstairs, deliberately by-passing the teeth destroying coffee and prison bread. I asked the man on reception if I could make an international phone call and charge it to my room. In November 2001, two of my old school friends, Siggy and Linda, were in Brisbane and came to stay with me. Unbeknown to me, Linda had been best mates with Maxine, the girl I had a real thing for when we were eighteen and nineteen. She gave me her phone number. I rang Maxine a few weeks later. She was really pleased to hear from me. I told her I would be in England the following May and I'd like to meet her for a beer. We had about eighteen years to catch up on.

I dialed the number with some trepidation. Maxine answered.

"Hi Max," I said. "It's Adam."

"I got your postcard," she said. "Are you still in the Falklands?"

"No, Buenos Aires. I arrive in Norwich on Thursday. Do you want to meet for a beer?"

She laughed. "You get around don't you? Well if you don't come and see me for a beer on the Thursday, you'll be dead by the Friday!"

I laughed too. "I'll call you from London."

Outside, I stopped at a street caravan and bought appalling breakfast and equally dreadful coffee. I left half of each and walked round the corner to find a similar establishment whose cuisine was considerably nearer the five-star rating than the one-star counterpart I had just tried. The proprietor could not have been more helpful and friendly, asking where I was from, what I was doing there, did I need directions etc. What a charming and friendly people and a beautiful and cultured place. What justice was there in screwing it up so badly?

I eventually found the office of TMP Worldwide with whom I was employed in Brisbane. Like most office blocks, there were security guards in the foyer who were immediately on their feet as I walked in. They seemed to do it to almost everyone. Although they didn't speak English, we fairly quickly established that I wanted to meet with TMP Worldwide, but they wanted to know why. Fortunately I brought some business cards with me and told them, "trabajo" (work). There were people coming downstairs from the offices in immaculate business suits, carrying brief cases and folders of papers. They looked at me, as the security guards did, with disdain.

"Quien," they asked me. "Who?"

I pronounced as best I could, "Cristina Bomchil, la Directore Generale."

They laughed. As if the Director General, would see someone looking like this. Wankers, I was having a good day and now they come along and ruin it.

I snatched the phone. "Llamar!" (Call her.)

One of the men dialed the number and read out the details on my business card. He threw my business card back down on the desk and indicated towards the stairs with a simple, "dos". Good job he didn't know what the word 'tosser' meant.

The reception was immaculate, as you would expect from a company that turned over US$28 billion. I announced to the receptionist that I had an appointment with the Director and handed over my business card. No sooner had I finished speaking than a small and slender vision of loveliness appeared around the corner, extending her hand.

"Cristina?" I asked.

"No," she said. "I am Lucila, Lucila Perolo, one of her senior consultants, please follow me."

She led me through the labyrinth that new offices always seem to be before you get used to them, and introduced me to some of the consultants, including her friend Dolores Sojo, who was equally attractive. We sat in one of their meeting rooms, discussing how their business operated. In lots of ways it wasn't too dissimilar from our own. One of the main differences was the state of the economy, which meant very few clients had money to spare for recruitment, that's if they could afford to take anyone on in the first place. The phone rang and Lucila said her boss could see us now. I was ushered into an imposing office. The directors in my own office sat at open plan workstations, the same as the plebs. This was more the style, dark oak desks, plush settees and huge plants. Cristina welcomed me in and I apologised for my appearance saying I had been trekking for four weeks. Lucila appeared with tea, coffee and biscuits on a silver tray. This was like the Hilton. We discussed the business situation. I wanted to know how their economy had gone so pear-shaped. Cristina was open with her opinions.

"Corruption, nepotism and gross financial mismanagement," she said. "Many people are put into the wrong jobs because of the people they knew, as opposed to their actual abilities."

She went on to talk about watching the decline of the country and being powerless to stop it, despite it being a democracy. There were people who had lost their life savings. Sums of up to $100,000 had disappeared, badly invested by the banks or simply stolen, from people who were about to retire with nothing to retire on. No wonder there was rioting in the streets and the banks were boarded up.

They asked about business in Brisbane and the services that other divisions in Australia provided. I told her that an expanding part of the business was Career Assessment and Development and went into a bit of detail. That had been something Cristina had been trying to break into, to support one aspect of the failing economy of her business.

Lucila had been to Australia the previous year to visit her sister in Sydney. She had loved it. We moved away from the business talk and they asked where I had been and where else I was going and what I thought of Buenos Aires. I had rehearsed this, knowing it would probably be asked. I told them after Tahiti and Easter Island, I had spent three weeks trekking in Tierra Del Fuego and was going on to the UK after this. I was careful not to mention that I was English, I saw nothing to be gained by doing so.

"You sound more British than Australian," Cristina said.

I tried to let it slide and not even register an acknowledgment. I mentioned to Lucila that I was having a drink with a friend that night, knowing that I would need one after meeting the pilots and would she and Dolores care to join us. She told me it was her birthday the following day and she would be working until about 8pm that night. I was surprised at them working so late but then found out they don't start until 9am at the earliest. I said I would call her anyway.

I said goodbye and left, ignoring the security guards. Across the road were lots of souvenir shops. They had some great artifacts and under different circumstances, I would have liked to have taken some home. In the first two I looked around, the proprietors tried to force stuff on me, so I left. I wandered aimlessly around for an hour or so, not really wanting to do or see anything, or go anywhere.

For the first time in weeks I was bored. I was starving and found a café. The menu was all in Spanish so I thought I'd chance my arm and ordered something without having a clue what it was. The waiter brought me a paper, which I thought was awfully civilised but I couldn't read it. I pointed to the section of the menu 'beverages' and asked for something I presumed was a fruit juice. It was, but sour. I ordered a Coke. Shortly after, the waiter brought me the meal. I couldn't even begin to describe it, but I thought I'd try it. It was dire. I ate a couple of mouthfuls but couldn't stomach it so I called the waiter back and ordered steak, egg and chips. I was pissed off as I could have got that in some greasy café in Great Yarmouth, or worse, Majorca. The steak though, was as good as the rest I'd had there, and it cost virtually nothing. They really know how to feed and breed their cattle over there.

CHAPTER 29

Las Malvinas War Memorial

After I'd eaten, I took in a few more sights and whether intentionally or not, I still do not know to this day, I ended up back at the Las Malvinas war memorial. I stood some distance away and looked at the beautifully sculpted marble architecture. As I stepped forward I saw three women, all of them in tears. The poppies I had left yesterday had fallen from the plaque, I picked them up and re-secured them.

I looked at the women and estimated their ages to be respectively, around mid twenties, mid forties and late sixties or early seventies. The middle-aged woman was comforting the older one who was sobbing and clutching a photograph. The younger of the three looked at me for a while and then came over, drying her eyes. She asked something in Spanish which I didn't understand, and I told her so, but used Spanish to do it. She showed me a black and white photograph of a man who looked to be in his mid twenties. "Papa," she said, and started talking again in Spanish, and again she started to cry. She stepped forward and I put my arms around her and she cried on me, like I had cried in San Carlos cemetery. Between sobs she was catching her breath and gasping the odd word. I didn't have a clue what she was on about, I presumed she was talking about him. She stopped crying and looked up at me.

"Que, que?" she asked.

"No entiendo Castellano," I told her.

"You don't speak Spanish," she said in near perfect English. "Well what are you doing here then, why did you put the poppies there? Were you in the Malvinas?"

This was dangerous ground; the family had obviously lost the bloke in the photograph.

I looked at her. For a minute I thought her face filled with hate. How would my sister have reacted if she'd been faced with one of the men who had killed her brother. I felt the tear run down my face, it dripped onto her jacket. She produced her well used and very damp handkerchief and handed it to me.

"You're British aren't you? You fought for the British didn't you?"

I nodded a confirmation. My voice wavered, there was a huge lump in my throat, my eyes blurred with tears.

"Please understand me," I said. "I came here out of respect, not to gloat over the outcome, but because every man whose name appears here left behind people like you three ladies. I know there are widows, parents without sons, and children without fathers here, just the same as in Britain."

"And you," she asked gently, "did you lose anyone? Relatives or friends?"

I nodded. "Yes, I lost my ship. It was my home and twenty men in her," I told her matter of factly.

That shocked her. "Twenty?"

Again I nodded, then, "tell me about your father," I said.

She went quiet for a moment, then the words tumbled out. "He was a soldier, I was only five, my brother was seven. Mama and Papa came to us one day and told us Papa was going to do his patriotic duty and defend the Malvinas. I was a little too young to understand, but my brother was ecstatic, he had already learned about it at school. Papa went away, we all went to see him off, there were hundreds and thousands of people waving flags, cheering and I remember the car horns blaring all the time. Papa hugged me and told me to be brave, and he told my brother that he was now the man of the house and to look after Mama. Then he was gone. We never saw him again."

She looked at the photo again and sobbed once more, her tears dropping onto the glass. I gave her a moment, then asked whether the two women with her were her family.

"No, we are not related," she said. "I met them here once. The older lady is always very upset. She lost her son, her only son, he was 18. Now she has no-one left in the world. The other lady lost her husband; she was only 25 at the time and pregnant. Her husband never saw his child."

I could understand that. At least one of the men lost in *Sheffield* had fathered a child he didn't live to see. The emotion was crushing me, suffocating me. How many other children had grown up not knowing or remembering their father, because he'd been killed in this senseless conflict? Even though it was a cool spring day I was flushed incredibly hot and I could feel the perspiration running down my back and soaking my clothes.

I wanted to leave. It was becoming unbelievably emotionally taxing. I knew I'd have to get my act together if I was to be composed when I met the pilots later that afternoon. I didn't want to sit in front of them and cry. Bugger it, I'd come this far and seen it through, there was no going back now.

The two older women started to move towards us. The girl spoke in Spanish. "No, no, don't tell them!" I said, but she ignored me and carried on.

They stopped and stared at me and I thought, oh Christ! What did she have to do that for? I really didn't know what to do for the best. The middle-aged woman approached me slowly, fixing me with a most unnerving gaze. I felt like a butterfly pinned to a board. I honestly thought she was going to hit me and a multitude of self-defence moves raced through my mind. She stopped a metre or so away from me.

"You were there in 1982, in the Malvinas with the British?"

It seemed pointless lying. I nodded. She backed away to the wall of the memorial and pointed to a name.

"Do you know who that is?" she demanded.

I shook my head. I wished I could have spoken, but the words wouldn't come.

"That was my husband," she said, icily. "We had been married only two years. He has a child he never saw. Are you proud of that?"

"Senora," I said, and meant it. "I am sorry for the loss of your husband. War is nothing to be proud of. But if pride must come into it somewhere, you should be proud that he died bravely, fighting for a cause he believed in and that he thought was just and right."

There was stone cold silence for a moment, then she spat: "Fighting bravely, you call it. He was on the *General Belgrano*, torpedoed and sunk without warning, outside the war zone, en route back home to Argentina. Doesn't that make it murder? Or piracy?"

I saw nothing to be achieved by arguing with her, I'd come here to recover from the fight, not start another one, I turned to leave. The young girl spoke quickly to her, and in harsh tones. The older woman broke down and started crying again.

"I'm sorry, I'm sorry," she said.

I shot a questioning look at the young one.

"I told her what happened to you too, and that you are here out of respect for our men."

The older woman spoke through her tears. "It is an honourable thing for you to do, to come here and pay homage to our lost loved ones too."

I nodded in reconciliation. "Senora, I have already told your friend, every man here left someone behind. You yourself are the same age as some of my friend's widows. This girl here is the same age as some of the children of the friends I lost. This other lady here is about the same age as my mum. I was the same age as her son. The only difference between us is the language we speak. We were all thrown together into the cauldron of war and look what it achieved."

I paused for a moment, then cast my arm toward the memorial wall. "There are memorials like this all over the islands, all over Britain, with names of young men like your husband and his friends, who were catapulted into the jaws of political motivation and they laid down their lives for it. They, and all the British men who were lost, were sacrificed upon the altar of politicians' ambitions. They all died together, and are now brothers-in-arms. Comprehendo? Brother-in-arms?"

"Si, comprehendo," she said between sobs.

"The reason for my visit here today is to honour their memory as fighting men. Especially those who were lost at sea. It doesn't matter what ensign they flew, they were still professional sailors. I am here to pay them the respect that they have earned."

I stepped toward her slowly, wishing that I was dressed a bit smarter and cleaner. "Look senora," I said, reaching out a hand. "I'm sure your husband would want you to be proud of him, his memory and the part he played. Let him rest, let go of your anguish and just honour his name."

She started to cry again and I stepped forward, and the two of us hugged. Her hair and scent reminded me of one of the girls I worked with.

"I did not think the British were so honourable as to come here and pay their respects," she said.

"Why not?" I asked.

She shrugged. "It is just what I had been led to believe."

"That's total bollocks," I assured her, without thinking.

"Bollocks? What is bollocks?" she said.

I was hard pushed not to burst out laughing. "It means... untrue."

I became aware of the older woman, who had moved close to us. I wondered if she spoke English and my question was soon answered. The younger one was talking to her and explaining. The woman looked even older now. She appeared to have aged by a decade in the ten minutes we'd been there. She showed me the photo. Her son didn't look old enough to be in the army. Odds on he'd been a conscript, probably the same age as I had been.

She started speaking, and the young girl translated. She kept her eyes fixed on the old woman, the old woman kept her eyes fixed on me. Her son had been killed before the British landed on May 21st. She still to this day does not know whether he was killed by British shelling, a Harrier bombing raid, or hypothermia. His body was never returned to Argentina and he has no known grave. If we hadn't landed they could have repatriated the bodies, or buried them in marked plots somewhere in the islands. This seemed to substantiate some of the claims I had heard.

She had stopped and was waiting for a response. I took her hands. They were thin and frail, and bone cold. I asked the young girl to translate for me.

"Your son was a brave young man who died fighting for a cause that he believed in. Wherever he is, he's at peace."

She looked at me with bloodshot eyes and the tears ran down her craggy face. I let go of her hands and turned towards the wall. As I did, the young girl embraced the old woman, and she cried the hollow cry of a desolate and lonely old woman. I had never felt so much sorrow and pity for anyone in all my life.

I went back to the far end of the memorial and ran my fingers across the entire length, across a fraction of the six hundred and fifty names. *Diego, Oscar, Luis, José.* And again I found myself thinking, the only difference is the language they spoke.

It seems to me that war has no real result other than suffering and tragedy. There are no winners – everyone loses one way or another. The war and the suffering go on, punctuated by the sobbing of the bereaved like these three women. It goes on long after the reason it started has been forgotten. I paused at the far end of the wall and turned to the three women. Their gaze met mine.

"Adios," I said, and they nodded. There was nothing else to say. Then I turned and walked away without looking back.

CHAPTER 30

Meeting the Enemy

I had to get my bearings and rendezvous with Nick. Once I had located the place to meet I bought a bottle of Coke and a Mars Bar. I wolfed them down and felt sick. My energy was sapped and I felt knackered. I had intended to take it easy the day I met the pilots, I had wanted to be as sharp as possible for the meeting. Not much chance of that now, I felt like I hadn't eaten or slept properly in days. This was not going according to plan and I hadn't even started one of the most important aspects of the trip. I was pissed off with myself for letting things get so pear shaped.

I didn't see the point in telling Nick about this afternoon's encounter with the three women. He might turn it into a story and embarrass the women. I spotted him at the pre-appointed place.

"Come on then let's get it over with," I said.

"Are you sure you still want to go through with it?" Nick asked. I didn't hesitate. "I've come this far, there's no turning back now." We set off for the Argentine Naval Officers' Club.

We met outside the Naval Club in Buenos Aires. I was in backpacker's jeans and boots so I knew there was no way we'd be holding a meeting in there. Strictly jacket and tie, very much based on Royal Navy standards, I found the irony almost amusing.

Captain Colombo was standing outside on the steps. I recognised him from somewhere but couldn't remember exactly where, a documentary or book about the conflict perhaps. It dawned on me later how much he resembled a cross between Eric Sykes and 'Blakey' from *On The Buses*. I can't imagine he had to chase many of his subordinates around with the catchphrase 'I 'ate you Butler, I'll get you' as they sniggered away to their fighters and bombers.

He was immaculately turned out in slacks and a blue blazer. I wished I had a suit. I was pissed off that some *Sheffields*, would have been ashamed of me turning up in that state. I strode in front of Nick and introduced myself. We looked each other in the eye and shook hands. There was a slight pause, for about fifty years it seemed.

"Please follow me," he said in perfect English. As we crossed the road to the designated meeting place, Captain Colombo, Jorgé, said, "In Spanish my name is pronounced 'Hawhay'. In English, the equivalent is George, please use whichever you feel most comfortable with."

I told him the Spanish was fine and mentioned that I had been practicing a bit for my stay in South America. He asked for the correct English pronunciation of Adam, and whether there was a Spanish equivalent. "I don't think there is," I said, so he settled for Adam.

We went to the basement of the Sheraton Hotel and Jorgé ordered coffee for himself and Nick while I settled for a mineral water. My throat had dried out so much it was sore and I immediately asked for another.

We sat down, Jorgé to my right, Nick to my left and the space opposite empty, awaiting the arrival of the other pilot. Jorgé opened the conversation with small talk about whether I had been to Argentina and Buenos Aires before and what my thoughts and opinions of the city and the country were. He thanked me for taking the time and trouble to come and meet him. He said that for him, this was a meeting of exceptional significance and asked me if it was the same for me.

I told him it was, that it was something I wanted and needed to do. As far as I knew no men had met under these circumstances but that wasn't why I had wanted to do it. There was another silence and I waited to see what Jorgé had to say. I thought there was bound to be some politics but the man proved me wrong. He was a man of dignity and integrity; a highly intelligent and educated man, fluent in four languages, a man worthy of holding a military officer's commission, and worthy of his position and rank – a truly worthy adversary.

He placed both his hands on the table and took a deep breath. This was difficult for him too.

"You must understand Adam," he said, "that I am a military man, as you are, and whatever happened, there was never anything personal. I don't hold anything against you. I know that just like us, you were 'simply carrying out orders'. I know that in the same situation you would do the same again, as would I."

He looked me squarely in the eye and I knew that he was seeking an exoneration or a forgiveness for the events of twenty years ago. I think he also realised it was forthcoming.

"Tell me about the events of May 1982 Jorgé," I said. For a moment, he looked as if one of his grandchildren had said 'tell me what you did in the war Papa', and he wasn't sure were to start. Then, the words tumbled out.

"I am 62 years old and the grandfather of five grandchildren. Flying was a very important part of my life and still is. I flew a mission on May 2nd which was curtailed by technical problems (if only the one on the 4th had been…). I selected Armando and Augusto myself for the May 4th mission against you, although we did not know who, or what specifically the targets would be."

His gaze was distant and I could see that he was re-living those days and events and I wondered how many times he had done that and like myself, wondered what might have happened had the outcome been different.

He swallowed hard, looked at me for a while and swallowed again. "Adam, I am very sorry for the loss of *Sheffield* and for the loss of the men in her."

I interrupted. "Jorgé, you must never be sorry for doing your job, doing what you were ordered to do, and for doing what you thought, and probably still do think, was right. If you are sorry for the loss of the men and for the sorrow and anguish their families suffered, and have done ever since, then for that I am grateful."

"Yes," he said. "I am sorry for the loss of the men and for their families' grief. But you must understand Adam, that it was war, regardless of what anyone else thought or said, it *was* war and in war, men die. They always have, they always will. I am sorry but that is the way it will always be." He was very emphatic in his points.

He leant forward, hands clenched on the edge of the table. His knuckles were white.

He was silent again, lost in thought. I emptied my water glass and before I had finished, he snapped his fingers and called out, "Si Senor, por favor". The waiter appeared at the table as I lowered my glass, and as he refilled it, I noticed my hand was trembling. I lowered my hands, clenched them beneath the table to try to stop the tremors, then I grabbed the glass and gulped down more water.

"Can I ask you some questions please Jorgé?" I said.

"Certainly," he replied. He seemed to have got his second wind. It appeared to me that he felt a sense of relief, certainly he was more relaxed, as though finally, he had been allowed to get something off his chest which had weighed heavily and preyed on his mind. Maybe like me, he was confronting his twenty year old demons and finally exorcising his ghosts.

"Did you agree with your government's orders of April 1982 to invade the islands?"

He hesitated as if to construct an answer; "I am still a very well known Naval Aviator, and I must ask you to keep my comments and responses to questions like this confidential between you and I." He gave me a questioning look.

"You have my word as a gentleman and a fellow military man," I assured him.

It sounded like a cliché but I meant it. Jorgé then went into detail on his opinion of the then military junta that ruled his country, and their reasons for invading the Falkland Islands, and whether he thought their reasons were valid. On occasion, he referred to them in the English vernacular, which sounded as unusual as Las Malvinas does coming from a Brit. Before I could ask another question he leant forward.

"Adam, let me ask you something. You cannot deny geography, physical geography. Physically where are those islands located? Nearer to you, or to us?"

I gave him the truth, that physically they were located nearer to Argentina, though that fact did not give any country a right to invade and attempt to take over.[14]

"Well that may be the case," he said, "but did you British not take those islands by force from Argentina in 1833?"

He certainly had a point, but I pointed out that not a shot was fired in 1833.

"So what did you intend doing with all those people then," I asked him. "Six generations of people steeped in English culture, speaking English, their way of life, even down to details like driving on the left? Did that give you a right to go in and dictate that everything they had ever known would disappear and change?"

He shook his head. "No. Nothing gives any country that right," he said, "but you must understand, the Malvinas is an emotional issue to the Argentinian people. We will never, never give up our claim of sovereignty over those islands. Even if we have joint sovereignty or just place a flag on there, we will never relinquish our claim."

---

[14] The Argentinians have since declared the islands part of the Tierra Del Fuego province.

I thought about telling Jorgé about my last day there only three days previously when I watched the Queen's birthday parade on Ross Road. I took photos of Islander children about the same age as my own daughter (seven) waving their little Union flags and celebrating the official day of their Monarch. I didn't see such a move as constructive and I didn't want any animosity to spoil the meeting, but no way was that loyalty to the crown ever going to change – not voluntarily anyway.

"Will you ever try to take the islands by force again?" I asked.

Jorgé thought for a moment, but then shook his head. "No," he said. "This is a different Argentina. Different from the days of the seventies and eighties. The youth of Argentina have grown up in peace and democracy. They would not stand for more aggression and violence now. Any officer who graduates with a commission now must speak at least one other language apart from Spanish."

Although he sounded convincing, I recalled the frenzy and fervour of national pride and excitement, the thronging masses, the ever swelling crowd in front of Galtieri in 1982 as he swaggered on the balcony of Evita's palace. He united their country like no-one had done for a long time and given that it was such an emotional issue and they all felt so strongly about it, would they all walk away if the chips were down again? There was a small corner of me thinking, 'I'd like to see you try that shit again'. A bigger part though hoped there wouldn't be another war over the islands, for lots of reasons, not least because I didn't want other people trying to get rid of the shit I was trying to dispense with.

"Hypothetically," I said, turning my thoughts back to Jorgé, "what would you have done if you'd won and retained possession of the islands? Would you have moved there? How many Argentinians would have moved there?"

He sighed and paused, then with a heavy shrug, he said, "I do not know. Personally I would not have moved there. I do not know who would. Half of Tierra Del Fuego is empty, the government is offering significant tax incentives for people to move there. I know, I know, I do not have the answers to those issues. But I can tell you that with the issue of joint sovereignty we would not try to change their lives but would respect their culture and history as it is."

Then I asked him one of the key questions I wanted an answer to.

"Jorgé, what sort of state do you think the islands would be in now?"

He gave me a wry look. "Probably the same as Argentina."

At the time of our meeting Argentina was on the verge of total economic collapse. From his response, I deduced that he meant the islands, instead of being almost totally self-sufficient and virtually able to support themselves for three years, such were their cash reserves, would by now have long food queues, closed banks, and poverty and rioting in the streets. He didn't comment further so I took it that he did not want to appear to be negative about his homeland.

Throughout this discussion, Nick had stayed silent. Jorgé turned to him now and asked him to go and see whether Mayora was at the club. As he rose and left, I sensed that Jorgé had wanted to get rid of him for a while so

---

Half of the Argentine population of 36 million live below the poverty line according to the latest census figures, reported Juan Carlos Del Bello head of National Census and Statistic Institute, INDEC.

Mr Del Bello said the number actually jumped from 14 to 18 million during the last six months as a direct consequence of the current situation with constant increase in food process, unemployment and frozen salaries.

During the current first quarter retail prices increased 21% reflecting the huge devaluation of the Argentine currency that rocketed from the pegged one dollar-one peso to three pesos to the US dollar in four months. 'The dramatic increase of the last few months has been caused by the huge 35.2% increase in basic food process, particularly last April when they actually jumped 17.7%' said Mr Del Bello.

According to Mr Del Bello in lower income families 46% of income is invested in food, and therefore the dramatic impact of the last month when beef, flour, oil experienced unprecedented increases.

A family couple plus two children, is now considered below the poverty line when their monthly income is below the equivalent of US$186, and indigence is defined when the group makes less than US$79 per month. According to INDEC, 6.5million Argentines are in the indigence category.

Regarding unemployment the latest official report dates from October 2001, when it reached 18.3%. However officials in the Ministry of Economy admit that in May the figure could be closer to 25%.

Five million Argentines under the poverty line live in Buenos Aires and its metropolitan influence area.

'With frozen salaries, rocketing food prices, it's hard to see how the situation in the short term can be reverted,' indicated Mr Del Bello

Source: Penguin News, Falkland Islands   17 May 2002

---

we could talk alone, away from anyone who had not been there and shared those experiences.

"Adam," he said, as Nick disappeared, "do you know who was the oldest man killed in the conflict?"

"Yes," I said, "it was Captain Ian North, the Master of the *Atlantic Conveyor*.

He nodded. "That is correct. I believe Captain North was about the same age as I am now. Some years ago I wrote to his family to express my regret at his loss. I did not get a response, but there again I did not expect one. Again it was my squadron who were responsible for the loss of the *Atlantic Conveyor* and the men aboard her. I once met Sandy Woodward in the USA. Do you know Sandy?"

"I know who he is obviously," I said. "He was the British Admiral who commanded the Task Force, but I have never met him."

"He is a man without much of a sense of humour," Jorgé told me, and that didn't come as any surprise.

"I introduced myself," he continued, "and we talked at length about the events of 1982 and he told me what a thorn in his side my squadron was. Do you know Sharky Ward."

"Yes, Jorgé," I said. "I know who he is. He was a Sea Harrier pilot and the Commanding Officer of 801 Naval Air Squadron, a bit of an 'ace' by all accounts and he kept you guys at bay on occasion. I think he was still on *Invincible* when I joined her in '83 but we're not exactly best mates."

Jorgé laughed. "I would very much like to meet Sharky Ward one day," he said.

"He's written a book about those events Jorgé, *Sea Harrier over the Falklands*. It would make very interesting reading for you. Nick Tozer tells me you think, irrespective of all the external factors surrounding the attack on *Sheffield* that you know about, you would have hit us anyway?"

"Absolutely," he replied. "I know the factors you mean, about the absence of your Anti-Air Warfare Officer, but they are, and always would have been irrelevant. If a ship is worked up to fight, it matters not if one officer is absent. There is, or should be another man immediately ready to step in and act in his position. If that is not the case then that ship is not ready to fight and defend itself."

I swallowed hard and felt myself flush red with fury. I took this as a personal slur on myself, my shipmates and on *Sheffield*. The ship held the trophies for High Seas Sea Dart Firings and Naval Gunfire Support. But because of this, we had all lived with this guilt for twenty years.

I took a deep breath, and answered in as controlled a manner as I could. "You're wrong Jorgé. If only one, just one of those factors from the equation had been removed, then things would have been very different, however, they weren't and they aren't."

"You know Adam," he said. "There are three things that would have made the outcome of the whole war very different. They were that you had the new Sidewinder missile and we did not. You had all your aircraft under constant positive radar control, and you knew where our aircraft were so you could vector the Harriers onto us. And you also had your Harriers on CAP (Combat Air Patrol) with a time over target of about forty minutes, whereas we had a maximum time over target of five minutes, only enough for one pass at our targets. Had those things been different, then I feel sure, the outcome would also have been."

"Maybe Jorgé," I said with a heavy sigh. "But they weren't different – for either of us."

He made to respond but then changed tack. "Armando should be here any minute. He speaks English but he is not fluent."

As though he'd heard him, Nick returned with Lt Cdr Armando Mayora, one of the pilots who had flown the attack mission against *Sheffield* on 4th May. Jorgé leapt to his feet and the two old comrades shook hands warmly, exchanging greetings in Spanish.

"This…," Jorgé said to me, pointing at Mayora and laughing, "is the bad guy!"

"No, no bad guy!" Mayora protested. I stood and we shook hands and exchanged pleasantries. As we sat down, a strange silence descended on the meeting. I wasn't sure why or what had changed in that split second, and I wasn't sure how to break it. I suddenly felt very uncomfortable. Nick broke the ice. "Armando only has forty minutes to spare," he said. I knew that would be enough.

"How old are you Armando?" I asked, turning to face him.

"I am forty eight," he said. "And you? You are the same age?"

I laughed out loud. I knew my shaved head added a few years onto me but I didn't think it was quite eleven. "No," I said. "I'm thirty seven."

As I watched, I saw both Colombo and Mayora do the same mental arithmetic, and they exclaimed simultaneously, "17! You were only seventeen in the Malvinas? So young. You were just a boy!"

I nodded at them. "There were a lot of boys down there, or at least they

248

were boys when they went, but they returned as men. I know that sounds like a cliché… you understand 'cliché' si?"

"Si, we understand," they responded. After a pause, Colombo asked, "Do you know who the youngest person there was? And the youngest person killed?"

Of course I could answer both questions, and told him so. "The youngest British person to serve in the war was 16 year old Junior Seaman Timothy Jones from one of the Castle Class patrol boats. I subsequently served with him on the destroyer *Nottingham*. The youngest man killed was a Paratrooper by the name of Jason Burt who was only 17.

They couldn't hide their surprise, and I read the look that said the British had sent their 16 and 17 year old boys to do the government's dirty work for them. I answered the unasked question. "Yes, they were – we were all volunteers."

"You know that there were many conscripts in the Argentine forces?" said Jorgé. I thought of the old cliché 'give me one volunteer over ten 'pressed' men any day' – a reference that a man who has volunteered for the military is going to be far more willing to fight and probably far better at it, than someone who has been forced into it against their will.

"Yes I know that," I said. I did not say that it wouldn't have made any difference because it probably would have done. Maybe the war would have gone on longer, maybe we would have taken more casualties, we'll never know but either way I knew we would still have won, the outcome would still have been the same. I saw nothing constructive being achieved by trying to inflict my point upon the two pilots.

"Armando," I said, turning my attention back to him. "Tell me about May 4th." He took a long deep breath and fixed his gaze on the ceiling. Then he looked at me, his face implacable. "That is a very important day for us. Not a day we celebrate, but a day that the Argentine Navy showed that it was, it is, a force to be reckoned with." He hesitated to see if his answer was enough.

"Go on," I urged him.

The two men looked at each other, and Jorgé raised his eyebrows. Armando nodded and Jorgé took over the briefing in true military style and detail.

"On the morning of 4th May, shortly after 05:00 hours, a Neptune Maritime Patrol Aircraft belonging to the Comando de Aviacion Naval Argentina, (CANA; Argentine Naval Aviation Command) took off from

Rio Grande Naval Base. The aircraft, callsign 'Mercurio' belonged to the reconnaissance squadron and was flown by Captain Ernesto Proni. Between the hours of 07:45 and 08:45 the aircraft had three contacts with British warships. Captain Proni was then ordered to avoid any further contact with you and proceed with a search pattern as if looking for survivors from the *General Belgrano*. When the news of his contacts reached CANA HQ, a Super Etendard mission was called. I personally selected Corvette Captain Augusto Bedacarratz and Frigate Lieutenant Armando Mayora here to fly the mission. I conducted the mission briefing. The Super Etendards (nicknamed SUEs by their crews) took off from Rio Gallegos at 9:45am, each carrying an underslung AM-39 Aerospatiale Exocet anti-ship missile."

Armando then took over the story again. "We already had a good idea where your ships where from the information we got from the original intelligence, from Captain Proni. Augusto was flying aircraft 0752/3-A-202 and using the callsign 'Aries'. I was callsign 'Boina' and was flying 0753/3-A-203. We climbed to about fifteen thousand feet and rendezvoused with a tanker, piloted by Commodoro Pessana at 10:00 and conducted air to air refuelling for the mission. Then we went low flying at about 400 knots to conserve fuel because the round trip was more than 800 miles. We were also in radio silence. At 10:30 Proni radioed us with updated information and coordinates. He then turned the Neptune for home and he never flew in the war after that, the aircraft was grounded."

"When we were 58 miles away from[15] you, we climbed to 450 metres and activated our radars for two sweeps but saw nothing. Augusto decided to continue searching and 32 miles later, when 26 miles away from the ships, we climbed and switched on our search radars and found two contacts, one large and one small. We believed the bigger of the two to be an aircraft carrier. We programmed the aircraft weapons systems with the coordinates, and dived back below your ships' radar horizons – we believed at the time we had still not been detected. We then climbed to 500 for the final time. There was tremendous noise and it wasn't until I saw fire from beneath Captain Bedacarratz's plane, that I fired my missile. We then turned our aircraft into steep tight dives to avoid any anti aircraft missiles that may be inbound and flew directly back here, home

---

[15] The reason they know this now is from hindsight reports from the British units that initially held them at this range on their own radars.

to Argentina. We did not know whether the mission had been a success until we heard the news announced by the British World Service that night."

I remembered my family telling me about gut-wrenching horror, disbelief and sheer shock as the news was announced. Hundreds of families panic stricken with worry, and for some the following morning the confirmation that the most terrible of their fears was borne out. Whomever their loved one aboard was, they would not be coming home. Armando paused awaiting my reaction.

"Did you celebrate, Armando?" I said, knowing the answer already. I knew he had celebrated, they all had.

"Yes we did," he said. The man sitting across the table from me had celebrated the deaths of twenty of my shipmates that he took a part in killing. I wondered if he really was a callous cold-blooded killer, with no remorse or sorrow in him.

"Did you celebrate when you torpedoed the *General Belgrano*?"

Initially I didn't reply. We had celebrated, we all did, albeit only momentarily before the realities set in. You were beating the adversary, the enemy, you were getting him so he couldn't get you. Armando wasn't a callous killer, he was a military man, a pilot, a man doing his job, nothing more than that. I remembered that military people must remain personally detached from the potential effects of their actions in case it affects their judgement and/or actions.

He paused, and I wasn't sure what to say. He then addressed a question to Nick in Spanish. Nick turned to me. "Did both missiles impact *Sheffield* in the same place?" he said.

Surely, I thought, after all this time they don't still believe that both missiles had hit *Sheffield*. It's widely documented and accepted that one missile had gone wide and ditched in the sea.

I took a deep breath. "Only one, *uno* missile hit us," I said.

Mayora looked confused, and the look, and Nick's unspoken question said, "What happened to the other one?"

"It passed our stern and headed towards HMS *Yarmouth*," I said. "We don't know what happened next. Some reports say it flew down the side, some across the stern or over the top."

"Over the top?" Armando asked, looking nonplussed.

"It's 20 year old hearsay," I said, "but I can tell you for sure it passed astern of us, headed towards *Yarmouth* and ditched in the sea."

251

The look on his face revealed confusion and disappointment, maybe because this was his missile. The senior pilot, Lt-Cdr Augusto Bedacarratz fired the one that hit *Sheffield*. Bedacarratz had a farm some distance from Buenos Aires and was unable to attend this meeting. He had sent his regrets.

"Armando," I said, "how do you feel about the loss of life in *Sheffield*?"

He hesitated. I imagined he understood and was considering his answer but Nick repeated the question in Spanish.

"Si, si..." Mayora raised his hand indicating that he was thinking. His response was long-winded, half in English and half in Spanish, which Nick translated. It basically equated to 'although I am sorry men died, I was doing my job and I'd do it again, without hesitation'. It was pretty near what I had expected.

Mayora looked directly at me. "My friend was killed in the Malvinas, how do you feel about that?"

I paused, not because I needed to think about how I felt but because of how it was. I swallowed hard, finding it difficult to believe that I was on the verge of getting upset at the fact that the man who had almost killed me had lost one of his friends. I was however, genuinely moved by the thought of grieving families. A lump came to my throat as I composed my response.

"Armando," I finally said, "I am really, really sorry for the loss of your friend."

I meant it.

Colombo rose from his seat. "Gentlemen, you must excuse me, I have to go."

He sounded as though he was excusing himself from a gentleman's club in Mayfair.

"Of course Jorgé, thank you so much for coming," I said.

He extended his hand. "Thank *you*, for coming to see us, for traveling all this distance and for making the effort to come to Buenos Aires."

We shook hands firmly, and warmly, then as he left, I sat down again with Mayora. He checked his watch.

"Do you still fly, Armando?" I asked him.

"No, not for a living anymore," he said. "I am now in sales and I have a presentation to do for a client." From Naval Aviator and war hero to salesman – it seemed a bit of a comedown and reminded me of two older men in the village where I grew up. They had been Spitfire pilots during the Battle of Britain, had shot down enemy aircraft, and had been shot down themselves. One had ended up a petrol pump attendant, in the days when such people existed, and the other, a painter and decorator. It seemed inglorious to such men, who deserved more.

Armando briefly described what he did, and as I had suspected, he was far more than a salesman, he was a senior executive in business development. He asked me how long I had stayed in the Navy, what I did after the conflict and why I actually left in the end. We made further small talk until very shortly it was time for him to go; he had stayed far longer than the forty minutes he'd initially allocated. He exchanged a few words in Spanish with Nick, who when I gave an inquisitive look, merely waved the words away, as though they were not relevant. Then Armando rose to leave, and extended his hand towards me. We clasped hands, then embraced, and he spoke to me in Spanish.

"No te preocupes?"

"No, no hard feelings," I told him, and after exchanging goodbyes with Nick, he turned and left.

I stood and watched him go, then after he had disappeared, I collapsed into my seat, exhausted. I felt as if I'd climbed a mountain carrying a pack mule. I noticed another glass of water had appeared so I picked it up and swallowed it, almost in one. Nick was talking to me, but I wasn't hearing him.

"Christ, I could murder a pint," I said, "let's find a pub. The one we were in last night will do." I got to my feet and looked around the basement bar; I hadn't taken much notice up until now. It was very British looking, dark oak or teak, stained panels, deep buttoned Draylon, classic paintings in ornate frames – very British. The two waiters were watching me. They were smart in waistcoats and bow-ties, Nick was in suit and tie and both of the pilots had been immaculately turned out. I caught sight of myself in the mirror and realised once again that my jeans and boots looked like they'd spent three weeks climbing mountains, clambering over rock runs and wading through peat bogs and seaweed, exactly what they had done. Just for once I had to agree with my mother, that when I have my head shaved, I look like I'd rob a bank or bash a granny.

CHAPTER 31

With Reckless Abandon

Nick and I found our way back to the Irish pub, O'Malley's, O'Reilly's, O'Grady's or whatever it was called. The barmaid was there and asked if I was going to be coming to the party with her on the weekend. I remained non-committal, not because I had any thoughts of going but because if I appeared keen, maybe I'd be in with a chance earlier, like before I left Buenos Aires. Even if I was around on the Saturday, there's no way I could go to a party in a house full of young Argentinians. When they sussed out I was a Brit, things could turn nasty and if one of them started mouthing off at me, I knew I'd be hard pushed not to mouth off right back, about my reasons for being in Buenos Aires. Then all hell would break loose.

Deciding the future with the barmaid was none existent, we headed off in search of The Kilkenny, the other Irish pub we'd briefly frequented the night before. The décor looked like Irish pubs world wide – dark stained beams, low lighting, with Gaelic signs and Guinness paraphernalia plastered around.

"So what do you think, what did you make of it?" Nick asked me.

I shrugged and told him the truth. "I don't know. It's all a bit too much at the moment."

"I saw you flinch when Armando asked about his friend. You swallowed hard and bit your lip. Were you upset about that?"

I didn't trust myself to answer. I knew when Jorgé planned the missions and Armando and Augusto attacked us, it was nothing personal. We were just a blip on a radar screen and it was us or them. Had we destroyed their aircraft and them with it, with our missiles, would we have lost a minute's sleep or shown any remorse? I can't imagine so. But we wouldn't have known the men, their families, their hopes, their dreams and desires. Had we known them personally, would we have been so nonchalant about killing them? But then, isn't that always the way war works? I had Nick call

Lucila, and she and Dolores came down. They both gave me a hug and a kiss when we met. Must be the Argentinian way I thought. It was Lucila's birthday the following day, she would be twenty six and Dolores said she was almost married. Hardly surprising, she was gorgeous.

When I came back from the gents, Lucila asked me, "so how long were you fighting in the Falklands for, Adam?" She actually used the English name, very unusual in South America, especially Argentina.

I was stunned and despite the background clamour in the pub, there was a sudden chilling silence as both girls looked at me. I wondered how Nick could have been so bloody stupid as to tell them. Living there, he knew how strongly they felt, and it was coming up to the twentieth anniversary. The girls were waiting for a response and I could feel the atmosphere building. From somewhere, the words came.

"It wasn't long and it was a long time ago, another drink?"

They declined. I grabbed the two empty pint pots and made for the bar, where I had them re-filled, despite the fact it was Nick's round. The Irish barman was chatting away to me but I completely ignored him and tried to think of a way to talk my way out of a potentially unpleasant situation. Surely the girls wouldn't get aggressive. What if they'd lost someone? Would we have a repeat of this afternoon's events? Another one would finish me. I'd had enough; I wanted to get back to the UK.

When I reached the table and sat down again, the conversation was in full flow in Spanish and immediately switched to English. I couldn't decide whether they were being courteous or merely switching subjects. After a couple of hours and a couple of Daquiris, the girls said they had to head off. There was much hugging, amidst promising of keeping in touch via e-mail, and with that they carried their slinky South American figures out of the door, with some of the young local guys watching them. No doubt they were wondering why two gorgeous women of that calibre had been with a middle-aged, bearded bloke wearing a tweed jacket with leather patches on the elbows, and a shaven-headed, goatee-clad scarecrow.

I turned to Nick. "What the fuck did you tell them that for?" I asked.

"Tell them what?" he said, looking bemused.

"That I'd been 'down south' in '82?"

He looked more bemused than ever then. "I didn't. I thought you must have when you met them this afternoon."

"Why the bloody hell would I tell them something like that?" I said.

We came to the conclusion that they must have made the connection themselves. Their boss Cristina had sussed me out as a Brit in the office; they'd made the connection, yet they'd still come for a drink with me.

"Fuck it!" I said aloud and sank my pint, feeling damned good for it. I knew I was on for a session.

I don't know how many drinks we had, or what time we left, not because I was too pissed to remember but because I didn't care. As long as I had money in my wallet, the beer was this cheap, the pubs stayed open and I was enjoying myself, then I was going to stay. I looked around and out of the top of the window I studied the frontage of the bar across the road, which had half an old longboat hanging out as a sign.

"Let's go in there," I said to Nick who looked surprised.

"Why?" he asked. I laughed and gave him my standard answer.

"Why not? Come hither youth, sup up."

We crossed the road and entered the bar, which was dark, but clean and tidy. A couple were seated at the bar and there was a group eating at the far end. In the centre was a spiral staircase, with curly metal railings. That was going to be a bastard to negotiate by the end of the night, I thought. Odds on, that's where the toilets are.

I checked out the beers at the bar but saw nothing I liked the look of.

"Hey shipmate, is that all you've got!" I asked the barman who walked past me to the end of the bar and switched on the light in a fridge full with Budweiser, Red Stripe and lots of other western beers including the one and only Newcastle Brown.

"'Bugger me!" I said. "Have you got Nuclear Brown fella?" I sounded like a school kid.

Without letting up on the boredom, the barman reached inside.

"Dos senor, por favor," I gave him in my best Spanish, now the worse for wear by at least half a dozen pints.

"That's one hell of an accent!" came a broad Australian twang from the other end of the bar.

I spun round to see a girl and a bloke. "You can't talk, sounding like that. Where are you from?" I said.

She and the bloke said in unison, "'stralia, mate."

"Me too" I said. "Whereabouts?"

"Tasmania," the girl said, drawing the usual response from me.

"Show us yer scars where they took your second head off, and your sixth finger. And the webbing from between your toes!"

256

She wasn't phased; she'd clearly heard it all before. The mainlanders have always accused Tasmanians of being inbred.

"I'm from Brisbane," her boyfriend said.

"No shit, I'm from Brisbane too," I told him. "Where exactly?"

"Wynnum, what about you?"

"Bugger me," I said. "I'm from Tingalpa! What a small world!" Wynnum was the next suburb, literally one minute's drive away from where I lived.

We swapped names, then Susan, Rick and I got down to the stuff that Brits and Aussies do so well, doing serious damage to the bar's beer reserves. They related their traveling stories of trekking around Tierra Del Fuego. They had also sailed around Cape Horn, which pissed me off, because I hadn't.

Nick was not a great drinker. I knew he'd be absolutely wrecked by the end of the night, and I didn't envisage *his* night going on too much longer. The four of us crossed the road to yet another British pub, The Cutty Sark, named after the clipper from the days of sail. We only stayed for one drink. It turned out to be a pick-up/escort type place and the beer was five times more expensive than anywhere else. We crossed the road back to another bar where the beer was going down well and there were some other travelers.

Eventually the question came from Susan. "What are you doing here in Argentina?"

We had been talking loudly to make ourselves heard above the din of the bar. I hesitated and looked around, I didn't want to shout something at exactly the moment the band stopped playing and find myself announcing my reasons for being there to the whole pub. When I judged it safe, I told them. They listened intently. They said they'd never met anyone who'd been in a war before.

"What's it like?" Susan asked.

What a strange question. I didn't really know the answer, but I told them what I could remember. "It's like every emotion you can ever feel. There is excitement, exhilaration, rushes of adrenalin and then terror. There is humour, madness, sadness, relief, anguish, and of course unprecedented violence… It's a bit like being married really."

Susan burst out laughing. "Sorry!" she said. "I didn't mean to laugh."

I laughed too. "It's OK," I told her. "There are many aspects of it that I can't describe. War is about fucking up lots of people's lives, physically, mentally and emotionally. In my opinion, it's usually for political reasons so, in short – war is a really really shithouse business and although I would never have wished it on anyone, speaking personally I would not have missed it for the world – ever!"

"That's weird," Susan said. "How can you describe such an awful, life threatening experience but not want to miss it given the choice?"

"The point is, I wasn't given a choice, and it taught me a lot. I think it has given me a perspective on the world, a perspective that only people who have been through the same thing can understand. It has made me the kind of person I am today."

"And what kind of a person is that then?" Rick asked.

I thought for a moment. "I don't know, Rick. It's not for me to say. The one thing I do know is, I haven't led a protected little life. I saw what the world was *really* like at an early age. It did me a power of good in comparison to those who have been spoilt and sheltered. Throw people like that into an experience like war and it will rock them so badly they won't survive."

"Did it make you a different person?" Susan asked.

I answered honestly. "I can't remember what I was like before the war. It's too long ago and I'd only been out of school six months when I joined the Navy. It's certainly had an impact on the way I look at things today."

She pressed me further. "Can you give me an example?"

"Easy. I live my life the same way I cook, and the same way I make love."

She grinned at me. "Go on then, I'm listening."

"With reckless abandon – all of them!"

She threw her head back and roared with laughter. "You mad bastard!" she said. "I'll drink to that."

We raised our glasses and chorused, "to reckless abandon!"

I sank my pint, relishing every drop, then banged the glass down on the bar. I didn't realise how hard until I noticed people looking up and staring. I looked from them to the glass and realised I'd cracked it. I signaled an apology to the barman but there was no ill-will.

"What was it like meeting the pilots?" Rick said. "Did you hate them?"

The whole thing was still too mixed up in my head for me to answer him, but I knew it was an immense relief, like being bursting for a pee then suddenly finding a toilet, the same kind of 'eye-watering' relief.

Eventually I told him, I had no problem with the men. The fact was, they were carrying out orders, as was I, and as were all people on both sides.

If I had a problem with any of it, it lay with the political instigators of the whole thing.

"That's a different conversation for a different time," I said.

The three of us drank some more, and danced some more, and I noticed that some of the clientele, who were very smartly dressed, some even in formal evening wear, were getting a little pissed off with the back-packing and traveling clientele, i.e. us, who were monopolising the dance floor and the bar area. I didn't give a shit.

"Are you coming to Anzac Day?" Rick asked me. A lot of Australians, wherever they are traveling make a point of attending a service somewhere in memory of the men killed at the Gallipoli landings in 1915, the campaign which forged the Anzac legend. It's a spirit which burns passionately in the Australian youth, even today. I wished there were more of it in Britain.

"I can't mate," I told him, not without regret. "I leave tomorrow morning. I'll be in transit to Blighty, arriving that morning. But I'll be there in spirit."

It was late, we were pissed, and we'd all had enough. We exchanged e-mail addresses and went our separate ways. I set off in the general direction of a taxi rank I had seen earlier. Turning the corner, I was confronted with the door of our favourite pub – The Kilkenny. I hesitated, would one more beer hurt me? No, I really should go home, I was leaving the following morning. That thought didn't stop me though. I stupidly and very immaturely gave in.

Homeward Bound

I awoke feeling tired, but not in the least bit hungover and I couldn't for the life of me imagine why. I took a quick shower, threw the remaining gear in my rucksack, did my final check for tickets and passports and said farewell to the shithole Juncal Palace I'd never set foot in again.

The bloke at reception had the nerve to ask if I'd like their atrocious breakfast. I passed, settled the bill with American dollars and walked out without looking back at the dump.

The rush-hour was in full swing. All this morning's contestants fully fired up and intent on winning the Wednesday destruction derby. Reminding myself it was my last taxi ride, for the final time I popped a brave pill and hailed a cab. Three of them screeched to a halt simultaneously to take my fare, horns blaring and fists waving. I wanted to shut out the racket; I'd had enough of this place now. Two cars behind them was another taxi. Hoisting my entire compliment of gear onto my back, shoulders, and anywhere else it would fit, I broke into what felt like a sprint but was more of a wobbly stagger to the cab. The driver was already out and grabbing my gear, no doubt realising there must be a distinct possibility of getting the airport with this one. Maybe he'd even be able to go the long way round and rip me off some more.

I reached the airport in one piece. There was a stack wrapping machine that you see in factories, for wrapping pallets of product. People were wrapping their luggage with heavy industrial cling film to prevent anything being stolen. I considered copying them but I knew that if baggage handlers want to steal, they will steal, regardless of industrial cling film or anything else. I had nothing worth nicking anyway. I'd borrowed my rucksack from my boss. I didn't fancy returning it with a massive knife wound in it, which is what would happen if I wrapped it, signaling that it contained stuff of value.

I checked in and found the bar. It was only 9am and already it was open. Excellent! I sat down with a beer and caught site of my reflection in the plate glass. Not a pretty sight. I'm hardly a Brad Pitt look-alike at the best of times but I needed a good soak in a hot bath and a close shave, a meal, a night's sleep and fresh clothes. I needed a hug from my little girl and to wake up in the bedroom that had been mine 20 years previously. The bedroom that had seen me leave school and then leave home to join the Navy twenty two years ago, the bedroom that had seen some of my earliest fumbling encounters with the female of the species when Mum and Dad were out.

The stench of camel shit cigarettes was everywhere. I hated being in Argentina and wanted to escape – immediately! I couldn't stop drinking; maybe I was becoming an alcoholic. This trip was supposed to heal me, not turn me back.

I found a comfy settee and flopped back into it. I put my boots up on the table, relaxed and calmed down. I'd been through a lot, physically, mentally and emotionally. I'd come through, and I was quietly pleased. I reflected on the past few weeks; some of the things that had happened, the places I'd been and the things I'd experienced, the effect(s) it had had on me, both good and bad.

War works in strange ways. I had seen reports of men who had tried to kill each other in battle and had then become close friends afterwards. Did I want to stay in touch with Jorgé or Armando, exchange Christmas cards and so forth? No I didn't. I had achieved what I'd set out to do. I respected their bravery and professionalism, they were military men. Their fellow pilots flying Mirages and Skyhawks suffered appalling losses from the British Sea Harriers and our warships' anti-aircraft missiles. Every day they got back into their aircraft and brought their attacks in at almost suicidal level to deliver their explosive cargoes. They had bottle in abundance, crates and crates of the stuff.

A waiter came by and picked up the empty bottle. He gave me a questioning look. I nodded. This procedure was repeated numerous times, then at last the flight was called. I was pissed out of my brains – again.

CHAPTER 32

Peace at Last

It was pouring with rain as the 737 lifted off from Buenos Aires. I didn't care. I looked out of the window and no sooner had we climbed out of sight of the Argentinian capital than I fell in to an alcohol-induced slumber.

The hostess was shaking me and asking in Portuguese whether I wanted the fish or chicken. I nodded at the first one. It was beef curry, good guess. I wolfed it down, drank a couple of beers and a small bottle of wine and immediately went back to sleep. I was awoken by the change in cabin pressure as the aircraft descended. My ears were hurting. I checked my watch – the news was not good. At this rate, by the time we landed, my flight for London would have just 15 minutes before takeoff. Even if I made it, the chances of my bag making it were slim. Bugger!

We came into Sao Paulo very smoothly. Like Buenos Aires, it appeared immense from the air and took ages to fly over to the airport. It was now dark and I had very little time to find my connecting flight to London. I didn't even know if it was in the same terminal or if there was more than one terminal. A flight attendant stood at the gate with a sign for 'British Airways'. I showed her my ticket.

"Hurry! Follow me. We don't have much time," she said.

We raced down various moving walkways and out onto the rainy tarmac. A van was waiting with the engine running. She jumped in the passenger seat and in typical South American style we took off at break neck speed. How we didn't hit an aircraft, or anything else I'll never know, and I thought the Argentinians were bad. Then I remembered a famous Brazilian driver, Ayrton Senna… I prayed that I did not share his fate. The woman threw the van around corners and underneath aircraft, and came to a sliding halt that the Blues Brothers would have been proud of. The flight attendant was out of the van and dragging me out with her before I even realised we had stopped. She even had my smaller backpack which was no light weight.

I saw the British Airways sign with some of the cabin crew milling around the doors and knew I'd made it. The check-in queue was at least five miles long and my chauffeur marched straight to the front, handed over my ticket and gave instructions to the check-in staff. I was dealt with and away. There was even a five minute wait before boarding, so as I needed to freshen up, I went into the toilets, had a quick wash, cleaned the fur off my teeth and changed my t-shirt. The shirt on the top of my bag was bright yellow, with a black embroidered outline of the islands. In bold capital letters underneath the crest were the words – **FALKLAND ISLANDS**. It felt good just to get even slightly cleaned up. The final boarding call for the aircraft came and I headed for the door. There were only two cabin crew standing by the entrance now. I saw the girl eye the emblem on my shirt. I handed my ticket to her colleague. He was obviously bored with welcoming the homeward bound tourists onto the plane as he dispensed with the usual niceties of 'welcome aboard' and said simply, "on the right". I turned right and headed towards the back of the plane. I found my seat and was attempting to locate some overhead space to stow my backpack when the stewardess who had been at the door appeared.

"Excuse me," she said. "Where did you get your t-shirt from?"

I thought it would have been obvious. "From the Falklands, like it says."

"Follow me," she said, heading back towards the front of the plane. We went through the now drawn curtain into the first class section.

"Here," she said, "have this seat." She indicated one of the big armchair type padded recliners. I didn't even have time to thank her before she was gone but I wasn't complaining. Being first class, the seat came with all the usual niceties, such as smiles, towels, refreshments and the crew pretending that they were interested in you. They could pretend all they wanted. It was free and it was good.

The aircraft sat at the end of the runway, waiting and waiting. I was wishing the pilot would get his finger out and get us rolling. Finally, the engines revved to a crescendo and I felt the aircraft strain forward. The noise from the underslung Pratt and Whitney's peaked, and the brakes were released. The 737 surged forward at an alarming rate, and I allowed myself one look out of the window at the rainy South American tarmac. The nose lifted in the air, and the noise of the wheels on the runway died away. Despite the fact it was nothing to do with the Brazilians, Chileans or anyone else, I pictured the whole South American continent and thought, 'fuck you lot, all of you'. I was going home.

The seat was comfy and the service was great, and I decided I could get used to it. The flight was uneventful and after the standard food and drink I dozed off. I woke up, gagging for a drink of water. The cabin was in darkness. I found my way back to one of the galleys, where the crew was passing the time, chatting and reading magazines. As I drew back the curtain, they all stopped talking and looked at me.

"Can I have a drink of water or orange please?" I said. I was chronically dehydrated from the flying and all the drink I'd necked over the last few days. The flight attendant who had shown me to first class was in there. Her male colleague passed me a tray holding two glasses of orange and two of water. I drank the lot. The look on his face said I should have taken one, maybe two.

He eyed the crest on my shirt. "Are you just on your way home from there?"

I nodded. "Yes I am. How long until we land?"

"About another four hours," he said. "We're ahead of schedule. I take it you were there in '82. What are the islands like?"

"Beautiful and still relatively unspoilt," I told him. "Why did you think I was there in '82? I could be a photographer or a wildlife enthusiast."

He screwed up his face. "You look like a soldier," he said. "We've taken a couple of others home recently. One was a Royal Marine. He was really quite disturbed."

"Yeah, he would have been," I said. "They all are. It's part of the training."

I swiped another orange and water and retired back to my own personal airborne settee.

The cabin lights came on with the usual announcements of breakfast, ETA and the like. It would have to have been one of the most comfortable long distance flights I've ever done. This was a very positive way of starting the last leg of my journey, a 'journey to peace' I decided.

We touched down in London. I was wondering whether my rucksack had made the life-threatening journey across Sao Paulo airport in time. I was pleasantly surprised to see the bright green bag come around the carousel first. I hoisted it onto the luggage trolley and prepared myself for the inquisition that I always get at customs. This seemed especially likely given that I was arriving from South America but this time the customs officers looked disinterestedly at me as I waltzed through. I'd have to try the yellow bandana, shaved head and goatee look again, it obviously did the trick.

Having cleared customs I opened the bag to check its contents. Bugger! I should have spent a few minutes and dollars having it cling-wrapped in Buenos Aires. Some light fingered baggage handler had made a small profit. They'd had away my Maglite torch, Swiss army knife and all the empty bullet cases I'd collected, plus the bits of aircraft wreckage and various other little odds and sods. The thieving bastards had had the last laugh on me after all. I tried not to be pissed off, I was almost home. I couldn't let anything spoil it now.

It was not far off midday as I made my way down to the tube station and found the circle line. Nothing much had changed; it was still filthy and covered in graffiti. I bought a bottle of water and a Mars Bar but there was nowhere to put the wrapper. All the rubbish bins had been removed years ago to stop the IRA putting bombs in them.

I shoved the wrapper in my pocket, I could have thrown it down amongst the litter blowing around my feet, no-one would have noticed. The train arrived, it was filthy, the seats were torn and it stank of stale urine. The passengers were a real cross section of the population with the normal complement of freaks and weirdos. No-one was smiling or talking. The Macarena tune rang on a mobile and I recognised the language as someone started gabbling away in Spanish. The train arrived at Liverpool Street and I made my way up to the old station where I had spent so much time on Friday evenings going to my Mum and Dad's for the weekend, when I'd been at sea.

There was an hour to wait for the train. I bought my ticket and nearly died of shock as I found out a two hour train journey to Norwich cost the equivalent of ninety Australian dollars. The same journey in Australia would cost about fifteen or maybe twenty. I found a phone and called Maxine and told her I'd be in town that afternoon if she fancied a rendezvous for a drink. She was all for it. I wondered what she looked like now and whether the years had been kind to her. I told her I'd call her once I'd got myself established at a pub in Norwich, and could give her a meeting place, I already knew where it would be.

The train pulled out of Liverpool Street late, what a surprise. It was also dirty, so nothing much had changed there either. We went past the dark and grimy buildings in the east end, which had always seemed so depressing. They hadn't changed or even been cleaned in twenty years. They were probably even more depressing to actually live in. Eventually we cleared the outskirts of London and the scenery gave way to the green fields of the Essex countryside. I sat there thinking how beautiful England was in the spring. We rattled through villages with small spired churches and country folk going about their daily toil.

We arrived in Norwich on schedule. I unloaded my gear and walked up a clean, refurbished platform and out of the Victorian station building. I got to the far end of the car park and turned round to look at the new station. They'd made quite a good job of it. Another surprise. I was weighed down with a serious amount of gear but I was determined that I would walk, it was part of the exorcism. The hill from the station up Prince of Wales Road towards Norwich Castle is not steep but it is long and winding. There was a time when I could have run it, in boots, carrying my pack mule-like load.

I walked round Castle Meadow looking up at the pale yellow sandstone walls of the tenth century Norman castle which is perched atop a steep hill. The grass growing on the slopes was a beautiful deep green, broken with the flowering of bright yellow daffodils. I silently recited some of the lines of Wordsworth's poem:

For oft, when on my couch I lie
In vacant or in pensive mood,
They flash upon that inward eye
Which is the bliss of solitude;
And then my heart with pleasure fills
And dances with the daffodils.

I wanted to pick some, a whole bunch and give them to someone special, but there was no-one in my life. I saw a couple walking hand in hand, laughing. I was jealous. Jealous of anyone who had someone special. This was the closest I had geographically been to my family in years but I felt very alone. My back was killing me, it was OK whilst I was walking, but when I stopped and stood up straight it started to hurt.

The last uphill struggle was to the rendezvous point with Max. An old pub called 'The Murderers' set on a cobbled hill in the shadow of the castle. There are various stories behind how it got its name and it's officially called

'The Gardeners Arms'. The sign says 'The Murderers', so 'The Murderers' it is. It was 4.00pm. I stood and eyed the collection of draught real ales and bitters, I was going to enjoy tonight. I got a pint of something wonderful, made the necessary phone call and retired to a table outside in the warm. I was so glad to be a man of such simple tastes. Two pints later and I had struck up a conversation with a couple of fellow drinkers. One was a wanker who'd just been to court that day, where he'd be fined again and was blaming the world for everything – a typical victim. The other was interested in where I'd been traveling; I had only got as far as talking about Tahiti when Maxine arrived.

The years had been kinder to her than they had to me. Her face and her eyes had not changed. They had that same sparkle that I remembered the first time I saw her the night after we got home in '82. I pictured her in that ridiculous white and blue polka dot rah-rah dress, with her Claire Grogan hairstyle. I still fancied her.

She gave me the biggest bear hug ever and asked, "Well, are you going to buy me a drink then?" She had such a mischievous grin.

"No," I said. "I'm going to buy you a lot of drinks." I meant it. We talked for hours, and worked out it had been maybe eighteen or nineteen years, neither of us could remember exactly the last time we'd seen each other. I told her I'd had the hots for her, but she told me she had the hots for my mate Brian. He in turn had the hots for my sister, who lived with an RAF bloke. A bit of an unsatisfactory result for a few of us really. All that time we hadn't even lived that far apart. She asked why I was so determined to see her again. I didn't know how to tell her, so I said nothing. I ran it through in my mind and made a mental note to confess to her at some point. Not having seen her for so long, I'd didn't know how she'd react straight away and may think I was just using her, which was not the case at all.

There were two parts to the truth. One was because I'd fancied her and we'd always got on well and so why not catch up after all these years. That is what I'd told her on the phone. The other was the healing part. She was the first girl I'd seen all those years ago and I wanted to re-enact that. I can't explain why. For the same reason I wanted to walk up the hill and not get a taxi, for the same reason I climbed all the mountains around Stanley. I just did.

We continued drinking, and were having a great time. We adjourned next door to The Bell, with the intention of getting something to eat. That didn't happen and we continued drinking. Sitting opposite us, but with her back turned, was a fat girl. The back of her jeans had ridden down and her exotic G-string was showing as it disappeared up the crack of her arse. We pissed ourselves laughing; it's the last thing I can remember.

I woke up and looked around. What strange décor. Although it was very dark I could make out shapes and silhouettes of lots of ornaments and artifacts, all Indian and sub-continent. I was freezing, although I did have a blanket. I was bursting for a pee. I didn't have a clue where I was or how I got there. I was crammed very uncomfortably on a small two-seater settee. I struggled to get to my feet and knocked something over. For a split second I held my breath, waiting for the splintering crash, but a dull thud came instead. I breathed a small sigh of relief; I was saving the big sigh for when I found the toilet. I could only find one door and that opened out into the front garden. My eyes were streaming by this time so it looked like the rose-bed would have to do, I just hoped no-one walked past. That finished, I returned to the room. In front of me was a door going through to the back of the house and a staircase on the right. How had I not seen that? I'd completely forgotten about all my gear. I took my boots off, climbed the stairs and went into the bedroom on the right. The double bed was empty. I crossed the landing into the other room. There was a figure in the bed. I walked slowly and quietly towards the bed, not wanting to alarm the occupant. My attempts at stealth, which more likely resembled a herd of elephants, had been wasted as they awoke with a start.

"What are you doing?" whispered a girl.

"Where am I?" I asked in all sincerity.

"You're in my house, where do you think? Adam it's me, Maxine. I've made up the spare bed for you, I couldn't wake you up downstairs, you fell asleep on the settee." I crouched down and looked at her. It *was* Maxine, a very tousle haired Maxine. Now it was all coming back. I thought about trying to get in with her, then thought better of it. I turned round and went and found the spare bed. I hadn't even said thanks.

"Hey, tea up." A very different looking Max put the tea down beside the bed.

"What a great hotel," I said. "Can I come again?"

"You cheeky bastard," she said. "I'll charge you next time. Right I'm off to work. There's bread if you want toast, don't leave a mess. There's a taxi number next to the phone, clean your whiskers out of the sink if you shave, and no going through my knicker drawer, understand?" Although she sounded fierce, there was a grin on her face.

"Thanks," I said. "I'll give you a ring sometime." I meant it.

She leant over and kissed me. She didn't move away straight away, and I had the urge to drag her into bed. I thought better of it. She was clean, tidy, dressed, looked respectable and I hadn't showered, shaved or cleaned my teeth properly in 24 hours. I put the thought away. If it was ever meant to happen, I had three weeks to let it. I'd waited 20 years; another couple of weeks wouldn't hurt me. Shortly after she left I grabbed my gear, had a quick freshen up and set off for my sister's on the other side of town some five miles away. It was raining hard. Bugger! It would be, wouldn't it!

I was determined to walk to Toni's, in the rain if necessary. The water seeped down my neck and in every other space it could find. I was freezing and soaking. It hadn't even been this bad in the Islands. As I walked past the pubs there seemed to be a lot of people in them but surely they couldn't be open at this early hour and they can't all have been cleaners. Coming down St Stephen's Street towards the scenes of last night's frenetic drinking, the wind howled and whistled up the street. How could it? It had been so beautiful yesterday. Turning the corner by the castle, the rain stopped as quickly as it had started. I trudged down through the cobbled streets of medieval Tombland and up Magdalen Street with my head down. I stopped briefly on the bridge over the River Wensum. The water was high and the weeping willows trailed lazily by in the slow meandering water.

I opened the back gate and saw my lovely sister through the kitchen window. She had been so understanding. I had made her life so difficult, and that of my parents too. She made to throw her arms around me but with so much gear hanging off me, it was difficult for her to find a place for her arms.

Toni asked the question I knew she was bound to ask, the question lots of people would be asking.

"Well, how was it, what was it like?"

I'd thought about what to say on the plane home. It would depend on who was asking and how much I wanted to talk about it. Obviously with the family, I would open up. They had carried a burden themselves and were entitled to an answer of sorts. I thought back to the night in New Zealand, when we sat up all night sinking the crate of beer between us. That had been the time I had decided to go ahead with the trip. It was Toni who had talked to me of 'closure'. I had never really heard the term before.

"Windy, very windy," I told her. It was true. The only other time I had come across wind so strong was in the middle of the North Sea. She accepted it without a further word, knowing we would discuss it in detail at some point in the next three weeks.

She rang my mum and dad and told them I was there. No-one had expected me until the following week. She made sure my daughter didn't find out I was back as I wanted to surprise her. I dived into my bag and dug out the two white furry seal pups I'd bought from the souvenir shop in Stanley, one each for Lucy and her cousin, Molly.

We arrived in Hickling, the Broadland village I had grown up in. Not much had changed since 1970. There were still no street lights, no white lines on the roads, no piped natural gas. It is a very peaceful and quiet place and somewhere I always enjoyed going back to. Toni slipped into the house with the furry seals. I crept in through the back door and heard my mum asking the girls if they knew what they were and where they came from. She carried on dropping clues and asking questions until Lucy exclaimed, "The Falkland Islands." So mum posed her a dilemma.

"If that's where they came from, how did they get here?"

I could see Lucy's brow furrowing as she tried to work out the logistics, as she was not expecting me for a few more days. When I heard her say, "Well I know Daddy's just been there," I walked in. For a split second her face was a picture of confusion. Then the penny dropped, she barged through shouting, "Daddy, Daddy, my Daddy," and grabbed me in a tightest possible hug. I lifted her up and held her to me. Her tears were wet against my face.

CHAPTER 33

Reminiscing

I spent a couple of days chilling, collecting my thoughts and reflecting on where I'd come from, both geographically and emotionally. I wandered alone down to Hickling Broad and called in for a pint to the Pleasure Boat Inn where I'd lived thirty years previously. The pub is painted pinkish, similar to Evita's palace in Plaza de Maya. The sailing dyke leading from the broad comes almost up to the pub front door. There were a couple of cruisers and yachts tied up in the dyke, not even the rigging halyards were moving. I sat outside on one of the bench seats enjoying the peace and serenity and it dawned on me that there was not a sound – total silence, no birds singing, no tractors, no boats, not even any wind. That is when I knew that I had found peace, at long last, that peace that had eluded me for so long.

I had found the inner strength and courage to confront and beat Post Traumatic Stress Disorder – PTSD, the mental cancer that had gnawed away at me, tormented me, invaded my head, heart, memory and mind. I had walked on the dark side of human nature and fought back from the edge of my existence.

Twenty years ago, we had brought freedom 8,000 miles to the Falkland Islands. Now the islands themselves had brought me my own freedom, delivering salvation from the wreckage of my mind. I was the one that had overcome. I remembered the struggle to the top of Two Sisters. I felt as if I could achieve anything. A warm pins and needles feeling radiated out from the centre of my body, down my arms and legs until my fingertips tingled. I closed my eyes to savour the moment.

The golden silence was shattered by the Mexican Hat Dance ringtone on a mobile phone. I burst out laughing. A group of youngsters were walking up the car park. They looked at me strangely. Maybe it wasn't normal to sit outside a pub by yourself laughing. I then sat and thought seriously for a minute; what constitutes 'normal?' In whose book, by whose standard? Did it matter?

I walked back from the Broad taking the road I'd ridden my pushbike along every morning and afternoon on my way to and from school when I was a boy. The trees had grown, there were a few more houses but not much else had changed. I had no doubt that I had found the strength I needed from my mum, dad, and sister. The resolve they had shown in standing by me and supporting me back in 1982 was what I had drawn on in the past few weeks. They had taught, encouraged and guided me, and when necessary, had been cruel to be kind. I could never have achieved this without them.

I finally got round to unpacking the remains of my rucksack. I had collected stones for Mum and Dad's garden; it's a really interesting garden with lots of little ornaments, intricacies and oddities. We labeled where each stone had come from and which unit had been involved in the action there, and mounted it in the summer house in the corner of the garden. I had brought Lucy a fossilised shell from West Falkland. I gave it to her and she studied it curiously. "What's it for?" she asked. I picked up the piece of quartzite crystal that I'd taken from the summit of the south spur of Two Sisters Mountain. I was going to keep this little piece of rock as a reminder of how incredibly alive I'd felt when I reached the summit. My thoughts were interrupted by Lucy. "Why have you got that beard, Daddy?" I didn't have a specific reason so I told her I wanted to see what I'd look like with a goatee; I asked her what she thought.

"You look like a goat," she said, with the attitude that only children can get away with.

I took the 'Danger Mines' sign I'd got from the bomb disposal office in Stanley, fixed it to a small stake and embedded it into the ground near the sign announcing the name of Mum and Dad's cottage – 'The Land of Green Ginger'. I then wandered up to the village shops, and by the time I got back, the sign had already acquired its first piece of graffiti. My sister had written underneath in thick black felt-tip, 'a pint!'

Bloody vandal. I laughed for ages.

Old Haunts, Portsmouth

On Thursday we drove down to Portsmouth for the reunion and memorial service. Once settled in Portsmouth, I rang Bob Mullen and arranged to

272

drop around and see him. He had left the mob recently as a Chief. It was good to see him again and find out about what some of the lads had been up to. His house was full of *Sheffield* memorabilia, I found it rather unnerving. In my own house I have a photo of each ship I served on, and one of 1987 Devonport Field Gun Crew. They are tucked away in the dining room so I don't see them every day. Each to their own; I respected Bob's decision to keep the history alive.

We watched a video made recently by a local Portsmouth TV station. Bob and one of the gunners had attended a school to give a talk on the war and its effects. It didn't make pretty watching. The man with Bob broke down. I was told that there were a lot of my old shipmates like that. They had never managed to fully recover from those events, and some had received treatment for a range of conditions associated with the war. Watching it made me realise how lucky I had been to come through it without losing the plot completely. It also made me more pissed off at the government for not doing something about it and helping those men.

I woke up in the B&B and had a chance to take stock of what an appalling shithole the place was. The guesthouse is on a piece of land just across from the station and ferry ports called 'The Hard' right outside Victory Gate. It was ideally situated to solicit custom. The landlord didn't give a shit about the state of the place. It was filthy, run-down and a dangerous fire trap. "If you don't like it, leave," the landlord said when we complained. We rang every other hotel and B&B we could find. It was Bank Holiday, there were lots of other reunions going on and there was not a spare room to be had in Portsmouth. How could he have the nerve to name this dosshouse, the most disgraceful accommodation in Pompey, after the lady of our nation's greatest naval hero?

We walked down to the sea wall and the round tower in Old Portsmouth. Mounted on the wall is a plaque with the names of all the sailors and marines killed in the conflict. As I bent down to read the notices I saw one from Allan Knowles Jnr. It bore a picture of the memorial on Sealion Island. Lucy and Molly asked what it was and why we were there. I had agreed with my sister that they would not go to the memorial service or be exposed to any of the grieving. Although Lucy had an idea, I didn't feel the need to expose her to it further and Molly knew nothing of it, there was no reason for her to at this young age.

My brother in law arrived that afternoon to look after the children. I went out with Toni and my old shipmate and Blues Brother Andy 'Brum'

Hansford from *Invincible*, one of the blokes from the SODS Opera that had so impressed Captain Layman. We wandered around what had been Brum's training establishment, HMS *Vernon*. All the divers, mine warfare and sonar rates had trained in *Vernon*. It was now cafés, trendy designer shops and harbour front restaurants called Gunwharf Quays. Brum did his own share of reminiscing. "That was the TAS mess, over there was the diving school, this was the classrooms." Where he'd passed his final exam was now an upmarket boutique.

That night we ambled up Queen Street, a road we'd trodden a thousand times before. The previous evening Bob had told me the lads would be in the Park Tavern. It was like stepping into a time warp. The place had hardly changed at all, and even the faces were the same; just a bit older, a bit fatter, balder, greyer and wrinklier. I recognised everyone but I knew none of them recognised me. The difference is greater when you go from a seven stone, non-shaving, seventeen year old, to a shaven-headed ex field-gunner, than it is when you go from mid twenties to mid forties. Bob announced to the gathered masses, "hey everyone, this is Junior Seaman Joe Lawton." Scouse Roberts the Leading Reg' and Eddie Whittaker the killick RO came straight over. The last time I had seen Scouse I remembered the panic on his face as he searched for the Master at Arms after the attack. Sadly, the Master was already dead. He still had a kindly face; I hoped life had treated him well.

"Is it true you've come all the way from Australia for this?" Eddie Whittaker asked.

"Yep, bloody right," I said. "I wouldn't have missed it for the world."

Eddie was impressed, we laughed about the time I nearly landed him in the shit when he was killick of the mess. I was temporarily billeted in the RO's mess and he presumed I was eighteen and drew beer rations for me; up until the Master at Arms found out. It was great to catch up with so many of the ship's company again. Some had done well; some had not been treated kindly by life. Lots were suffering from varying degrees of Post Traumatic Stress Disorder; it is a hideous and insidious condition. I was very aware of the damage the condition can do. There were stories of alcoholism, drugs, violence, multiple divorces and acute anxiety, chronic depression and extreme obsessive compulsive disorders, all as a result of the events of 4th May 1982. *There but for the grace of God, go I,* I thought.

Brum, Toni and I carried on doing the rounds of the Portsmouth pubs that we knew from old. The Mighty Fine, City Arms, Mucky Duck, and for the first time in fifteen years we ended up in Joanna's nightclub in

Southsea, otherwise known as the Royal Navy School of Dancing, where you learn to do that dance exclusive to the RN, 'The Pissed Matelot Stomp'. Sure enough Bob turned up with some of the lads.

I wanted to catch up and have a chat with Leading Seaman (now Warrant Officer) Gilly Gilchrist. After the war, many of us had ended up in HMS *Dryad* awaiting our next ships. One night after too much beer, there was an altercation and this time I was actually an innocent party. Stupidly, when I was questioned I gave a statement dropping Gilly in the shit. I had always regretted it and knew I should have pleaded ignorance.

In the nightclub I raised the subject with him. He asked if I'd let it bother me for all these years and I admitted it had. He told me he'd forgiven me years ago, and put it down to the naivety of a Junior. This was decent of him, given that it cost him a month's wages and a year's seniority at the time.

We talked about my recent trip back to the islands and the meeting with the two Etendard pilots. He asked about the men and what they had to say. I told it how it was. They were doing a job – just like us.

Saturday 4th May 2002

My mum and dad arrived and settled in to the hovel we were forced to stay in, much to their disgust. I was livid. My brother in law took the kids to his sister's in Fareham. I complained about the filth and danger and the landlord's attitude to the visitors centre just across the road. The people there said they refuse to recognise it, never recommend it and if possible dissuade potential guests from staying there. We took Mum and Dad down to the memorial plaque near the Round Tower and walked along the sea wall for a while. Whilst at the memorial I saw a big bloke who looked familiar, he was wearing sunglasses so I couldn't be sure.

I knew he must have something to do with the events or he wouldn't have been at the Falklands memorial but I was still hesitant. I didn't know why, it wasn't like me. I chanced it. "Excuse me," I said. "Are you Swanny Rivers?"

The bloke looked round. "Yes I am," he said, taking his sunglasses off. "Who are you?" He hadn't changed much and didn't look that much older.

"I'm Joe, Joe Lawton," I told him. "I was a baby RP." He was there with his own family and was then working as a postman in Suffolk. He'd always been a quiet bloke, massive but quiet, one of the world's nice guys.

Making our way round to Gunwharf Quays, our entire family piled onto one of the boat trips around the dockyard, to view all the warships. 'Fanny boats' as they are known, have been running for decades, I remember the rude remarks we used to make about all the tourists. Usually that all the women aged between sixteen and sixty were gagging for it, and any male who went on a boat trip to view ships and sailors would have to be a confirmed poofter. Once we had done all the viewing and were on the way back, I walked to the back of the boat with Lucy. I took out two poppies and two Argentine coins and gave one of each to her. She asked why we were doing this and I explained it was in memory of all the sailors who had died in the war. She gently let them slip from her little hands into the foaming white wake below.

"What about yours, Daddy?"

I wrapped the wire stem of the poppy around the Argentine peso coin and cast it high into the air astern of the boat. I turned away before it fell into the harbour, a long way behind the boat.

We returned to the hotel to get ready for the reunion. What was this going to be like? Here I was at the age of thirty seven, about to be one of the youngest members of a very exclusive club, not the sort you would volunteer to join though. We stopped for a pint in The Ship's Leopard on The Hard. The first blokes I recognised were outside the pub. One had been a killick tiff, and later a Chief when I was in Leander Refit Group in Rosyth. Another had been a killick WEM. The bastard didn't look as if he'd aged a day. And there was the bloke who maintained the *Sheffield* website.

We walked the distantly familiar route up Queen Street towards HMS *Nelson*. In front of us was a group of teenage girls pushing little ones in buggies and swearing. Some things about Pompey hadn't changed.

We arrived at the main gate of HMS *Nelson*; the last time I had been there was to be discharged in 1987. A taxi pulled up and my divisional Petty Officer climbed out. Like everyone else so far, he didn't recognise me. We were directed to the hall for the reunion, and at the foot of the stairwell were photographs of the establishment's CO and Executive Officer who had been a Chief Marine Engineer on *Ardent*. I recalled two mates who'd survived *Ardent's* sinking mentioning how badly injured he'd been, yet he still survived. He owed his life to a young AB who had been in radar training at the same time as me. The Able Seaman had been awarded the George Medal for saving the Chief's life. I was told afterwards by a couple of ex-*Ardents* that he had sold his medals and dropped out of sight. No one had heard from him since.

CHAPTER 34

HMS Sheffield Reunion

Saturday 4ᵗʰ May 2002

It was twenty years to the day since I had seen some of these men. The faces had not changed that much, but all had acquired lines and wrinkles, all had thinning hair or were bald, and some were grotesquely fat. Everyone seemed pleased to see everyone else, though very few recognised me, the previously scrawny kid. I spotted Scouse Riozzie and Doddy. I didn't know, but Doddy was also unfortunate enough to be staying in the same hovel as us. Scouse was sitting down with his wife and I went over and sat down right in front of him. He looked puzzled at first, so I gave it to him simply.

"OK then, recognise this face?"

He looked blank. I wasn't surprised; he would've been the first one who did.

"Who was the youngest RP on board?"

His brow furrowed for a minute, then he mouthed the words, 'Joe Lawton'. "No!" he said at last, "I don't believe it! You were such a skinny little bastard. Look at you. What happened?"

I laughed. "Oh, you know how it is Riz. I grew up I suppose."

Doddy and Riz recounted the times that they used to hit me with twelve inch plastic rulers in the operations room. I laughed about it but it bloody hurt at the time. I'd previously seen Riz in Dryad in '83 when he was there on a course. I was up there with Command Team Training on HMS *Nottingham*.

Tanzy Lee was a couple of years older than me and had graduated from 'Junior' status when I joined. The older blokes had someone new to direct their crap at, and he was no doubt secretly glad. He produced some photos from the Gulf trip that he'd sent home prior to us sailing south.

I'd already seen Captain Sam Salt but he was always surrounded by people. I decided I would bide my time to speak to him, but Tanzy grabbed my arm and shoved his way through the crowd. He introduced me. "Do you remember Joe Lawton, the youngest onboard?" That wasn't strictly correct. Of the three under-eighteens at the time, I was the oldest. 'Sky' Larkin was younger than me and JMEM Bailey was too, he had been the Captain on Christmas Day in Muscat.

It hadn't been that many weeks since I'd last spoken to Captain Salt, and he remembered our conversations about my intention to meet the Argentine pilots.

"What were they like?" he asked.

"Like you and me sir, men doing a job."

I knew he knew that. He had told me that himself when we first spoke about my intentions, when I asked for his thoughts, his opinion or permission, whatever it was I was seeking at the time. I couldn't remember.

Tanzy produced the photos. "Look at this one sir," he said laughing. "Joe looks like he's about twelve."

Sam studied the photo. "Joe, you were only five years older than twelve. It isn't that different is it?"

I'd never thought of our age being so close to that of schoolboys. Less than two years before, I'd still been in a classroom about to sit my 'O' levels. Some of the brighter kids my age who got into grammar school were still there when the first bombs fell and the first guns fired. "Good luck for the future," Sam said, and we shook hands.

I spotted André Lahiff. We'd been Bosun's Mates together for the latter half of the Gulf patrol in the months before the voyage south. He'd been on the piss with Andy 'The Gorilla' Myers during the afternoon and could hardly stand. I'd been to André's for a weekend in Blackpool in about '86 when I was living in Scotland. That was the last time we'd seen each other although we'd exchanged the odd letter and later e-mail. He'd done well, had completed an MBA and was the Marketing Manager for Royal Mail in Leeds. The ship's PTI (Clubs), Steve Iacovou, hadn't changed to look at. Slightly thinning, slighter build, but still Clubs. He was with Ricky Morana. The last time I'd seen Ricky was when I was laying him on the deck of the emergency operating space with a massive lump of metal jutting out of his head, blood everywhere. Just like Clubs, his hair had thinned, he didn't have the body that women would kill for that he used to have, but I could still recognise him in the street.

I bumped into my Divisional Officer, Sub Lt Colin Haley. He was now a Commander. I drew him outside for a chat. In the six months I was on board, I got in the shit and was run in front of the Jimmy twice. Just after the second occasion I went to Sub Lt Haley to have my "Form 264" (review) completed.

"There are all the indicators that you are going to be a problem rating," he told me. I couldn't believe it. I got top marks in my seamanship class and came third in my radar class. I told him during that review that he was wrong about me, and I wanted to make a good impression. He just said I'd gone about that in a strange way.

The Jimmy had shaved his beard off, but I'd recognise him anywhere. He had dished me out two sets of No9 punishment. I asked him if he knew who I was. "No," he said. "But you were obviously young then." He was the only one who had made the connection; I thought I looked a lot older than I was. We talked a bit about where we went in the Navy afterwards. He'd been one of Flag Officer Sea Training inspection staff and came on board *Invincible* in about '83 or '84. I spoke to him briefly then.

I knew John Strange as soon I saw him. I had wondered if he'd been burnt beyond recognition – the last time I'd seen him he was. It gave me goose pimples talking to him when I'd seen him in such a state and he was given virtually no chance of making it through the night, never mind another twenty years. I asked him how old he'd been at the time. "38," he said, which was almost the same age as I was then. He looked well and I was glad to see it. Just then Riz and Doddy reappeared and hijacked me to the back bar. My two greatest tormentors from 2nd Port watch started to ply me with shorts. Riz actually apologised for being such a bully to me but said it was my own fault for being such a mouthy junior. Fairly accurate.

An old fat bloke was there. "Who's that?" I asked Bob Mullen.

"It's Bod," he replied.

"Bod? Who's Bod?" I couldn't work it out, and I couldn't recognise him.

"Bod," he said. "B.O.D. Boring Old Don. It's Don Chamberlain."

I pissed myself laughing. Poor old Don. Another face I recognised belonged to Ralph Coates, a fellow native of Hull, or more accurately a pub in Beverley. He and another AB called Jerry Taylor had been the 966 air trackers opposite Ollie Hardy and myself. I went down to the Royal Tournament in London in '90 and '91 and had seen Jerry there running field gun for Pompey. He hadn't recognised me either – no surprises there.

Ralph had done well. He was a senior officer in Hampshire Fire Brigade and had almost completed his MBA.

I was standing near the bar with my dad, himself an old seadog with white hair and white beard. Someone I didn't recognise staggered up to him.

"I'd recognise that face anywhere," the bloke slurred to Dad, telling him how great it was to see him again and shaking his hand. My dad and I just looked at each other and burst out laughing.

The comedian Jim Davidson came on stage. Jim has been a patron of the Falklands charities since '82 and prior to that, a great supporter of the British Forces. As usual he put on a great show and took the piss out of all the appropriate people, Prince Charles, Margaret Thatcher etc.

Sunday morning dawned and I could hear the shrill whistle of the Bosuns' calls announcing 'Call the Hands'. I dressed in the smart charcoal suit my brother-in-law had brought over from Australia for me. There was no way I could have put that in a rucksack.

It was only a short walk inside the dockyard to St Anne's church where the memorial was being held. Already, a lot of the ship's company were waiting, some faces I hadn't seen during the previous night's mayhem. Very few were still serving, and most were in civvies. I was having a chat with Scouse Morrison, the same Able Seaman Scouse Morrison who'd been refused the VC10 home from Ascension for being too pissed. He was now Lieutenant Commander Morrison. I asked him why he didn't come in uniform.

"Because back then, I was 'Scouse', not Lt Cdr Morrison," he said. "Now I think it's important that at times like this, I should be remembered as Scouse. How can the lads remember me like that if I'm here wearing two and a half rings?"

Scouse was a good bloke, sensible, switched on. That's why he was a two and a half ringer. He'd never given me any shit when I was a junior, he'd always helped and advised. Maybe he'd got shit as a junior and remembered what it was like.

During the service there was a man in his twenties who sobbed continuously. He must have lost his dad when he was just a kid. Was he the child who had cried "I want my daddy" at the 1982 memorial? After the service, the church emptied and everyone was milling about outside. I went up and spoke to Chris Kent about one of the lads I'd had a few beers and a chat with over the weekend's proceedings. I told Chris I was worried about him, and asked if there was anything he could say or do that might help him. He said he was worried too and would have a word with him later that day. Some of the ship's company were heading down to a pub in Southsea for a big piss-up. Shep Woolley the comedian was coming, Gilly Gilchrist organised it. If I hadn't been heading off on the last leg of my own mission, I'd have joined them on theirs to get absolutely hammered.

Afterwards, we all went down to the memorial plaque near the round tower for wreath laying. I spent a while there with my family then left them to make their own way home while I headed off for the Falklands Chapel in Pangbourne.

The Chapel is set in wooded, peaceful grounds and is a beautiful building. Outside was the collection of stones and rocks, one collected from the home area of each of the men who died. I retrieved those I had brought from the islands, carefully labeled with their location of origin. Goose Green, Sealion Island, Blue Beach, Tumbledown Mountain. I laid them with the other stones and entered the church.

All the names of the fallen are in the foyer, with the guest books. There are no ranks here, just names. I wandered around for a while; I've never been that interested in churches, especially modern ones, but I found the best collection of Falklands books I'd ever seen in one of the offices.

Each of the prayer kneeling mats had the name of one of the 255 men who failed to return from the campaign embroidered on it. I looked at a couple of them and knew that I wasn't going to be able to hold it together much longer. I selected a prayer mat with the name of Frank Armes on it. Frank came from Norwich and had been a stoker on HMS *Coventry*. He was only nineteen. I knelt down and let go with the last lot of my grief. I was shaking and just couldn't stop it, and in truth, I didn't want to. I had held it in for 20 years and only very recently learned to let it go. This would be my only chance and I would never be like this again, I was absolutely sure. A hand squeezed my shoulder. I tried to dry my eyes before I looked round. There was a middle aged woman and a priest there.

"I won't ask you if you're OK, but if we can help in any way…," the woman said. I tried to say 'thank you', but though my lips moved, there was no sound. I have no idea how long I sat there, crying. I was determined though that once I left there, there would be no more. It would be finished with, and I had a holiday to enjoy. I'd done my grieving, I'd paid my respects, nothing could bring the men back, and nothing could change what had happened. It was time to move on, time to get on with the rest of my life.

As I was on the way out, the woman and the priest were in the foyer. I recognised the woman from somewhere, but I couldn't think where. She may have been someone's widow. I shook hands with them both and thanked them for the opportunity of seeing the place. They offered me tea and cakes but I wanted to get out of the place and head north. I drove away from the chapel, deliberately not checking the rearview mirror.

AFTERWORD

Closure

10th May 2002

My 38th birthday. Twenty years ago today, HMS *Sheffield*, the first Royal Navy warship to be lost in action since the Second World War, had slipped below the South Atlantic waves. She is now an official war grave, resting in one thousand fathoms of water. She will never be disturbed, neither should she be nor the men who rest with her. I had cried more tears in the last five weeks than I had done in the last twenty years. I was all cried out.

Now it was over. I had one last thing to do, alone. It was time for a ritual cleansing; disposing of the gear that I'd worn when exorcising my ghosts. I walked out into the garden where my daughter and niece were playing with their fluffy baby fur seals I had brought them from the South Atlantic.

I dumped the jeans and boots I had worn hiking around the Falklands and Argentina into the dustbin, followed by the thick socks and the t-shirt I had worn to meet the two Argentine fighter pilots. I looked at the pile of now filthy and crumpled clothing, then jammed the lid back on the bin, and stood up, inhaling the crisp English spring air.

Breathing out, I let my shoulders slump, and leaned against the fence. The back door was open and my dad was pouring two pints of his special home brew. With the squeals of delight of the two little cousins behind me, I knew for certain that for me, after twenty years, the war was finally over. I had not only survived the war, I had also survived the peace. I turned and went back into the house.

RIP
Rear Admiral Sam Salt
19 April 1940 – 3 December 2009